LADAKH and Adjoining Areas

Leh Area

Taru
Nyemo • Phiyang
Skara Leh Sabu
Stutuk Choglamsar
Shey
Stok Tikse Sakti
Chushot
Matho Stakna Chemrey
Karu
Hemis
Martselang

Shahidulla and Yarkand
Suget Pass
C H I N A
akoram Pass
Daulat Beg Oldi
apshan Kizil Langar
Dipsang Plain
aser-La Kataklik
Paramik
Mandaltang Winter Route
Tiggur
Deskit Satti
Khardung-La
Phiyang Agham
tuk
Leh Shey
Shey Tikse
Chemrey
Stakna
Karu
Hemis
tselang
Upshi
Gya
alang-La
Puga
Lunga-Lacha-La
Bara-Lacha-La
RADESH

K A S H M I R

AKSAI CHIN

CHINA

TIBET

Pangong Tsho
Chushul

Indus River

Hanle
Demchok
CHINA
TIBET
To Gartok and Lhasa

LADAKH
Crossroads of High Asia

LADAKH
Crossroads of High Asia

JANET RIZVI

DELHI
OXFORD UNIVERSITY PRESS
BOMBAY CALCUTTA MADRAS
1989

Oxford University Press, Walton Street, Oxford OX2 6DP

New York   Toronto
Delhi Bombay Calcutta Madras Karachi
Petaling Jaya Singapore Hong Kong Tokyo
Nairobi Dar es Salaam
Melbourne Auckland
and associates in
Berlin Ibadan

First published 1983
Second impression 1986
First published in Oxford India Paperbacks 1989

SBN 0 19 562390 8

Filmset by Arun and Rajive Pvt. Ltd., Chandigarh
Printed by Rekha Printers, New Delhi 110020
and published by S. K. Mookerjee, Oxford University Press
YMCA Library Building, Jai Singh Road, New Delhi 110001

For SAYEED
who loves Ladakh as much as I do

Contents

Preface

This book is intended as a background and an introduction to a
little-known corner of the Buddhist world, existing in isolation in
India. After being closed to outsiders for thirty years, for military
and strategic reasons, Ladakh was partly opened in 1974, and
immediately became an important destination for the serious
student of Buddhism and Tibetology. It also holds attractions for
the lover of mountains, and the traveller who simply wants to
extend his horizons; in addition it has become part of the Asian
itinerary of footloose western youth.

In spite of its many features of interest, no comprehensive
account of Ladakh has been published in English in the nine
years since it was opened, and authentic and up-to-date information is hard to come by. I have written this book in an
attempt to fill the gap. In it, I have tried to place on record some
of the important facts about a part of the world which has been
little studied up till now, and which has often been regarded as
no more than an undifferentiated appendage of old Tibet. I
believe, on the contrary, that Ladakh has its own vigorous social
and cultural identity, of which the Tibetan tradition is only one
component; and that it is important there should be an account
of it before it is eroded by contact with the modern world. For
the benefit of the visitor to Ladakh, I have also included some
descriptions of places, particularly of the major *gompas*, or
monasteries, within reach of Leh; and I should like to think that
the book as a whole will give him some indications as to what he
might keep his eyes open for, and help him to place what he sees
in its historical and cultural setting.

I lay no claim to originality, much less to having conducted
anything in the nature of research. Many of the facts about
Ladakh are available to anyone with access to the literature of
Buddhism, or of central Asian and Tibetan travel, and the rest to
anyone who has been lucky enough, as I have, to live there for
some years. These, taken together, are my qualifications to write

about Ladakh; of them, the second is of far greater importance. I
lived for two years in Leh, and during that time formed a deep
affection for the land and its people. My husband, Sayeed Rizvi,
was Development Commissioner, or head of the district administration; as well as sharing my affection for Ladakh, he acquired in
the line of business a wide knowledge of the country as it is today,
a good deal of which rubbed off on me. This, and the fact that I
was living there, going about and meeting the people (though not,
to my regret, able to converse with them in their own tongue) gave
me something of a 'feel' for Ladakh, whose physical, social and
mental atmosphere I found deeply sympathetic.

In our day (1976–8) Ladakh was a single district, in area
India's largest, in population one of its smallest. In June 1979 it
was split in two, the town of Kargil becoming the headquarters
of a district of the same name. Most of this book was written
before the bifurcation took place; even now it is hard for me to
think of Ladakh as more than a single district. Our home was in
Leh, and it is central Ladakh, the core of the present Leh
district, with which I am most familiar, and on which I have laid
most emphasis. I could indeed have confined myself to the
present Leh district; but to do that would be to omit all mention
of some particularly interesting regions in Kargil district—
Zanskar, one of Ladakh's most beautiful and isolated valleys;
Da-Hanu, where the Buddhist Dards pursue a way of life unique
in the world, and Shagkar-Chigtan, a nominally Muslim area
rich in Buddhist survivals, and with a wealth of oral literature
unsurpassed anywhere else. It would also be to ignore the
underlying unity, historical, cultural and linguistic, which has
for centuries bound the often sharply differentiated regions of
the two districts together. Nevertheless, I am conscious that, not
wishing to tread where I was unsure of my ground, I have not
done justice to Kargil, and to that extent my picture of Ladakh is
less than complete.

We are no longer in Ladakh; but Ladakh was an experience
which has remained with us. A few of our Ladakhi friends, we
hope and believe, have become friends for life; and for me the
writing of this book, started before we left, has been a valuable
means of preserving that experience, and keeping in touch with
Ladakh.

Janet Rizvi

Acknowledgements

My first thanks must be to the people of Ladakh, among whom I lived for two years, and who treated me with unfailing kindness and generosity. From my contact with them is drawn most of the mosaic of facts and impressions that make up this book.

An invaluable contribution was made by many friends, both Ladakhi and non-Ladakhi, who shared and indulged my passion for 'Ladakh talk', endless hours of it, in which issues were raised, and ideas hammered into shape. Special thanks in this connection to Beera and T. K. Mitra, Trevor Morlin, Camila Perez, Helena Norberg-Hodge, James Crowden, Tadzin Joldan and Abdul Majid.

Abdul Hakim and G. M. Kakpuri set the ball rolling by giving me access to their notes. The typescript was read at various stages in the drafting by the late Sonam Narboo, Tashi Rabgias, Deen Khan, Kamal and Pami Singh, and my mother Margaret Clarke, all of whom made valuable suggestions. My aunt, Janet Adam Smith, went through it from the point of view of readability and style, and in its present form it owes much to her. Jamal Rizvi and Adil Rizvi helped with the index. The editorial and production staff of Oxford University Press took enormous pains over the book's content and presentation, and to them I extend my warmest thanks.

My husband, Sayeed Rizvi, briefed me on Ladakh's developing economy; and Prakash Gole replied promptly and fully to my queries on bird life. Professor Luciano Petech was equally generous in the time and attention he devoted to my request for information on specific issues in Ladakhi history; and I am further indebted to him for permission to use the quotation from Hui-ch'ao, on page 37. Andrew Roberts took time off from the real business of his life, African history, to chase up references and Xerox material for me in the library of the School of Oriental and African Studies, London. Akbar Ladakhi freely and generously put at my disposal his unrivalled understanding of Ladakh both past and present, besides translating the poems at the end of Chapter X. Whatever I know about Ladakh's secular culture, I owe to him.

I am indebted to Pinto Narboo for a title whose appositeness in conveying what I feel to be *the* important thing about Ladakh is little short of inspired.

The Joldan family gave me most generous hospitality on my return trip to Ladakh to tie up ends and see as yet unvisited *gompas*. Abdul Majid devoted much time and effort to organizing my *gompa* visits, and the ease and comfort in which these were accomplished were due to him, and to my driver, Norbu. My *gompa* visits in the Kargil region were organized by G. M. Kakpuri.

Lastly, I must thank those who, by keeping things going on the domestic front, freed me for the task of writing. My parents-in-law, Mr and Mrs S. Q. Rizvi, not only absolved me of the duties usually expected of the *bahu*, during long winter sojourns with them, but also came to baby-sit and take over my domestic responsibilities, when I left Mussoorie for my return trip to Ladakh. Routine chores during the period of writing were undertaken by Dorje and Hamidullah in Leh, and Raufan Bua in Srinagar and Mussoorie. Without their cheerful service this book could certainly not have been written.

Introduction
Where Many Roads Meet

Ladakh, which is one of the newest of the few 'new frontiers' left in the world, still retains some of its aura of mystery and inaccessibility. It is perhaps the place which bears the closest resemblance to old Tibet—a Tibet which, though still alive in the hearts of countless Tibetans both inside and outside their country, has in a physical sense ceased to exist since the start of the long years of Chinese occupation. Along with Sikkim and Bhutan, and remote parts of Nepal, Ladakh is one of the last places where Tibetan Buddhism continues to be practised as a living religion, as it has been for a thousand years; in landscape it probably resembles Tibet more than does either Sikkim or Bhutan. This book deals with Ladakh alone, but it will surely enrich the reader's appreciation of Ladakh—and the visitor's even more—to remember from the outset that a good part of what is said here applies to the whole Tibetan cultural area, and much of the physical area too.

The landscape, for a start. Since 1974, Ladakh has been one of the few trans-Himalayan areas open—even if not fully open—to outside visitors: as such it presents a scene which, while it may appal or enthral the newcomer, will probably be unlike anything he has encountered before. This scene has a good deal in common with much of Tibet. It is true that southern and eastern Tibet, with their mountain pastures where enormous herds of cattle and yak are kept by nomadic herdspeople, and their fertile tracts along the Tsang-Po and other great rivers, must surely lack Ladakh's barren moonlike quality. But south-east Ladakh is a continuation of the fearsome massif of central and north-west Tibet, with its bare mountains, its high-altitude plateaux, and its salt lakes. And even towards Ladakh's north-west, the landscape, while perhaps less extreme, represents a continuity with this—a basic similarity, in contrast to the comparative lushness of Bhutan and southern Sikkim. Visitors who have read Michel Peissel's account of the journey he made in 1964 to Mustang, the remote kingdom just north of Annapurna, projecting out of Nepal like a promontory into Tibet, will be immediately struck by the resemblance between the barren grandeur he describes and the landscape they are confronted with here. Whether he flies in sti aight from the plains, or takes the road from Kashmir, the traveller cannot fail to be aware that, coming from India (which is the only approach possible today) he is entering a completely different environment. In a geo-physical sense he has left India and entered Tibet.

That Ladakh was part of the Tibetan religio-cultural empire—though never subject to Tibet politically—is a recurrent theme in this book, and need not be gone into here. But it is exciting to find observers of other centuries, and in regions hundreds of miles away, making reports on customs both secular and religious, which might have been written of Ladakh today. Apart from the Jesuit and Capuchin would-be missionaries of the 17th and 18th centuries, the first European to have written an account of Tibet was George Bogle who, under a special commission from Warren Hastings to explore the possibility of opening trade relations between Tibet and British India, spent the winter of 1774-5 with the Panchen Lama at his seat at Tashilunpo in southern Tibet. Bogle's account rings many bells. On his way he saw 'devil-dances' in Bhutan, which were surely the same as the dance-dramas performed in the monasteries of Ladakh today (so did Michel Peissel on the very day of his arrival in the capital of Mustang 190 years later). All along the way he gave and received, in ceremonial greeting, the white 'handkerchiefs' or scarves which in Peissel's Mustang, as in Tibet proper, are known as *katas*, and in Ladakh as *kataks*. Bogle is reticent about what he must have observed of the temples, images and rituals of Tibetan Buddhism. But Peissel's descriptions of what he saw in Mustang tally in almost every detail with the religion practised in Ladakh. The mural paintings of the 'Guardian Divinities' and the 'Wheel of Life'; the scroll paintings called *thangkas*; the images, including some of gigantic size, round which have been built two-storey shrines—all these, as described by Peissel, could have been in any monastery in Ladakh.

But as striking as the identity of religious observance (no greater, after all, than over an area of comparable size in pre-Reformation Europe) is the similarity of many social customs and attitudes. Bogle seems to have been the first to describe the Tibetan system of fraternal polyandry (he claimed credit for coining the word); and Peissel found it actively practised in Mustang—also the custom known as *khang-bu*, or 'little house', whereby the elders of a family, as soon as the eldest son has reached the years of discretion, retire gracefully from participation in affairs, and taking only enough of the property for their own sustenance, yield the headship of the family to him. Neither of these customs is current in Ladakh now, except occasionally in remote villages in the mountains or the plateaux of the south-east; but both are described in nineteenth century accounts. What remain characteristic of Buddhist Ladakh are the high status and complete emancipation enjoyed by women which, while not specifically commented on by Bogle, are implicit in his descriptions of his own relationships with Tibetans of both sexes; and which struck Peissel forcibly during his stay in Mustang. A related feature is the absence of anything like a caste system among the Tibetan Buddhists. Class distinctions do exist, in the form of a consciousness among all concerned that a few families form an aristocracy of birth. This is as true of Ladakh today as it was of Bogle's Tibet and Peissel's Mustang. But it in no way dominates social intercourse; indeed one of the most attractive things about Ladakhi life is the self-confidence of people not belonging to the privileged class, and the lack of arrogance of those who do. Perhaps it is after all part of the complex of Buddhist attitudes that a person is assessed for what he is, and not primarily on the basis of his membership of a particular class, or sex.

Tibetan influence spreads from these intangibles to details of dress and custom as well. The Ladakhi dress is an adaptation of the Tibetan *chuba*, the men's version being perhaps the most elegant of all its variants. Other similarities may be a function of the continuity of the physical environment. The staples of the diet of all the Tibetan peoples are the same: *tsampa*, or parched barley flour, and *chang*, a mildly alcoholic drink made from fermented barley, both of them derived from the main crop of the Tibetan plateau; and butter-tea, which reflects the availability of butter from the huge herds of cattle, sheep and yak that roam the upland pastures. Tea itself, in the form of 'bricks' of slightly dampened and compressed tea-leaves, must have been obtained through imports from China along established trade routes from a very early period. The same technology too is found all over the huge area of greater Tibet: water-mills identical to those described by both Bogle and Peissel are in common use in Ladakh today; so is the simple but effective system of irrigation by channelling water to the fields from mountain streams—almost the only source of moisture in this whole region, where hardly any rain falls, and people must depend for water on the melting of the snow on the heights.

The point need not be laboured further. Ladakh is, and always has been, part of the great Tibetan cultural empire; and this will constitute its main interest for a large number of people—perhaps the majority among those who make the effort to visit it. And yet the visitor should not make the mistake of thinking that he has indeed stepped straight into old Tibet. In spite of the identity of religion and the similarity of language and custom, Tibetans now living in Ladakh as refugees hardly feel themselves even half-way home. For there is much more to Ladakh than only Buddhism and 'Tibetanness'. Geographically it was an outpost of Tibet, and as such open to influences other than the Tibetan. Central Ladakh was the bastion of Buddhism against which at last the tide of Islam beat in vain; western Ladakh, while not completely turning its back on the earlier ways of life and thought, accepted the new religion and much of the culture that went with it. Nor did central Ladakh itself remain untouched by outside forces, of which Islam was only the most insistent. Its position as a major entrepot at the centre of a network of important trade routes gave Leh in the old days something of a cosmopolitan air, and this is reflected even now in the mixed racial composition of its population; while the speech of the Leh people, basically a Tibetan dialect as everywhere in Ladakh, is enriched by an admixture of foreign words, mainly Persian and Urdu. There is a wealth of folk literature in Ladakh, some derived from the ancient pre-Buddhist past of Tibet, such as that based on the national epic, the Kesar saga, and some seeming to spring from the native genius of the people. This has been influenced, particularly in the western region, by poetic forms like the *ghazal*, developed in the context of Islamic culture, and these have percolated through to central Ladakh too. More accessible to the visitor (if he is lucky and a match is being played during his stay in Leh), the game of polo—in its original form, not as 'improved' by the

British—exists in the western Himalaya in an area more or less co-extensive with the spread of Islam. It has been kept alive in central Ladakh by the settlement of Shia Muslims, originally from Baltistan, at Chushot, a village 15 kilometres up the Indus from Leh; but it generates wild enthusiasm among Muslims and Buddhists alike, and adds a unique excitement to summer in Leh.

Nor was the Islamic connection the only one modifying the 'Tibetanness' of Ladakh and the Ladakhis. On the political level, the Dogra conquest of 1834–42 brought Ladakh within the orbit of India; and though till 1959 the lamas continued to look to Lhasa for religious inspiration, the new generations of secular Ladakhis started going to Srinagar and the universities of British India for higher education. Thus the modern world, first brought in a small way by the devoted work of Moravian missionaries, made its more permanent mark via India; Ladakh became an integral part of the Indian polity in 1947 with the accession to India of the princely state of Jammu and Kashmir of which it formed a part. Since then, but more especially in the last ten years, it has been involved in the nation-wide programme of development and modernization which has been the hall-mark of independent India's economic effort. In the context of India's ambivalent relationship with China, Ladakh's geographical position gives it a strategic importance which is reflected by a massive military presence. Troops are stationed both in the accessible areas of western and central Ladakh, and far to the east and south-east on the inhospitable plateaux of Chang-Thang towards the Tibetan border—regions on which, before their arrival, the world south of the Himalaya had hardly impinged. Though not yet fully assimilated into the life of the people, India is a palpable presence in Ladakh, and one that is there to stay.

It is the combination of the spirit and atmosphere of Tibetan Buddhism with elements of other cultures that gives Ladakh its characteristic and piquant flavour. But all said and done, in central Ladakh it is Buddhism that predominates. As the visitor will carry away a memory of mountain, ridge and peak stretching away endlessly, so, when he thinks of the people and their imprint on this awe-inspiring landscape, his impression will be of *chorten* and *mani* wall; of lamas and Buddha images, *gompas* and *gonchas*. If he looks with a perceptive eye, he will notice faces where, on a basic Tibetan pattern, can also be discerned traces of other racial elements; most of these faces will belong to Muslims. Indeed, not the least valuable contribution of the settlements of Muslims in the Buddhist heartland of central Ladakh—once Islam had renounced the possibility of converting it by the sword—has been to give the opportunity for the practical expression of Buddhism's tolerance towards other faiths. Here the spirit of Buddhism has not been betrayed.

Ladakh :
Mountain and Valley

I
The Road to Leh

Although a scheduled air service has been introduced between Srinagar and Leh, there remains a great deal to be said for coming into Ladakh by road. The road journey is admittedly tiring; but it has this advantage, that it mitigates the violence done to the human system by a sudden transition from a lower altitude to Leh's 3,500 metres: it imposes a process of acclimatization naturally. Further, the road journey provides a kind of orientation. Ladakh is not only physically remote—Leh is 440 kilometres from Srinagar by road, though a good deal less as the crow flies—it is also remote in atmosphere, landscape and culture from anything most travellers are likely to have encountered before. Not the least of the contrasts that Ladakh presents is that with its nearest neighbour, Kashmir. The visitor who has made a thorough exploration of the Kashmir valley will find that his familiarity with it provides no point of reference in his discovery of the Buddhist heartland of Ladakh. This being so, it may give a feeling of unreality, a feeling that Ladakh is somehow unconnected with the rest of the world, to plunge straight into this strange environment, by air from Srinagar or Delhi. The road journey, as it tempers the effect on the body of transition to a great altitude, similarly tempers the effect on the mind and senses of transition to an unfamiliar landscape and culture.

But more than this, the road journey has its own rewards. It passes through what must be in its stark way some of the most spectacular mountain scenery in the world; and the road itself surely rivals, in some of the acrobatics it performs up and down the mountain sides, any in the Alps, the Andes, or elsewhere in the Himalaya. It might even be argued that the only satisfactory way to enter Ladakh would be on foot or by pony. The receptive traveller may well regret the distance that the four wheels of his vehicle put between him and the landscape, and in particular how

he is cut off from its sounds: the sigh of the wind, the roar of
rushing water, the whistle of the marmots, the cry of the birds.
Today few could afford the luxury of a leisurely twelve-day
march from Sonamarg. Indeed with trucks and buses careering
along the road, such a march would hold little pleasure. Happily
the scope for mountain walking elsewhere in Ladakh is enormous.

The road to Ladakh may be taken to begin two hours' drive
from Srinagar, at Sonamarg, the last tourist resort up the Sind, a
tributary of Kashmir's main river, the Jhelum. A few hundred
metres beyond Sonamarg, at a bridge carrying the road across the
Sind to its right bank, there is a prominent notice with this striking
message: 'DRIVE CAREFREE: BEACON TOILS DAY AND NIGHT' This
claim is no more than the literal truth. 'Beacon' is the code name
of that section of the para-military Border Roads Organization
which deals with Kashmir and Ladakh. All along the road from
Sonamarg to Leh is the evidence of Beacon's toil. The road is
under a constant process of maintenance by BRO detachments
consisting of men drawn from the four corners of India, supplemented by locally recruited labour of both sexes. And while
during the summer months when travellers from outside are
passing, their working conditions are tolerable, it must be remembered that these men are on the job all the year round: only the
Zoji-La, the pass between Kashmir and Ladakh, is blocked all
winter, while within Ladakh snowfall is relatively scanty, and it is
possible to keep the other passes on the highway open most of the
time. But this is done at a staggering cost, not only in money, but
also in human hardship. When the temperature may be minus
30°C in Leh, living and working conditions on the top of the
Fatu-La, a wind trap at a level 600 metres higher than Leh, hardly
bear thinking of; and the BRO detachments live mostly in bunk-
ers and tented encampments. The work of opening the Zoji-La,
involving weeks of effort in clearing a path through metres of
snow, is only the most spectacular of the feats routinely
achieved by the men of the Border Roads Organization—feats
that are truly heroic. On their efforts, not only the tourist traffic
and its infrastructure, but much of the life of the people of
modern Ladakh, and all the amenities they enjoy, ultimately
depend. They should not be taken for granted.

To return to the road. A few kms beyond Sonamarg, it begins

to rise, and soon to ascend in hairpins (known as the Captain Bends, after the memorial to a BRO captain who lost his life there) towards the top of the Zoji-La (3,450 metres). It almost defies belief that in November 1948, during the Indo-Pakistan war for Kashmir, a column of tanks made its way through a near-blizzard, up this punishing ascent, to attack and dislodge the Pakistani forces who held the pass. So improbable was their appearance that when the Pakistanis reported it to their command behind the lines, the latter refused to believe them, and replied that 'the so-called tanks must be camouflaged jeeps'. A previous assault had failed, for infantry supported only by howitzers could make little impression on an enemy strongly entrenched in so commanding a position. The credit for the success of this one, which saved Ladakh for India, must be shared among the intrepid tank crews, using their vehicles at an altitude and in conditions never before attempted; the engineers who constructed a track for the tanks, in the shortest time and under the enemy's fire; and commanders who had the dash and imagination to conceive this brilliantly unorthodox solution to an intractable military problem.

As we begin the ascent towards the pass, we are still recognizably in Kashmir, with its mountain flora, and fir and birch trees. Opposite the steeply rising road, and far below, the Sind river, which it has just left, takes a right-angled turn away in a southeasterly direction along a delectable valley with a footpath, which is the lesser-known route to the holy cave of Amarnath, an important Hindu place of pilgrimage. Away down, at the confluence of the Sind and the tributary whose course we are now following three hundred metres above, is the village of Baltal, which used to be a staging post on the old foot- and pony-road. A hard climb they must have had of it, from Baltal up to the pass. The summer route, whose alignment is still visible, zig-zagged up parallel to and a little below today's motor road; the winter one led up the ravine that marks the course of the stream—frozen and covered with snow at that season.[1] After the climb, the road flattens out,

---

[1]There is an exciting account of what must have been one of the last winter crossings of the Zoji-La, in February 1948, by the team which was to built the first airstrip in Ladakh, in Ved Mehta's *Portrait of India* (Penguin edition, London 1973), pp. 283–8. In the old days, runners used to take advantage of breaks in the weather to cross the pass more or less regularly during winter, carrying mail.

and the ascent to the pass is so gentle that it would be easy to miss the top if it were not marked. The watershed is inconspicuous, and it is only a little later that one realizes that the stream beside the road is flowing in the same direction as one's journey.

The Zoji-La, in fact, has been aptly described as less a pass, in the usually understood sense of the word, than a gigantic step cut through the wall of the Great Himalaya to the high valleys and plateaux beyond. But if the watershed is hardly dramatic—the drama of this pass having occurred in the steepness of the climb on the Kashmir side—the same cannot be said of the change in the landscape. The scenery on the Kashmir side is Alpine; over in Ladakh it has become stark. Literally, there is not a tree in sight; and though we have not yet come to the complete aridity of most of central Ladakh, the vegetation is confined to short grass and low bushes. Here the traveller who keeps his eyes open may be lucky enough to spot marmots—mountain-dwelling rodents about the size of a beaver—whose luxuriant fur and clumsy-seeming gait are belied by the ease and completeness with which they can disappear into their burrows, and frustrate any attempt to examine them more closely.

The Zoji-La marks not only a geo-physical, but also an ethnic and linguistic divide. It is true that the people of Dras, the first major village over the pass, are Dards, an Indo-Iranian stock akin to the Kashmiris; but as the road continues towards central Ladakh, there is increasing evidence, in the people's features, of the quite different racial element represented by the Tibetans. Similarly, the Dard language, spoken at Dras, which belongs to the same language-group as Kashmiri, gives way to the Ladakhi language, a dialect of Tibetan.

All along the road at this point are poles marked off in metres from the ground, to measure the depth of the winter's snow. For in contrast to inner Ladakh, this area experiences heavy snowfall. Travellers early in the season, when the road has been cleared but the snow has not yet melted completely, may find themselves driving between snow walls that overtop their vehicle. This is less picturesque than it sounds: by the time the bulldozers have done their work, the snow is distinctly grubby, though here and there white gleams along the lines of rather ephemeral graffiti. The Great Himalaya forms a barrier to the entry of moisture-laden clouds to the rest of Ladakh, but here they find a way in through

the gap of the Zoji-La, and the resultant heavy snowfall renders
this area entirely inaccessible in winter. It must be an incredibly
hard life for the people here (as in Zanskar, to the south-east,
which becomes similarly snowbound, and where winter is said to
last for seven months out of the twelve): Dras has the local
reputation of being the coldest permanently inhabited place in
the world outside Siberia.

For some time before Dras, the road has been following the
upper waters of the river of the same name; at Dras village the
valley opens out into an upland plateau—or rather a series of
alluvial plateaux at different levels. Plantations of willow, here as
at a few villages further on, add to the impression of relative
lushness given by the fields and meadows near the river, in
contrast to the bleakness of the surrounding hills. The road
continues to follow the waters of the Dras for another two hours'
journey, passing its confluence with another major stream, the
Shingo. As the valley narrows to little more than a gorge, the
vegetation diminishes and the landscape grows starker. At the
meeting of the Dras with the Suru river, coming in from the
south-east, the road turns up the latter, and within a matter of
minutes Kargil is reached—the second city of Ladakh, with a
population of about 2,500, and the natural halting-place for the
night.

Kargil looks very different from the areas traversed hitherto.
At about 2,750 metres, and with a winter snowfall much less than
that towards the Zoji-La, the climate allows of a lush growth of
crops, including wheat, and fruit trees, wherever there is water.
Areas within reach of irrigation being a small part of the whole
are thus intensively cultivated; and the brightness of the green
fields and trees—or alternatively the rich golds and reds of their
autumn colours—make a pattern of elongated shapes, often
mere strips along the water-courses, in startling contrast to the
immediately adjoining bare brown hillsides. This contrast will
become familiar as the traveller penetrates farther into Ladakh.

The town itself is a drab little place, to which the main contribution of the twentieth century would seem to be the perpetual
traffic jam in its streets and alleyways. Straggling along the river-
bank, a steep mountain-slope rising on its other side, it occupies a
strip of land too narrow for the construction of a bypass; consequently the Srinagar–Leh highway runs slap through its main

bazaar. The Kargilis hold fast to their traditional faith, a strict and puritanical form of Islam's Shia sect; yet while many of them seem to regard the travellers who use their town as a staging-post with barely-veiled suspicion, or at best indifference, others display all the warmth and openness the visitor will come to recognize as the hallmark of the Ladakhis.

Although Kargil is only about twenty kilometres from the Indus as the crow flies, the road does not make straight for the river at this point, but continues on a course roughly parallel with it, crossing two passes higher than the Zoji-La, and making a wide curve to join the Indus at right angles at Khaltse, 100 kilometres down river from Leh.

As the road crosses the Suru and ascends the brown hillside to the plateau opposite, it can be seen that the apparent barrenness is modified by the presence of low creeping vegetation; this occurs on nearly all the seemingly bare hillsides, and even provides sustenance for sparse populations of sheep and goats, domestic on the lower slopes, and wild on the heights. If all goes according to plan, the desert plateau opposite Kargil may be transformed in a few years, with the completion of the Kharbathang irrigation canal, a major Government project, which will bring water from the upper reaches of the Wakha river. The road descends from the plateau to the village of Pashkyum, whose fields, extending over the width of the valley bottom and watered by channels taken off from the Wakha river running through, are refreshingly green. The valley narrows almost to a gorge, and high on the opposite side can be seen the Kharbathang channel, which will eventually bring water to the plateau behind. The traveller may already have noticed the 'private enterprise' irrigation works which, visible in the form of strips of green, follow the contours of the hillsides, sometimes at amazing heights above the valley bottoms.

About an hour's drive from Kargil, the road emerges into the smiling pasture and arable land around Mulbekh. This is the first predominantly Buddhist area reached; hence the relatively unconstrained manners of the women on the road and in the fields, and the fact that they are wearing the *perak*, the turquoise-studded headdress peculiar to the Buddhist women of Ladakh. Here, in contrast to the fashion of central Ladakh, the *perak* is surmounted by a small pill-box hat. Right beside the road, but partly obscured by a small shrine that has recently been built round it, is an enormous rock-engraving, dating perhaps from the eighth century, of the Maitreya—the Buddha-to-come.

From Mulbekh, the road leaves the Wakha river valley, and turns left up the valley of a tributary. At least, this is what one would assume it to be, and what it must have been geological ages ago. A wide pebbly river-bed runs down the centre, and the sides of the valley are seamed and contoured with the beds of its tributary streams. Everyone has seen terrain shaped by water into exactly comparable formations. But here there is no water. That ages ago there was water in plenty cannot be doubted; but the water has gone. Ladakh is a land from which, geological ages ago, upheavals of a violence beyond anything we can conceive drained off the abundant water of rivers and lakes: this is everywhere apparent, but nowhere so vividly, so weirdly, so disturbingly, as on this section of the road, the approach to the Namika-La. Here and there the same kind of low creeping vegetation appears, with even an occasional tiny patch of green, growing tenaciously out of some random accumulation of moisture from the melting of the meagre winter snows. This only serves to accentuate the otherwise all but complete aridity; and inspires wonder at the determination of life to establish itself, given the slightest chance, even in the most unpromising environment.

The road contours up one side of this valley, and at its head crosses the Namika-La, a pass of 3,700 metres. The name means Pillar of the Sky, and refers to the great rock formation that stands sentinel over it. The descent zig-zags down a mountainside which the eye made sensitive by the weird landscape on the other side of the pass can clearly perçeive to be another from which the water has been taken away; but not so completely. Stream-beds have at least a trickle of water flowing down them, and a corresponding hint of green on their margins; and the valley into which the road debouches is open and cultivated. This is the village of Bodh Kharbu. The road follows the Kanji river up towards the Fatu-La; downstream is the area of Shagkar-Chigtan, rich in historical association and folk culture.

In olden times this was the gateway to central Ladakh. It must have been here, around the year 1600, that a Balti army lay in wait for Jamyang Namgyal, after perhaps tricking that inept king into crossing the Fatu-La in winter; and having outmanoeuvred and defeated him proceeded to overrun central Ladakh; and it was here that forty years later his son Sengge Namgyal, Ladakh's most famous ruler, met a force sent from Kashmir by command of the Great Moghul himself, the Emperor Shah Jahan. The area's strategic importance is attested by the existence of ancient fortifications. A little beyond where the road turns into the Kanji valley, on the opposite side of the river, stands the ruined castle of Stag-tse, while at the foot of the ascent to the Fatu-La the road passes the old fort of Heniskot.

Even before Sonamarg, and increasingly after his entry into Ladakh, the traveller becomes aware of the surrounding mountains, and their amazing saw-tooth outlines against the sky. These become ever more spectacular on the approach to and traverse of the Fatu-La, the last and, at 4,100 metres, the highest of the three passes into central Ladakh. From the top of the pass the view opens out into a panorama of ridge, peak and valley, mostly composed of the ramifications of the Zanskar range (through which the road has been passing ever since it left Kargil), but affording an exciting glimpse ahead of a snow-outlined ridge of the Ladakh range, north of the Indus. Even in the middle of summer, however, the temptation to linger and drink in the view is rudely cut short by the bitter wind that howls over the pass without respite.

From the pass the road hairpins down to Lamayuru; this is surely one of the most picturesque and dramatically situated villages in India, if not in the world. A track runs down from the road to the village, clinging to the spur of a steep hillside, at the bottom of which, in a narrow valley, are the fields on which the life of the villagers depends. The flat-roofed, white or earth-coloured houses are piled almost on top of one another, in seemingly the most precarious way; the whole structure (for so it seems to be, rather than a group of independent buildings) is crowned by a *gompa* or monastery, its white walls picked out in red, itself rising in tier upon tier above the village. On the sides of the ravine below there is a multitude of astonishing rock and earth formations: these exist elsewhere in Ladakh too, but nowhere are there so many, with such fantastic shapes. They are alluvial or lacustrine deposits, laid down when a far greater volume of water than now filled this narrow valley; their tortured forms are the result of millennia of wind erosion.

But the descent from the Fatu-La is by no means finished at Lamayuru; for in one bound, so to speak, the road has to drop nearly 1,200 metres from 4,100 to 2,900, the level of the Indus at Khaltse. A short distance beyond Lamayuru the road starts to descend steeply once more—and what a descent! From above, virtually the whole of the next stretch can be seen in all its serpentine length of bends, loops and whorls, down to the bridge across the stream—the Wanla river—600 metres below. Truck-drivers call this stretch the Jalebi Bends—aptly, for it indeed calls to mind the *jalebi*, with its fantastic curls and whirls.

Spectacular though it may be as a piece of road-design and engineering, the Jalebi Bends are undeniably tedious to negotiate (at least for the passenger; for the driver they are a challenge). But the tedium is relieved by the view of the mountainside opposite—on the other side, not of the narrow Wanla river, but of the Indus itself—appearing now on the right hand, now on the left, as the road loops and bends its way down. It presents an amazing range of colours: not only the brown and grey one expects of a rocky mountain face, but red, russet, dull purple, ochre, pink, even green. It is hard to believe that so many colours can occur naturally and in such profusion in non-living matter.

And so at last on to the straight, across the Wanla river, which the road follows down a few kilometres to its confluence with the Indus. The Indus, historically and geographically one of the great rivers of the world, from which the very name India is derived; the Lion River, Sengge-ka-bab to the Ladakhis, which has already come 800 kilometres from its source near holy Lake Manasarowar in western Tibet—where, as tradition has it, it emerges from a lion's mouth; the Indus which will empty itself into the sea near Karachi, 1,600 kilometres on, after receiving the flow of the Shayok, the Hunza and Gilgit rivers, the Kabul, and greatest of all the Panjnad, the combined waters of the five rivers of the Punjab: at this point it is comparable in size to one of the medium-sized rivers of Europe—the Arno at Florence, perhaps. It gives a satisfying sense of geographical continuity to reflect that, however divided by range upon range of mountains, every one of the rivers and streams the traveller has crossed or followed for some distance since leaving Srinagar, is part of the immense river system of which this is the central artery, and which drains the area extending from Chitral in the north to the Great

Indian Desert in the south; from Lake Manasarowar in the east to
the Arabian Sea in the west.

Now we reach the village of Khaltse, and are entering the
heartland of Ladakh; the outward signs of Buddhism are everywhere. On the outskirts of every village are *chorten*—the Tibetan
version of the *stupa* of ancient Indian Buddhism. *Mani* walls have
their facing stones engraved with prayers and invocations—*Om
Mani Padme Hum*; and strings of prayer flags flutter like faded
bunting in the breeze.

For the rest of the journey the road follows the Indus up its
right bank—but not too closely, for at some points the river swirls
through deep gorges, and the road must perforce climb up on to a
neighbouring plateau. This happens beyond Saspol, the first big
village after Khaltse, and famous, like Khaltse, for its apricots. Its
smiling fields and orchards are in striking contrast to the bare
brown plateau beyond, with only the low prickly vegetation of the
desert, which is crossed before the road descends once more in a
dizzy series of hairpins to the twin villages of Basgo and Nyemo.
Towering above Basgo, an erstwhile royal residence, is a fantastic
system of wind-eroded pinnacles in dull red rock; towards the top
of these are an ancient half-ruined fort and temple. In the 1680s,
the fort held out for three years when besieged by the combined
Tibetan–Mongol army that invaded Ladakh on the orders of the
Fifth Dalai Lama.

Beyond Nyemo, the road rises again, following for a short
distance the line of the river, hundreds of metres below, and
affording an exciting glimpse of the meeting of the Indus and its
biggest Ladakh tributary, the Zanskar river. The Zanskar Valley
is divided from the Indus by the range to which it has given its
name; the river, in turning north to join its parent, has cut itself a
mighty gorge through the mountains, and contributes to the joint
stream a volume of water rather greater than that of the Indus
itself.

The road now turns away from the river for the last time, and
crosses one more barren plateau. When it descends once more to
the Indus, past the village and *gompa* of Phiyang, a couple of
kilometres off to the left, the valley opens out ahead into a broad
plain. If, as will most often happen, it is getting on towards
evening as the traveller approaches Leh, the rays from the low
sun will be coming from behind him with a soft light, casting into

relief with long shadows every contour of the mountains rising on either hand, and illuminating the higher snow-covered ridges in the distance. The Indus meanders in a number of channels through the wide bed it cut for itself in the alluvium brought down by its tributary torrents, at a period when both mainstream and tributaries carried a far greater volume of water than they do now. The ancient river-bed is green with cultivation; but the slopes on the far side are dry and barren, at this point and for thirty kilometres upriver, with the exception of some oases watered naturally or by small-scale irrigation works. In ten years or so their potential fertility may be realized with the completion of the High Martselang irrigation scheme, a major Government project still at the planning stage, which will bring water to the entire tract.

As the road approaches Spituk hill on the right, with its *gompa* just below the summit, and the green fields of Spituk village below, the scene is marred by military depots on either side; past Spituk these occupy much of the plain between it and Leh, which can be spied eight kilometres ahead, a collection of flat roofs among trees, dominated by the massive bulk of the now-deserted palace. Just beyond Spituk on the right is the airfield; on the left, after four or five kilometres, military installations give way to the fields of Skara village—so near Leh as to be almost a suburb. At last the road wriggles through the outskirts of the town, round a last spur, and up a small steep ascent. At the top of this is a large gaily-painted *chorten*, marking the beginning of the city proper; far above, on the summit of the palace hill, the small fort and temple of Namgyal Tsemo are silhouetted against the sky. With this, and the drive along the surprisingly broad and gracious main bazaar of Leh, still shaded by the remains of a splendid poplar avenue, the journey has ended; and the Ladakh heartland lies waiting to be discovered.

II
Profile of a Landscape

The most striking and obvious features of the Ladakh landscape are the mountains, and the aridity. To the uninstructed eye, the mountains may appear as a formless jumble; but the map shows that the main ranges and valleys form a system of parallels, behind and in the same direction as the Great Himalaya—south-east to north-west. Taking them from the north, the ranges are, first the Karakoram, to the north-east of the Shayok and Nubra valleys; and to their south-west the Ladakh range, an extension of the Kailash range. After the eastern Himalaya, the Karakoram has the highest peaks in the world, including K2, second only to Everest—though these are well out of Ladakh, and are approached from Baltistan. The highest mountain in the Ladakh Karakoram, indeed in the whole of Ladakh, is Saser Kangri (7,680 metres), on an outlying spur of the range between the upper reaches of the Shayok and Nubra rivers. A notable feature of the Saser spur is a system of glaciers, rivalling in complexity, if not in length, those of the K2 massif. The advance and retreat of these rivers of ice has over the centuries modified the alignment of the trade routes that penetrated these formidable mountains.

The Ladakh range has no major peaks; its average height is a little less than 6,000 metres, and few of its passes are less than 4,800 metres. It forms in Ladakh proper the northern boundary of the Indus valley, though when the Indus enters Ladakh in the south-east, it is actually flowing on the northern flank of these granite mountains, which it crosses by a great gorge it has cut for itself near its confluence with the Hanle river. The Indus valley, from this point down to where it enters Baltistan, is the geographical backbone of Ladakh; historically and culturally, from about sixty kilometres upstream from Leh to 100 down, it has formed Ladakh's heartland.

The Indus valley is bounded to the south-west by the Zanskar range, a most convoluted mass of mountains and valleys in which the visitor, as he traverses them on the road between Kargil and Khaltse, may be pardoned for failing to discern any pattern or coherence at all. It is cut by transverse valleys carrying the waters of tributary streams to the Indus; the greatest of these is the Zanskar river itself, whose clear waters join the silt-laden Indus near Nyemo, thirty kilometres down-river from Leh. Other such streams which the traveller has crossed, or followed for some distance on his journey into Ladakh, are the Dras, Suru and Wakha rivers, all of which combine a little below Kargil into a single stream (the Dras has its origin high in the main Himalayan range); and, on either side of the Fatu-La, the Kanji and Wanla rivers. The summits of the Zanskar range are in the region of 5,500 to 6,200 metres; the one which the visitor is likely to become most familiar with is the elegant Stok Kangri just across the Indus from Leh.

The Zanskar range falls on its south-western flank to the Suru and Zanskar valleys. The Suru valley is easily accessible from Kargil; it opens out about fifty kilometres upstream into an unexpectedly green and fertile belt around the village of Sankhu. The road, newly constructed beyond this point, and still painfully rough, fit only for jeeps and trucks, leads on in the same generally south-easterly direction another 150 kilometres or so, over the 4,400 metres Pensi-La, into the 'lost valley' of Zanskar. This road has already made a lot of difference to Zanskar, opening it up in a small way to the modern world during the summer months at least; in winter the only route in and out remains the highway made by the frozen waters of the Zanskar river, down to the Indus valley at Nyemo.

To the south-west of the Suru and Zanskar valleys rises the Great Himalaya itself; though, crossing it by the great depression of the Zoji-La, the traveller is hardly conscious of traversing the greatest range of mountains in the world. Certainly at this point its summits are puny compared with the giants of the eastern Himalaya, or with Nanga Parbat, 150 kilometres to the north-west. Nevertheless, if he continues up the Suru valley some fifteen kilometres beyond Sankhu, the traveller will see the graceful mass of the twin peaks of Nun-Kun towering, at 7,130 metres, a good 900 metres above their neighbours.

There is, then, a geographically coherent pattern in the disposition of mountain, valley and river, and a satellite's eye view would reveal their parallelism, which travellers of earlier times had to find out the hard way. The pattern is not everywhere obvious on the ground; particularly among the crumpled masses of the Zanskar range their apparent confusion makes one think with wonder and respect of the merchant travellers of olden times. Without the resources of modern transport and surveying, they worked out routes from north to south, from east to west, of this inhospitable land, making it an essential stage on the network of trade-routes that criss-crossed south and central Asia.

The aridity of Ladakh is part of a general severity of climate, and, to put it briefly, is caused by the barrier which the Great Himalaya forms to the moisture-laden clouds of the Indian monsoon, and also to the winter snowfall whose melting clothes with vegetation the ranges to the south—the Lahul range, and the Pir Panjal. This is demonstrated by the height of the snowline which, on the two inner ranges, the Ladakh and the Zanskar, varies between 5,600 and 6,100 metres while on the Lahul range, by contrast, it is about 5,000 metres.

Tens of thousands of years ago, Ladakh's climate was moister and milder than it is now. The existence of fresh-water fossils, and other geological evidence, indicate that the salt-water lakes in south-eastern Ladakh are the remains of a former much more extensive fresh-water lake system, reaching perhaps as far as Leh; and great alluvial and lacustrine deposits in other regions, for instance around Lamayuru, prove the existence in past ages of quantities of water out of all proportion to the small streams we see today. It has been estimated that perhaps a quarter of Ladakh was once covered with lakes, the evaporation from which would have caused a rainfall incomparably higher than the present average of seven to thirteen centimetres annually. As a result, the very appearance of the landscape would have been entirely different from today's picture. Today—and nowhere so clearly as on the approach to the Namika-La on the Kargil—Leh highway—we see a landscape whose contours have been formed by water, but in which water is now a negligible part. Huge gorges through the mountains can only have been cut by terrific torrents rushing down them over untold ages; now perhaps a small stream finds its way down the middle of the chasm—a stream whose insignificance seems to mock the grandeur of the water-wrought formation through which it passes. Had the water continued to flow, to do its work of weathering and eroding the granite and sandstone, the limestone and shale of which the mountains are made, the shape of the land would be different. Everywhere the story is the same. From his first entry into Ladakh, as he drives along the road, the observant traveller can see continual signs of the waters that flowed countless millennia ago, and that flow no longer. The question he will ask himself is, Why? The answer is far from clear. Certainly, as in the Kashmir valley, lake waters have been drained off, gradually or cataclysmically. Can this have been due to erosion? earthquake? or to the processes by which the Himalaya and its attendant ranges were formed, originating in the drift and collision of whole continents? Some of the rocks themselves are very ancient, far older than the mountains of which they are a part; but research into Ladakh's geological history has hardly started, and much work remains to be done before a reasonably firm hypothesis can be reached.

Thus geological ages ago, rivers and mountain torrents, fed by the melting of enormous quantities of snow and by abundant summer rainfall, must have provided ample natural irrigation to cover the valleys and mountain slopes with at least the vegetation of alpine areas. But today Ladakh is a desert—a high altitude desert. What little water there is has been fully exploited, given the limitations of traditional technique. The traveller has already noticed the irrigation channels, constructed in past centuries without the resources of modern engineering and machines, which follow the contours of the hillsides high above the valley bottoms. Schemes to increase the amount of cultivable land through further irrigation can now only be taken up by those economic development agencies which have at their disposal huge quantities of money and technical expertise. Along every watercourse, natural or man-made, clings a strip of cultivation; in places where water is relatively abundant, the ubiquitous browns and greys of a parched landscape are relieved by the green of wide fields, punctuated by the bushy growth of willows and the spires of poplars; or the gold of harvest and the crimson leaves of the apricot trees in autumn. Aptly have these spots, made fertile by the availability of water, been characterized as the oases of Ladakh. It seems to be an irony of nature that this land, through which flows in its upper reaches one of the world's great rivers, should be a desert, dependent for its water on whatever little moisture might be left in the clouds after their journey across the Indian plains, and their collision with the Great Himalaya.

The result of all this is a set of ecological limitations that are unlikely to be overcome. This desert will never blossom like the rose. Exercises in development, like irrigation schemes, tree-planting and exploration for ground-water, even if successful, will do no more than scratch the surface of the problem. Water in abundance is simply not there and, unless the barrier of the Great Himalaya could be conjured away, never will be there. This landscape may be modified, it can never be transformed.

In Dras and Zanskar snowfall is heavy, and both regions remain virtually cut off from the rest of the country in winter, the frozen river forming Zanskar's only lifeline for at least six months of every year. In summer it is accessible from various directions, as there are routes in over a number of passes, from Kishtwar on the southern flank of the Great Himalaya, as well as from central Ladakh via Lamayuru. The only jeep road is from Kargil up the Suru valley. Dras is better situated, being on the main summer route into Ladakh. In both Dras and Zanskar summer is pleasant, and the air lacks the fierce dryness of those parts of Ladakh where there is almost no winter snow. But the warmth of summer lasts all too briefly, and the cold begins to be intense even before there has been enough snow to block the passes and cut off all contact with the outside world.

In the valleys of central Ladakh and Nubra, on the other hand, and even more on the high plateaux of Chang-Thang, precipitation is minimal, and almost all the water actually available comes from the melting snows on the heights. Because of the poverty of the vegetation, the proportion of oxygen in the air is less than in many other places at the same altitude; and there is little or no atmospheric moisture to temper the effects of the rarefied air. Consequently, the force of the sun's rays is actually greater than on the Indian plains; but the degree of radiation from the earth is also much higher.

The result of this is a climate of extremes in which, it is said, a bareheaded man sitting in the sun with his feet in shadow, may suffer from sunstroke and frostbite at the same moment. Little heat is stored in the earth, and temperatures fall rapidly as autumn approaches. Similarly, while in the warmest days of sum-

mer, nights are cool, in winter, even when the shade temperature
remains well below freezing, the sun still gives real warmth. The
strength of the summer sun is sufficient to ripen the crops very
quickly which is just as well, as it is not warm enough for sowing till
May, and the harvest must be gathered in by September to
avoid the first frosts. This refers to the Leh area, at about 3,500
metres; 100 kilometres down the Indus, and 600 metres lower, at
Khaltse, the harvest of *grim* (naked barley, the staple crop) is
gathered in by mid-July, and there is time for another crop,
usually of turnips.

It is hard, after all, to give a generalized description of the
landscape of an area of 98,000 square kilometres with an altitude
range of 4,000 metres. Even the valleys and plateaux are up to
4,500 metres. Already on his first entry into Ladakh the traveller
will have noticed the varied contours of the mountains—round-
ed in outline near the Namika-La, fierce and jagged elsewhere—
and the startling contrast between the barren mountain slopes
and the valley bottoms made green and fertile by water. The
transition from the desert to the sown is abrupt—never any strip
of herbage, only a dry-stone wall divides them. Again, a distance
of fifty kilometres travelled, if it also means an ascent of 600
metres, brings about a change of climate which involves at the
same time a change of season: late in May, for instance, when the
crops are being sown at Leh, they are already half-grown at
Khaltse; a month or two later there will be golden fields down the
Indus, while at Leh the barley is still green, and the harvest two
months distant.

Until restrictions on travel to areas in the north, east and
south-east are lifted, and until unrestricted but nearly inaccessible
parts like Zanskar are further opened up by road, the picture
carried away by most visitors is probably that of the semi-desert
landscape of central Ladakh. There are, indeed, people who are
appalled by it—who see the starkness but not the grandeur; the
barrenness, but not the way in which this is softened and balanced
by the cultivated oases wherever there is water. It is true that the
landscape is harsh and uncompromising, that potentially fertile
soil is left untilled for want of water, and that whole areas are a
stony waste. It is true that there is nothing to check the winds that
scour the earth, fretting it into often grotesque forms. And yet
there is great beauty in this stark scene. The rivers which in

summer when the snow is melting run brown and muddy with silt, become crystal clear as winter approaches, and take on the most amazing shade of ultramarine, as vivid as the turquoises on a Ladakhi woman's *perak*. Every horizon is bounded by mountains biting into the sky with jagged, saw-like teeth; and from some vantage-points (there is one such at the fifth kilometre-stone out of Lamayuru on the way down to Khaltse) a vista opens up of ridge upon ridge, stretching away as far as the eye can see—and as much further as the informed imagination will take them. On some of its faces, the rock itself shows an astonishing range of colours—grey, brown, dull red, purple, pink, russet, green, black. And all these can be found in the microcosm of the pebbles at the traveller's feet.

There is no getting away from the mountains. Between Saspol and Leh, and again up as far as Hemis (to name only tracts on the well-trodden tourist beat), the very processes by which they were formed can be discerned in the layers of sedimentary rocks, tilted at all angles between the horizontal and the vertical by the strains and pressures of unimaginable upheavals in the earth's crust. Their aspect changes with every shift of light: the low evening sun throws into relief the contours of the south-east to north-west running ridges, like the flank of the Zanskar range across the Indus from Leh, so that their vertical as well as their horizontal structure is revealed; and then, in the soft light, the last lingering regret for the vegetation that is not there is eventually stilled, and the landscape achieves a harmony with itself which is perfectly satisfying.

Humbler beauties at nearer hand are seen against this ever-present background. A wild-rose bush covered with a profusion of blooms, red, pink, or occasionally yellow; the graceful feathery flowers of tall tamarisk bushes; clumps of dwarf iris, their form no less perfect than that of their full-grown cousins in more temperate climes; the virginal blossom that appears before the leaves on the apricot trees at the close of winter: all this fragile loveliness acquires a heart-breaking poignancy from its setting of bare earth and rock, and the savage grandeur of the ridges. The robuster beauty of green and golden fields, or apricot orchards, the branches heavy with ruddy fruit or crimson with the leaves of autumn, gains too in the imagination by its nearness to the wilderness. A landscape where cultivation, or at least vegetation, stretches to the horizon, lets the mind sink into acceptance: this is how things are. But in the Ladakh desert that is not how things are, any more than in the Sahara: here the bones of the earth not only protrude through the mantle which life has cast over them, as they do in the mountains anywhere, but are given only the scantiest covering. Here the beauty of line predominates rather than beauty of texture.

Man's imprint on this scene of contrasts has in the main been a pleasing one. Each oasis has its village, the houses as often scattered singly among the fields as clustered together in a group or strung out along a road; and these villages blend well into the landscape. The flat-roofed houses of sun-dried bricks echo the colour, though not the line, of the mountains; and where, on a slope, a cluster of houses is crowned by the piled-up structure of a *gompa* or monastery (as at Lamayuru), the effect can be breathtaking. Leh itself is but the largest of such villages, the houses clinging to the mountainside above the bazaar, dominated by the great bulk of the palace, while away up the ridge on the Namgyal Peak—the Peak of Victory—is the Namgyal Tsemo temple, the focus for the reverence and respect of the town's Buddhist population.

The Ladakhis themselves complete the picture. The people of central Ladakh might have been created to fit the stereotype of simple, cheerful, open, honest mountain folk. Children laugh and wave to strangers. Women smile and, in contrast to the constraints under which they live in the neighbouring predominantly Muslim countries, have an ease of manner which is by no means incompatible with real modesty. Among men and women alike, there is a conspicuous absence of status-consciousness: of any exaggerated awareness of the cleavage between the sahibs of the world and the rest. In for instance Leh bazaar, this naturalness and ease of manner are palpable; and the traveller unless he is very unlucky will find them in all his dealings with the Ladakhi people.

III
Creatures of the Wild

No exhaustive study has been done of Ladakh's wildlife, though there have been preliminary surveys. Of birds, well over a hundred species have been noted and identified, and a good many of these may be spotted by the knowledgeable visitor, while there are a few which will strike even the most ignorant.

As he crosses the Zoji-La, the traveller cannot but be aware of passing from one geo-physical environment to another; the character of the wildlife too changes accordingly. The Great Himalaya forms a dividing line between the Indian subcontinent and the rest of the Eurasian land-mass to the north; and Ladakh, in its fauna as in other respects, has more in common with Tibet, Central Asia and Mongolia than with India. However, as far as birds are concerned, migration forms a link between the Indian and the Tibetan regions. The migratory bird which the visitor is most likely to notice is the hoopoe; even more common, though less conspicuous, is the Indian redstart. Perhaps the greatest surprise among the bird life is the brownheaded gull, which is seen along the Indus in summer, and which breeds along the margins of the Star-tsapuk Tso, Chang-Thang's fresh-water lake. This too is migratory, staying from May till September, or even later, on the fringes of the Tibetan plateau to nest and breed, and returning to the coasts of India when the cold weather sets in. Other migratory birds which breed in Ladakh are the brahmini duck (ruddy shelduck), the barheaded goose, and the great crested grebe: these too make their nests in Chang-Thang, round the fresh-water inlets to the brackish lakes. At present few travellers get permission to visit these areas.

The same is true of Chushul, the region immediately adjoining the Pang-gong Lake to the west, and Hanle, south of the Indus on Ladakh's eastern border, where there are plenty of interesting birds, and which have recently been found to be the western limit of the breeding area of the Tibetan or black-necked crane, one of the rarest birds in the world. Two pairs were observed in 1976 by an expedition led by the *doyen* of Indian ornithology, Dr Sálim Ali. In 1980 there were as many as six pairs, of which one successfully reared a couple of chicks. No ornithologist visited the region in 1981, but the Army authorities reported sightings of three pairs, one of which was nesting. The Tibetan crane is a high-altitude bird, with a short migration range; but nobody knows the winter home of the pairs found in Ladakh in summer. So far this rare and endangered species seems to be holding its own, no more; sadly, its continuance in Ladakh, and indeed its survival at all, are very doubtful.

Migratory birds apart, the species found on the Tibetan plateau fall into two categories: those found in all the elevated regions of Asia, but not at lower altitudes; and those found mainly in desert regions everywhere, without regard to latitude or altitude. Examples of the first are the Tibetan crane, the Tibetan raven, the red-billed chough, the Bactrian magpie, the snow-cock, and the chukor or mountain partridge; while characteristically desert birds are the sand grouse, sand plover, desert wheatear, horned lark and twite. The most characteristic bird of Ladakh is perhaps the Bactrian magpie, a handsome fellow, whose black feathers have a greenish sheen, and who sports a white breast and wing-bands, and a long fan-like tail.

Among cosmopolitan species common to the Himalayan and Tibetan regions, and sometimes to the plains of India as well, are the ubiquitous house-sparrow, the carrion crow and the chukor. All these may be seen in and around Leh, close to human habitation—the chukor mainly in the fields—as may the Bactrian magpie, and in summer the hoopoe and the Indian redstart. The pied wagtail, a dapper black and white bird, is common near water. Birds that see the winter out, at least at the altitude of Leh, are the sparrow, the crow, the magpie and the grey tit. Flocks of hill pigeons may also be noticed well into the cold weather. They are locally migratory, and descend to lower areas of Ladakh in winter. Of the larger birds, the lammergeier or bearded vulture which is a scavenger and found near human habitations at high altitudes may be seen very occasionally. Eagles may still exist in the heights, as may Tibetan snow-cock, but sightings are rare. The only birds of prey noticed by recent expeditions are the kestrel and the buzzard, both in the far reaches of the Chang-Thang plateaux.

While the bird-watcher may find a fair amount to reward him in even the limited area of Ladakh open to visitors without restriction, the person interested in spotting animals in the wild will probably be less fortunate. In any case, he is not likely to see much unless he takes to the mountain paths and passes on foot; and even then he will regret that he could not set out on his expedition one or two hundred years earlier. For the sportsman with a gun has wrought havoc among the wildlife of Ladakh's mountains. It is true that at no time since Ladakh was discovered by the sportsman and other sahibs in the mid-nineteenth century has shooting been allowed indiscriminately. Even so, under the Maharaja's rule forty licences a year were issued and the nature of the terrain made it impossible to enforce any restriction so it is certain that a lot of poaching went on. By the Jammu and Kashmir Wildlife Protection Act of 1978 the shooting of some species is now forbidden absolutely, and of others severely limited; but enforcement agencies hardly exist and the law is certainly still honoured in the breach quite as much as in the observance. Where writers of even fifty years ago tell of fairly abundant populations of various species of wild goats and sheep and of snow-leopards, now the former are certainly much reduced in numbers, while the snow-leopard is officially on the list of endangered species, and may be heading for extinction. For this last state of affairs, the sportsman may not be entirely to blame. In the old days, when he still reigned as king of the mountains, the snow-leopard took a terrible toll of the villagers' flocks; and they, in retaliation, developed various ways of trapping and killing him.

Pashmina, the raw material of the 'cashmere' shawl, is produced from a particular kind of goat domesticated by the nomadic herdsmen of the Chang-Thang plateaux; but some of the different species of wild goat produce a similar kind of soft fine wool, from the warm under-coat which nature has provided to enable them to survive in winter; those animals which have it in sufficient quantities to make it worth the trouble and risk of collecting, have in the past been mercilessly trapped and hunted. Cunningham tells us that ibex in great numbers used to be 'snared at night and shot in the grey dawn of the morning, when they venture down to the streams to drink.' But it is the Tibetan antelope or chiru, whose local name is *stos*, which produces the wool prized above all others for shawls, known as *toosh*, or even *shahtoosh*—royal *toosh*. This surpasses pashmina to perhaps the same extent as pashmina surpasses ordinary sheep's wool. A pure *shahtoosh* shawl is actually softer than silk—and so fine that it can be passed with ease through an ordinary finger ring. Yet at the same time it is unbelievably warm. The demand for *shahtoosh*, and its enormous value in monetary terms—today the price of a plain *shahtoosh* shawl[1] runs into thousands of rupees—have led to the decimation of the Tibetan antelope population. It is even now possible to buy in Srinagar shawls claimed to be genuine *shahtoosh*, the raw material for which has come, whether legally or illegally, from Ladakh.

Ladakh's mountains and high valleys are the habitat of various species of wild sheep and wild goats, all of which have been prized by the sportsman for their magnificent horns. Best known among the goats are the ibex and the markhor (which also roams the ranges of the outer Himalaya, including the Pir Panjal). The sheep family is represented by the barhal or blue sheep, the shapu (*ovis vignei*), and the argali or *ovis ammon*, whose scientific name refers to its enormous curved horns, calling to mind Zeus Ammon, Zeus in the shape of a ram, whose shrine was in the Libyan desert and who was the tutelary deity of Alexander the Great. Shapu live on the lower hills, while the barhal frequent the higher slopes where, early this century, they could sometimes be seen in herds of fifty or a hundred. The *ovis ammon* is found much higher up near the snow-line, and the ibex favours rocky terrain. All of them tend to move down to a lower level in winter, when the shapu used to be seen right down in the fields. Of these, the only ones that most visitors today might have even a chance of seeing—and a slender enough chance at that—are the barhal and the shapu. In the last few years the army authorities in Leh have started a small zoo, which has a couple of barhal, besides wolves, marmots, Pallas's cat, an eagle-owl and other species.

The remote and lofty plateaux of Chang-Chenmo, to the north of the Pang-gong Lake, and Chang-Thang, may still be the home of small herds of the Tibetan gazelle and the Tibetan antelope. It is not known whether or not there are still a few head of wild yak, which are said to live only at altitudes above 4,500 metres, and to

[1]*Shahtoosh* shawls are never dyed or embroidered—that would be sacrilege. In spite of their drab colour they are very elegant, because they drape beautifully.

look like a larger and shaggier version of the domestic yak. Seen fairly often by those few who get permission to visit Chang-Thang are herds of kyang, the Tibetan wild ass, which are however too shy and too fleet to be approached. Though on the endangered list, this species seems to be holding its own.

Of the smaller animals, marmots are plentiful on the hill slopes, even quite close to the road, in the Dras area and elsewhere; the best time to hope for a sight of them is soon after the road opens, when they are perhaps still slightly drugged with sleep after their long hibernation. They show no alarm at the sight of vehicles, or even of people emerging from them; but anyone hoping to get a closer look will be disappointed, because for all their clumsy appearance and waddling gait, they vanish when approached, very fast and totally, into a network of burrows. There are plenty of voles and hares; the large mouse mentioned by Moorcroft may perhaps actually have been the mouse-hare.

Among the beasts of prey, wolves and foxes are fairly common, and there is a wild cat, Pallas's cat, which in captivity looks deceptively like the domestic one. Also mentioned by various authorities are the lynx, the wild dog and the brown bear, of which a few are said to exist in Dras, Suru and Zanskar. It is believed that the few remaining snow-leopards are to be found in the mountains adjoining the Suru and Nubra valleys. The snow-leopard is a magnificent beast, and it is a tragedy that his survival should be so much in doubt. But no greater a tragedy than that relating to the *ovis ammon*, the wild yak, the Tibetan antelope, the ibex, the Tibetan wild ass, the Tibetan crane, and the brown-headed gull, all of them endangered species. It is sad to reflect that even the remoteness of their mountain habitat has not preserved them from the threat of extinction.

Ladakh Past

IV
The Old Kingdom

The history of Ladakh was first researched and reconstructed by the German scholars Emil and Hermann von Schlagintweit, Karl Marx and A. H. Francke. Marx and Francke were members of the Moravian mission, and combined an academic approach to Ladakh's past with a knowledge of the country and its traditions that could only have been gained as the result of many years spent living in close and constant touch with its people. For the most part they used rock inscriptions and the records available to them in Ladakh or originating there, the main body of which, known collectively as the Ladakh Chronicle, was published with an English translation by Francke in 1926, in volume II of his *Antiquities of Indian Tibet*. He had already published in 1907 his *History of Western Tibet* in which, however, the results of his later research are missing. The weakness of Francke's work is that it relies mainly on Ladakh-centred sources, and thus gives a picture that is one-sided and sometimes misleading.

In 1977 Professor Luciano Petech, of the Istituto Italiano per il Medio ed Estremo Oriente, published his book *The Kingdom of Ladakh c. 950–1842 AD*, in which he incorporated not only the material used by Francke, but also the results of a lifetime's familiarity with the far more numerous sources of Tibetan history. In these, references to Ladakh provide a valuable corrective to the occasionally inaccurate picture given by the Chronicle. He also used Chinese and Persian texts, as well as the findings of recent research into particular subjects relating to Ladakh's past. The result is (until the evaluation of further sources known to exist but not yet subjected to critical study) the most accurate possible reconstruction of Ladakh's political history. It is on Professor Petech's work that the following sketch is for the most part based.

From the racial composition of Ladakh's people, which exhibits a blending of the Indo-Iranian and the Mongoloid, it is possible to infer waves of immigration into the country. The 'bottom' layer probably represents the Dards from further down the Indus, who are mentioned in the writings of classical authors like Megasthenes and Ptolemy. They may at an early period have colonized the whole of the country we now know as Ladakh. For the most part the original Dard way of life has been overwhelmed, in the central and eastern regions by the later dominant Tibetan race and culture, and in the west by Islam—though the Muslim Dards in the Dras area still speak a Dard dialect.[1] But down the Indus from Khaltse, in the Da-Hanu area, there exist Dard villages which have preserved a culture and a way of life that are distinct from those elsewhere in Ladakh—or anywhere else in the world. For the people of the Dard homeland, the Gilgit and Astor valleys away down river to the north-west, as well as those in Dras, have at some point embraced Islam; but here in the lower Indus portion of Ladakh are the only Buddhist Dards left in existence. And yet their Buddhism is a very different matter from the Buddhism of central and eastern Ladakh. Their customs differ markedly from those of the Tibetan-descended population of those areas; and their cosmic system, as expressed in the hymns of their triennial Bono-na festival, show distinct traces of the pre-Buddhist animistic religion known as Bon-chos.[2]

The earliest Tibetans to migrate into Ladakh may have come as nomadic herdsmen, after the fashion of those who still roam the bare upland plateaux of Ladakh, as well as over the border in Tibet; but wholesale immigration from Tibet may have waited for the establishment of, first the loose suzerainty of Tibet over the countries contiguous to it on the west—what we now know as Ladakh, and probably Baltistan too—in the eighth and ninth centuries; and more positively for the establishment of a Tibetan dynasty in Ladakh in the middle of the tenth century.

These races, and possibly others, met and mingled, and in time became blended into a new community with its own characteristics, though in central and eastern Ladakh Tibetan traits were predominant, culturally as well as racially. The process must have continued down the centuries, since Ladakh was criss-crossed by trade-routes, along which journeyed caravans composed of representatives of many of the ethnic groups of south and central

[1]See below, p. 116.   [2]See below, p. 145.

Asia. Given the slowness of travel through the mountains, and the long delays imposed by the closing of the passes in winter, some must have stayed on, and others left half-Ladakhi children behind them.

As far as political history is concerned, Ladakh as a separate entity can hardly be said to have existed before the establishment of the kingdom about AD 950. Before that it seems to have shared the fluctuating fortunes of a wider area comprising the western part of the Tibetan plateau, and the upper Indus valley at least as far down-stream as what later became known as Baltistan. In the eighth century this area was surrounded by strong and aggressive, not to say expansionist neighbours. To the south-west was the empire of Lalitaditya, greatest of the Hindu kings of Kashmir; to the east Tibet, unified the previous century by its most powerful ruler, Sron-tsan-gam-po, and gradually extending its administration westwards; and to the north China, with its first occupation of central Asia. The texts are silent as to whether parts of Ladakh fell under Lalitaditya, though it seems not unlikely; but there is evidence of the ambitions of China and Tibet clashing in the upper Indus valley, and as far down-river as Gilgit. Eventually the tide turned in favour of Tibet, with China being forced by pressure from other quarters to withdraw from central Asia; and by the middle of the eighth century a loose Tibetan suzerainty seems to have been established, which lasted probably up to the collapse of the central Tibetan monarchy in 842.

We get a glimpse of the area in the travels of Hui-Ch'ao, a Chinese pilgrim who made the journey from India to central Asia in 727. He mentions three kingdoms lying to the north-east of Kashmir, which are

under the suzerainty of the Tibetans... The country is narrow and small, and the mountains and valleys very rugged. There are monasteries and monks, and the people venerate faithfully the Three Jewels. As to the kingdom of Tibet to the East, there are no monasteries at all and Buddha's teaching is unknown; but in the [three above-mentioned] countries the population consists of Hu, therefore they are believers. (Petech, *The Kingdom of Ladakh*, p. 10)

This confirms that at this date the area which includes Ladakh was under Tibetan suzerainty; also that it was inhabited mainly by people of non-Tibetan stock (Hu meant roughly Indo-Iranian,

and could apply perfectly well to the Dards), and that they had
accepted Buddhism, as in Tibet proper at this time many people
had not.

The religion of Ladakh's earliest inhabitants was presumably
some form of the Bon-chos, more a collection of cults than a
unified religion, pantheistic and shamanistic, and perhaps including a form of ancestor-worship—with the ibex, of which
numerous rock-carvings have been found in the Kargil area and
around Khaltse, as an important religious symbol perhaps denoting fertility. It is certain that Buddhism first entered the western
parts of what is now Ladakh, not from Tibet, but from Kashmir,
perhaps as early as the first or second century AD, when there are
indications that parts of it may have been incorporated in the
Kushan empire. The Buddhist influence continued to filter in
from Kashmir, which was one of its important centres; and rock
engravings in deep relief (as opposed to the shallow relief of the
later style) found at various places in the Kargil district—Zanskar, Dras and Mulbekh—certainly belong to the pre-Tibetan
period of Buddhism. The best-known is the Bodhisattva Maitreya
(Chamba) at Mulbekh, right beside the main road; the most
recent research indicates that it, and others like it, may date from
about the eighth century. In style they are purely Indian.

At the beginning of the tenth century, we may imagine a situation in which Buddhism was flourishing in western Ladakh
(roughly the present Kargil district, and even as far as Khaltse),
and may or may not have penetrated the upper portion of the
Indus valley and points east and north, where in any case it must
have existed, if at all, side by side with the older religion. The
decline of Buddhism in north India may already have resulted in
the immigration into Ladakh of numbers of Indian Buddhist
monks, bringing their own traditions of iconography and
worship. This movement would have been only one aspect of the
close cultural and religious links between Ladakh and north-west
India—particularly Kashmir—which may have been maintained
for close on a thousand years, from the Kushan era, in the first
and second centuries AD, to the twelfth century—well into the
period of rule by an originally Tibetan dynasty.

Tibetan rule in Ladakh began as a direct result of the break-up
of the Tibetan empire in 842. Buddhism had been accepted as the
state religion of Tibet only in the reign of Sron-tsan-gam-po in

the seventh century; and even by the middle of the ninth century had not gained undisputed hold throughout the country. Indeed, the collapse of the dynasty and the disintegration of the empire were due to religious friction between Buddhists and adherents of the older Bon religion. King Lang-dar-ma, eighth in the line of succession from Sron-tsan-gam-po, abandoned the religion established by his fathers, and made every effort to root out Buddhism in favour of the Bon-Chos. After he had been murdered by a holy hermit, who could find no other way to save the faith in Tibet, the political situation became confused. It was during this prolonged period of confusion, and probably between 75 and 100 years after the assassination, that Lang-dar-ma's great-grandson Nyima-Gon, accompanied by representatives of some of the *haute noblesse* of central Tibet, migrated westwards, and established his rule, probably in the provinces immediately to the east of present-day Ladakh. The circumstances in which the migration took place are unclear, but may be assumed to reflect a power-struggle among the Tibetan aristocracy going on in the political vacuum left by the collapse of the dynasty. Whatever political intrigues and manoeuvrings may have been involved, the fact remains that Nyima-Gon, the founder of the Ladakh dynasty, was at the same time a legitimate representative of the ancient Tibetan royal house, the line of Sron-tsan-gam-po.

The Chronicle indicates that Nyima-Gon's kingdom had its centre well to the east of present-day Ladakh; and though he allotted to the eldest son, Pal-gyi-Gon, the area from the Zoji-La roughly to the present eastern border—approximately the area we think of as Ladakh today, minus the province of Zanskar— this seems to have implied what Petech calls a theoretical right of sovereignty, the actual conquest being left to Pal-gyi-Gon. The Chronicle tells us that at this time Upper Ladakh was ruled by the descendants of the mythical hero Kesar (who probably had their capital at Shey); and Lower Ladakh was divided into a number of small independent principalities. The whole area had broken free of whatever dependence on Tibet had been implied in the earlier loose suzerainty, and may still have been inhabited mainly by the original Dard colonizers. Whatever Tibetanization had taken place as a result of the earlier political relationship was now to be reinforced and confirmed by an immigrant ruling class, eventually making of Ladakh a country inhabited by a mixed population, the predominant racial strain of which was Tibetan, speaking a form of Tibetan, and, while politically independent, subordinate to Tibet in religion, and the culture that is dependent on religion.

In the first two centuries or so after the conquest, however, the kings of Nyima-Gon's dynasty, intent on establishing Buddhism in their new dominions, looked not to Tibet, where there were not yet any old-established Buddhist traditions, but to north-west India, particularly to Kashmir. To the import of Indian Buddhist traditions into the kingdoms of western Tibet, and their establishment there, Tibetan historians have given the name of the 'second spreading' of Buddhism. (The 'first spreading', in Tibet proper, of which the Indian sage Padmasambhava was the leading figure, came to an end with the events of AD 842.) The principal surviving monument in Ladakh to the second spreading is the monastery of Alchi, seventy kilometres down the Indus from Leh, opposite the village of Saspol. Here is an astonishingly well-preserved series of wall-paintings, dating from the eleventh or twelfth century, in a style that owes nothing to Tibet, but is entirely Indian; thus Alchi provides one of the best opportunities to study the Indian influence on the iconography and religious architecture of this period. Nothing like the Alchi murals survives in Kashmir, where successive waves of Muslim invasion have obliterated all traces of the pre-existing Buddhist culture. But they have their counterpart in the *gompas* of Spiti, once part of Guge, the country allotted to Nyima-Gon's middle son; and some observers have detected a resemblance, in spirit if not in detail, to the wall-paintings of far-off Ajanta. Without any shadow of doubt they are Indian in inspiration, and perhaps in execution too; they have nothing in common, stylistically, with the Tibet-derived forms of the images and paintings in the later *gompas*.

It was not indeed the kings of Ladakh, but the representatives of one of the junior lines of Nyima-Gon's dynasty, who seem to have initiated and been most active in the second spreading. The ruler who contributed most was a grandson of Nyima-Gon—king Yesh-es-od of Guge. Guge was the area to the south-east of Ladakh and north-west of Lake Manasarowar; but owing to the failure of one of the two cadet lines of Nyima-Gon's family, Yesh-es-od seems to have ruled over Zanskar, Spiti and Kinnaur as well as Guge proper. His name is associated with two great scholars and missionaries, Rin-chen-zang-po and Atisa. Rin-chen-zang-po was one of a number of young scholars sent by Yesh-es-od to Kashmir and other Buddhist centres in north India to study and absorb the traditions of Indian Buddhism, iconographic as well as strictly religious, and then come back to western Tibet to propagate them. As far as the kingdoms of western Tibet are concerned, he may be regarded as the single most influential agent of the second spreading; he is honoured with the title of *Lotsawa,* translator, which gives a clear enough pointer to the nature of his achievement. Tradition connects his name with a number of monasteries in Kinnaur and Spiti, the greatest of which is at the village of Tabo; in Ladakh there are the remains of foundations dating from Rinchen-zang-po's time or soon after (the eleventh and twelfth centuries) at Chigtan in the Kargil district, at Lamayuru, and at Nyarma and Basgo in the Indus valley, as well as at Alchi. Of all these, only Tabo and Nyarma, which is not far from Tikse, and is now a collection of ruins, are definitely attributed to Rin-chen; but it is reasonable to suppose that others of a like period came into existence, if not with his direct participation, then at least under his inspiration. Alchi was founded by a member of one of the Tibetan noble families that had accompanied Nyima-Gon on his westward migration; he had studied at Nyarma, and thus Rin-chen's influence can be traced at least at second hand.

Yesh-es-od's association with the great Buddhist teacher from eastern India, Atisa, had a less immediate impact on western Tibet, but was the direct cause of almost revolutionary developments in Buddhism as practised in Tibet as a whole, and hence, in the long run, in western Tibet too. For it was a result of persistent invitations from Yesh-es-od, though not until the reign of his successor Chang-chub-od, that Atisa left the famous monastery of Vikramasila to travel, first to western Tibet, and thence to central Tibet, where he spent the last twelve years of his life. And it was as a result of Atisa's mission that the Vajrayana form of Mahayana Buddhism, with its esoteric and mystical aspects, including forms of the Tantra, was introduced into Tibet, where it quickly became the accepted form of the religion. Atisa also founded the Ka-dam-pa monastic order, precursor of the later important Ge-lugs-pa. He spent two years at Tholding, then the capital of Guge, where, on his first arrival, the only monk who did not rise to his feet in respectful greeting was the aged Rin-chen-

zang-po, who must have felt his nose badly out of joint. The
story goes that eventually even he was conquered by Atisa's
intellectual brilliance, and ended up sitting at his feet.

About the earliest kings of Nyima-Gon's dynasty, little is known
beyond their names. The statement in the Chronicle that the line
of descent was unbroken from father to son is open to question,
because one of the kings, fifth in the line from Pal-gyi-Gon, has a
Sanskrit name, Utpala, which may—though it is by no means
certain—indicate an intrusion. Chronology is doubtful; but at
about the same time as Utpala may have reigned, Aryan-speaking
tribes overran Guge and other parts of western Tibet, founding
new dynasties; Utpala himself is mentioned as an aggressive king,
conquering Kulu, Mustang, the province of Purans between Mustang and Guge, and parts of Baltistan. The inclusion of Guge is
probably meant to be assumed. The exact nature of a connection
between Hindu encroachments known to have taken place
around the same time in western Tibet, and the conquests of
Utpala, has not been established. At all events, in Guge the dominant Tibetan culture reasserted itself; and if indeed an intrusion
took place in Ladakh too, the same must have happened, either by
the return of the original dynasty, or by the complete Tibetanization of the hypothetical Hindu one.

Apart from Utpala's conquests and some records of castle-
building, the few achievements the Chronicle mentions in this
early period are all in the field of religion: the foundation of
Likir monastery; the copying of lamaist treatises in gold—the first
record of the introduction of Tibetan Buddhist literature into
Ladakh; and introduction of the system of sending novices to
central Tibet to complete their monastic training. In these two
events we have—perhaps 150–200 years after Yesh-es-od—the
first indications that Ladakhi Buddhists were looking to central
Tibet rather than to India for their inspiration. Lha-chen Ngorub, the king in whose reign we hear of the novices being sent to
Tibet, is the first ruler whose period is established from an independent source. He sponsored, along with the kings of Guge and
Purans, the building of a monastery near holy Mount Kailash by
the newly founded Dri-gung-pa monastic sect, in 1215. This, the
beginning of the thirteenth century, would correspond with the
period at which, from the Buddhist point of view, India was

ceasing to have anything to offer. Kashmir was falling into political turmoil; gradually Buddhism was being eradicated throughout India, in face of the advance of militant Hinduism; and from the north-west the first ominous rumblings of the Islamic onslaught were making themselves heard. For reasons which may for ever elude satisfactory explanation, Ladakh, deprived of the inspiration of Indian Buddhism, chose to seek and accept guidance in religious matters from Tibet, thus setting in train the process by which it was to become part of the Tibetan religious and cultural empire, rather than to develop its own distinctively Ladakhi form of Buddhism.

The chronology of the kings after Ngorub is uncertain, because the number of names mentioned before the next reliable chronological cross-reference is far too small to fill the known lapse of time, and so we must assume some names missing—faded from popular memory, perhaps, and thus lost to the later compilers of the Chronicle. In any case, the achievements of even those kings mentioned are confined, as far as the record goes, to some building activity; the period from the early thirteenth century to the early fifteenth century is for us virtually a blank.

However, as a sidelight it has been suggested that by a curious quirk of history it may have been a Ladakhi prince, Rinchen— billed in the Chronicle as Ngorub's son, but, if we assume that some kingly names are missing, more probably his great-, or even great-great-grand-son—who became the first of the Muslim kings of Kashmir. Certainly at some point during this blank period in Ladakhi history, during which a prince Rinchen (the title *Gyal-bu* used of him may indicate that, though a king's son, he never ascended the throne) receives a bare mention in the Chronicle, there appears in Kashmir an adventurer known as Rainchan Shah, or alternatively Rainchan Bhoti (Rainchan the Tibetan), who took advantage of the political vacuum there to gain power and have himself proclaimed king. He must have been a man of outstanding energy, great ambition and few scruples; for part of his method was to marry the daughter of the commander-in-chief of the nominal king, and later to murder his father-in-law. His Buddhism was not at this date, the first half of the fourteenth century, acceptable in Kashmir; and since he was not eligible to be accepted into any caste of Hinduism, he embraced Islam. The cynicism of his conversion is masked by stories of his devotion to his spiritual mentor, one Bulbul Shah, the sight of whose worship is said to have inspired in Rainchan the conviction that Islam was the true religion. Be that as it may, taking the name of Sadr-ud-din, he seems to have restored some kind of order in Kashmir, and is highly praised in the second Kashmir chronicle, the *Rajatarangini* of Pandit Jonaraja. The story ends in anticlimax, however, as he died of natural causes after a reign of only two and a half years.

A piquant enough tale as it stands, it gains by the identification of Rainchan Shah with Gyal-bu Rinchen. This can only be conjectural, and is disputed by Professor Petech on chronological grounds. But the similarity of the names, and the possible coincidence in time (admittedly achieved only after a little juggling with the insufficient data on this period provided by the Chronicle) make it a conjecture which, as well as being attractive, need not be dismissed as totally implausible. Before bowing out of Ladakh history, Gyal-bu Rinchen appears to have done his duty to his line by producing an heir, for the next king is mentioned as being his son.

The history of old Ladakh may be conveniently divided into 'earlier' and 'later' periods, the divide coming in the early fifteenth century. From this time, though even now some gaps remain, there is enough source material to give us a much clearer picture of events than is possible for the earlier period. The Chronicle itself begins to give fuller details, and in addition we have an increasing number of Tibetan sources, as well as the histories by Muslim chroniclers of the neighbouring countries where Islam was beginning to make inroads.

The Muslim conquests of Kashmir and central Asia meant that Ladakh was now partly surrounded by countries representing this new, aggressive and potentially hostile force. The first Muslim invasion was a raid, probably in the reign of king Trags-bum-de, and probably in the 1420s, led soon after his accession by the great sultan of Kashmir, Zain-ul-Abidin. It seems that, in search presumably of plunder and tribute, he penetrated into western Tibet as far as Guge. For nearly two centuries after this, till about 1600, Ladakh was subject to raids and invasions from Kashmir, central Asia, and latterly Baltistan, which was converted to Islam at some time during this period, though at exactly what time and in what circumstances it has not been recorded. A complicating factor for central Ladakh was the partial conversion, towards the end of this period, of Purig, the area around Kargil comprising the Suru Valley, Pashkyum, Mulbekh, Bodh Kharbu and Shagkar Chigtan, which consisted at the time of a number of small princi- palities bound in a loose quasi-feudal relationship to the Ladakhi monarchy. Central Ladakh itself seems in the end to have had a daunting effect on the invaders who, discouraged perhaps by the harshness of the climate or the difficulty of the terrain, seem never to have flung on it the full fury of the *jehad*. For the population of central Ladakh remained true to the ancient faith; and it is inconceivable that, if at any point they had been subjected to sustained pressure from the sword of Islam, and resisted it, there should be no memory of what would have been a traumatic experience, either in the Chronicle, or in popular tradition.

The early fifteenth century sees the arrival in Ladakh of the reformed monastic order of the Ge-lugs-pa or 'yellow hats', founded by the Tibetan master Tson-ka-pa (1357–1419). Envoys despatched by him to Ladakh were welcomed by king Trags- bum-de, at whose command the first Ge-lugs-pa monastery was founded, at Spituk, eight kilometres down the Indus from Leh; 'though', the Chronicle adds, 'in reality he did not build it, but it came into existence by a miracle.' (This remark has been added by the monkish chroniclers to their accounts of the foundation of several of the *gompas*.) From now on we see the strenghening of institutional links with central Tibet already established in the reign of king Ngorub, who introduced the system of having lamas complete their studies in the various monasteries there. Thus most of the *gompas* that exist today were founded at diffe- rent times after this as representatives of one or the other order of monks already established in Tibet.

At the beginning of this period we find two kingdoms in Ladakh, one centred on Leh and Shey, the other down the river with its capitals at Basgo and Tingmosgang. The two kings seem to have been brothers who had thus divided the kingdom between them; it has been assumed that legitimacy lay with the Shey line of king Trags-bum-de. Nevertheless it was Bhagan, a grandson of the Basgo king, who reunited the country by deposing the repre- sentative of the Shey line; and though this palace revolution did not mean any break in the direct line of descent from father to son, Bhagan is regarded as the founder of a new dynasty, the second and last to rule Ladakh, which took the surname of Namgyal, Victorious.

At this point we run into another chronological difficulty. Bhagan deposed Trags-bum-de's son, whom we know to have reigned in the middle of the fifteenth century; but Bhagan's son is given in the Chronicle as Tashi Namgyal, and Tashi's reign has been established from independent sources as taking place in the third quarter of the sixteenth century. Again we must assume some names omitted from the Chronicle, either through a straighforward lapse of popular memory and tradition, or on purpose to eradicate the memory of events felt to be best forgotten. Since in the Chronicle every event is related to the reign of a particular king, the omission of several names implies silence on the events that may have taken place during the period of their rule. However, in this case the gap is somewhat filled by references to Ladakh in the memoirs of Mirza Haidar Daughlat, an adventurer from central Asia who first invaded Ladakh in 1532. He penetrated as far south and west as the Suru Valley; parts of the country apparently came under him, for he mentions a rebellion against his officers in Nubra in 1535. The Ladakhi king, whoever he may have been, seems to have reached an agreement with the invader, for Haidar used Ladakh as a base for an invasion of Tibet about 1533. He was forced to retreat when within eight days' march of Lhasa by the difficult terrain and the bitter cold; he stayed for two more years in Ladakh, making his headquarters at Shey, before pulling out in 1536. Further raids followed in 1545 and 1548; on the latter occasion a nominal administration in Mirza Haidar's name was set up, but it did not survive his death in 1551. It may be that temporary domination by a Muslim power was reason enough for the compilers of the Chronicle—a work of piety as far as they were concerned, rather than of history as we think of it—to keep silence on this period.

There are some indications that at this time, as in the reigns of Trags-bum-de and his brother, the country was again divided into Upper and Lower Ladakh; but the reign of Tashi Namgyal (approximately 1555–75) sees it not only reunified but, if the Chronicle is to be believed, in an expansionist phase, with Purig brought firmly to heel, and a temporary suzerainty established over Guge. That Tashi was an energetic and ruthless king is evident from the story of his accession. He was the younger of two brothers; and excluded his elder brother from the throne by having his eyes put out. But the qualities that brought him to power, morally however reprehensible, were not without value to his government for he obviously strengthened his weak and previously divided kingdom, which cannot but have suffered some demoralization after the sporadic occupation of Muslim forces under Mirza Haidar. The Chronicle tells us that he repelled yet another invasion of Muslims from central Asia, and, having erected a temple dedicated to the guardian deities on the Namgyal Tsemo Hill overlooking Leh, he placed the bodies of some of the defeated enemy under the images of the Lords of the Four Quarters. The last of a series of not very effective attempts at invasion from Kashmir also took place about this time.

A special interest attaches to Tashi Namgyal, as being the first king of Ladakh whose portrait is extant. It is part of a court scene, on a tiny scale beside the huge representations of the Guardians, which adorns one wall of his Temple of the Guardian Deities on Namgyal Tsemo peak. This temple is part of a complex, including a fort, probably the whole of which was built by Tashi; it is the first recorded royal residence at Leh. Tashi was also responsible for the monastery at Phiyang, about fifteen kilometres to the west.

Tashi Namgyal died childless, and was succeeded by Tshewang Namgyal, the eldest son of his blinded brother. He seems to have been an energetic and able king, for he is said to have extended his rule eastwards as far as Mustang, south over Kulu, and west over Baltistan, which at that time may have included Gilgit, and even far-off Chitral. He planned to go to war against the Muslim kingdoms of central Asia, but desisted in the face of representations from the people of Nubra that war on the northern border would seriously damage the transit trade on which they were dependent. These conquests, if indeed they were such and not simply raids for plunder and tribute, must have lasted for only a very short time. Tshe-wang maintained and added to the royal residence at Basgo, where he ordered the building of the Maitreya Temple which still stands.

Tshe-wang Namgyal was succeeded by his brother Jamyang Namgyal. It must have been during his reign, in the very last years of the sixteenth century, that the first recorded visit of a European to Ladakh took place. This was a merchant from Portugal,

Diogo d'Almeida, and he stayed for two years. He found the
capital at Basgo; and strangely enough he described Ladakh as a
rich country. The presence of this enterprising Portuguese testifies to the importance of trade in the life of Ladakh, at this time as
always.

Of greater consequence, there occurred at this time, probably
about the year 1600, the most determined attempt on the part of a
Muslim power to bring Ladakh under the sway of Islam. Jamyang
intervened in a quarrel between the chiefs of Chigtan and Kar-
tse—sultans, as they now styled themselves, having recently
embraced Islam. He assembled an army to go to the aid of the
sultan of Chigtan; but it may be that the whole situation was an
elaborate plot on the part of a cabal of Muslim rulers, for no
sooner had Jamyang crossed the Fatu-La than he was confronted
by the forces of Baltistan under the ruler of Skardo, Ali Mir. The
Baltis outmanoeuvred the Ladakhi army at every turn, and overran the whole of Ladakh, plundering its riches and destroying its
religious treasures with iconoclastic zeal. (Thus, apart from Alchi,
probably as early as this time abandoned as a religious centre, and
a few others in remote villages in the mountains, the *gompa*
buildings and their treasures that we see today all date from after
this period.) Jamyang was taken prisoner to Skardo; and it must
have seemed that Buddhism was about to suffer the same eclipse
in Ladakh as it had in the neighbouring countries to the west and
north. However, for reasons which the passage of time has
obscured, the Baltis withdrew, and Jamyang was restored to his
throne, though only on condition of marrying one of Ali Mir's
daughters,[3] and disinheriting the sons of his previous marriage in
favour of any children of this one. (Needless to say, popular
tradition backed up by the Chronicle, has invested this episode
with a romantic gloss, involving an affair of the heart between
Jamyang and the Balti princess, Gyal Katun, a secret marriage or
perhaps an illicit pregnancy, and a dream in which her father saw
a lion jump out of the river and enter her body: 'at that very time
Gyal Katun conceived'.)[4] If this was intended as an expedient to

[3]Another of Ali Mir's daughters was married to prince Salim, heir-apparent to
Akbar, later the Emperor Jahangir. Though she shared her position with several
other princesses, this shows that Ali Mir must have been a ruler of more than local
importance.
[4]See below, p. 148, for a ballad on the birth of Sengge Namgyal.

insinuate Islam into Ladakh peacefully from the top, it was singularly unsuccessful. The Ladakhis reconciled themselves to their new queen by recognizing in her an incarnation of the Buddhist goddess, the White Tara—an ingenious way of turning the tables on the monotheists; and indeed the foreign genes seem to have infused new vigour into this rather undistinguished branch of the Namgyal family.

The Muslim connection notwithstanding, both Jamyang and his son Sengge Namgyal—Sengge means lion, and the name is related to his grandfather's dream; the lion king was to become the most famous of Ladakh's rulers—were convinced Buddhists, and adopted policies towards the strengthening of Buddhism. Jamyang is said to have relieved his Buddhist subjects of taxation, and to have ordered the copying of a number of holy books, and Sengge carried on the work, though it was impossible to repair all the ravages of the Balti invasion. Jamyang issued an invitation to the famous Tibetan priest, Stag-tsang-ras-pa, to visit Ladakh, but it was not taken up until well into Sengge's reign, when lama and king came to be thought of as a pair, adding to the glory of Ladakh, one in the religious and the other in the secular sphere.

Sengge Namgyal probably ascended the throne about 1616 as a minor, his mother acting as regent. In the early years of his reign, his authority faced a challenge from his younger brother Norbu Namgyal, who even seems to have succeeded in wresting the throne from him for a year or two before his own premature death. During this time Sengge, promising to devote himself to religion, retired to the distant village of Hanle where, under Stag-tsang-ras-pa's guidance, he built one of the biggest and most famous of Ladakh's monasteries, the first to be attached to the Drug-pa, one of the old 'red-hat' sects to which Stag-tsang-ras-pa belonged and which, under the patronage of the Namgyal family, was to assume such importance in Ladakh as to become a serious rival to the reformed Ge-lugs-pa.

After disposing of this threat to his power, Sengge, determined perhaps to restore the glory of his country and his dynasty, tarnished as it was by the events of his father's reign, resumed the expansionist activities of his uncle Tshe-wang Namgyal, and enlarged the Ladakhi empire to its greatest extent. He did not let his genuine devotion to Buddhism interfere with his *realpolitik*, but found excuses to go to war to annex the ancient vassal kingdoms of Zanskar and Guge, by now independent countries. His conquest of Guge, recorded in the Chronicle and in the biography of Stag-tsang-ras-pa—which is a more reliable source for the events of this reign than the Chronicle—is confirmed by the evidence of the Jesuits who had, improbably enough, opened a mission in 1626 at Tsaparang, the capital of Guge. Antonio de Andrade the founder and for two or three years the head of the mission, described in detail the background and actual events of the Ladakhi conquest, which took place in 1630; indeed it was this which, depriving the Jesuits of the support extended by their patron the king of Guge, brought their activities in Tsaparang to an end.[5] The Guge king was carried off into honourable exile in Ladakh; Guge was later handed over to a younger son of Sengge Namgyal.

Against the Muslim powers to the west Sengge seems to have had less success. He marched to Purig, with the idea of regaining the provinces lost by his father, and the Chronicle records a sweeping victory over a combined Mughal–Balti army at Bodh Kharbu. But Stag-tsang-ras-pa's biography passes over the event in discreet silence; according to Mughal records, the Ladakhis were defeated, and Sengge had to sue for peace on the promise— never fulfilled—of paying tribute to the Mughal empire through the governor of Kashmir. These events took place in 1639, and mark the beginning of the Mughal claim to suzerainty over Ladakh. According to the French traveller Francois Bernier, Sengge, in his pique at this defeat, closed the trade route from Kashmir, and forbade any person to enter his dominion from that direction, the embargo lasting up to the time of Bernier's visit in 1663. Bernier is our only source for this; but he has no axe to grind, and the way he puts it—laying emphasis on the traffic that used to cross Ladakh before the blockade was imposed—carries conviction. If he is to be believed, this was an act of incredible folly: a classic example of cutting off the nose to spite the face. It surely indicates a total failure to grasp economic realities, for to close any one important route obviously cost Ladakh its position at the centre of a network of routes, and so a large part of its revenue. Indeed, the decline in Ladakh's fortunes that set in after his death in 1642 may reasonably be attributed to the 'economic suicide' (in Professor Petech's phrase) committed by Sengge Namgyal.

[5]See Appendix I: The Jesuits in Western Tibet.

Apart from his actual and supposed military successes, Sengge Namgyal is best remembered for his association with Stag-tsang-ras-pa, and the various monasteries that were founded by the latter under his patronage. Hanle was the first of these; the other great foundation was Hemis, to this day the best known and reputedly the richest of all the Ladakh *gompas*. Chemrey, usually attributed to Sengge, was actually erected after his death as a funeral act of merit. As well as the monasteries, Sengge's reign saw religious life in Ladakh enriched by a number of *mani* walls—which may have been introduced by Stag-tsang-ras-pa—and statues, including the gigantic Buddha-image in the temple at Shey; while every few years religious missions to Tibet carried rich offerings in the form of gold, silver, turquoises and precious stuffs.

Sengge Namgyal left a permanent imprint on Leh, in the shape of the nine-storey palace which dominates the town. It is not mentioned in the account of Leh written by the Jesuit Father Francisco de Azevedo who visited it in 1631, and was in fact impressed by the meanness of the surroundings in which he found the king;[6] so it seems likely that it was built in the last years of the reign. The construction of the palace may be taken to reflect the growing importance of Leh, vis-à-vis the ancient capital of Shey. For it may have been about now that Leh, conveniently situated on the approach to the Khardung-La, the main summer route to Yarkand, began to assume importance as a trading centre. In earlier years when perhaps conditions were more unsettled than the Chronicle and other sources actually indicate, Shey, which has a magnificent strategic position, would have been the obvious choice for the capital, and the same might hold good for the period of the Muslim invasions. The shift in the balance of importance towards Leh may perhaps have been the outcome of a more peaceful atmosphere, in which mercantile considerations took precedence over strategic ones—and which, ironically, might have given Sengge the idea of using his power to cut the trade routes as a political weapon against Kashmir. In spite of the memory of the Balti invasion only a very short time before Sengge's birth, it may be that his vigorous personality, and his achievements at home and abroad before the disaster at Bodh Kharbu, which happened only three years before his death, imparted a sense of security and self-confidence to the Ladakh polity, one

[6]Ibid.

result of which was the development of mercantile Leh at the expense of embattled Shey.

Sengge Namgyal died at Hanle in 1642, on his way back from an expedition against the Mongol occupiers of Tsang, the Tibetan province adjoining Guge to the north-east, who were making threatening moves against Ladakh. He cannot have been much more than forty. After his death there was an interregnum, during which his widow, Skalzang Dolma, a princess from the uplands of Rupshu, acted as regent for sons who must still have been minors. In 1647 a partition was effected in which Ladakh proper went to the eldest son, Deldan Namgyal; Guge to the middle one, a lama known only by his religious name, Indrabodhi Namgyal; and Spiti and Zanskar to the youngest, Demchog Namgyal. Deldan's reign lasted till 1694, and embraced that of his son, Delegs Namgyal, who may never in fact have enjoyed full kingly status. The custom of the Ladakhi and other Tibetan dynasties was that the heir-apparent, on reaching years of discretion, should be associated with the work of government, so that in many cases two reigns seem to overlap. Often the king, if he reached old age and saw his son in his prime, would abdicate in the latter's favour. By this admirable system gerontocracy was avoided, and the ruler, except in the case of premature death, as happened with Delegs, would normally have youth and vigour on his side.[7]

Fifteen years after his accession, Deldan faced a major problem—that of relations with Kashmir, and through Kashmir with Mughal India. Sengge Namgyal's defeat at Bodh Kharbu and his unfulfilled promise of tribute (implying acceptance of vassal status, however reluctant) had left an entirely inconclusive situation, which the Mughal as would-be suzerain could not be expected to tolerate indefinitely. The matter was brought to the notice of Aurangzeb when he visited Kashmir in 1663; on that occasion Deldan renewed his father's promises of tribute and loyalty, and added that he would build a mosque, and have the *khutba*, the prayer for the secular authority, recited and coins struck in the name of the Emperor. This promise too looked like remaining a dead letter, until a couple of years later its fulfilment was partly enforced by a show of military might on the border with Kashmir, backed by support from the Emperor's loyal vassal, the chief of Skardo. From this time, 1666–7, dates the erection of the mosque

[7]See below p. 120, for the analogous social custom of *khang-bu*.

in Leh, the first in central Ladakh. The added pledge to encourage Islam in Ladakh was certainly not taken seriously, nor does it seem that the tribute was paid regularly, or at all. However, further exchanges with Aurangzeb showed that whatever reservations the Ladakhi king may have had, the Emperor regarded him as his vassal. Although it is not mentioned in the texts, it may be assumed that one result of Deldan's negotiations with Aurangzeb was the lifting of Ladakh's suicidal trade embargo against Kashmir.

His relationship with Aurangzeb, reluctantly accepted as it was, did not inhibit Deldan from adopting a forward policy to the west, with the primary object of regaining the lost province of Purig though such a policy was bound to bring him into conflict with his fellow-vassal, the Emperor's watch-dog, the ruler of Skardo. A force marched to western Ladakh in 1673, and was apparently successful in subduing the Purig principalities of Heniskot, Stag-tse, Chigtan and Kar-tse. Elated by this success, Deldan turned his attention to Baltistan, and the following year sent in an army whose success enabled him to instal puppet rulers in three of its principalities. This was overreaching himself; and a Mughal army arrived from Kashmir, numbering according to the Chronicle about 200,000 men; this too was roundly defeated. For these events we have only the word of the Chronicle, supported by a document of the following reign but uncorroborated by any non-Ladakhi source. There is probably a substratum of fact in their story, but some statements are obviously wild, like the Ladakhis defeating a Mughal army of 200,000; and the story of the unbroken success of Ladakhi arms need not be taken literally. However, it does seem that at about this time Purig was brought back within the orbit of Ladakh.

With his powerful neighbour to the east, Tibet, Ladakh's elder brother in terms of religion and culture, Deldan's relations were not happy. As a result of the influence of Stag-tsang-ras-pa, the Drug-pa monastic sect had become predominant in Ladakh, and enjoyed the special patronage of the royal family. At more or less the same time in Tibet, the reformed Ge-lugs-pa sect achieved political as well as religious dominance under the fifth Dalai Lama, supported by the tribe of Oelot Mongols. There did exist an agreement between Deldan and the Tibetan authorities that, on a reciprocal basis, the Drug-pa should be well treated in Tibet and the Ge-lugs-pa in Ladakh. But mutual suspicions remained, and it is possible that Deldan's acceptance, however unwilling, of Mughal suzerainty contributed to the worsening of his relations with Tibet.

This was the background to the quarrel that broke out between the two countries in the late 1670s. Tibet went to war with Bhutan, another stronghold of the Drug-pa; and though Bhutan proved perfectly capable of looking after itself, defeating the Tibetan army and sending it back in disarray, Deldan thought fit to send a letter to Tibet, taking up the cudgels on Bhutan's behalf. This perfectly uncalled-for intervention provoked a strong reaction on the part of the Dalai Lama, who evidently thought that he might as well profit by the occasion to bring this troublesome ruler to heel. In 1679 a small expeditionary force marched west, composed mainly of cavalry from Mongolia's steppes, and met the Ladakhi advance guard in some inconclusive skirmishes in different parts of Guge. The Ladakhi forces entrenched themselves in various fortresses, but retreated before the main Tibetan army which arrived in the summer of 1680. The Ladakhis were decisively defeated in a battle on the approaches to the Chang-La; the king and his general fled the field, and the Tibetans continued their westward march without resistance, until they came upon the remnants of the Ladakhi army blocking their advance at the defile of Basgo. Basgo is obviously a superb defensive position against attack from the east, with the road down the Indus forced to leave the line of the river and climb steeply up on to the neighbouring plateau; and, as their ruins still testify, the fortifications must have been nearly impregnable. They are also said to have had a perennial water supply. There the invaders were held for three years, and finally repulsed only when a relief army advanced from Kashmir in response to an appeal from Deldan.

But this timely help was not given gratis. The Kashmir army, now in occupation, agreed to withdraw only on conditions that confirmed Deldan's half-hearted acceptance of Mughal suzerainty nearly twenty years earlier. The tribute, long promised but apparently never paid, was exactly laid down as 18 piebald horses, 18 pods of musk and 18 white yak tails every three years; while in return 500 bags of rice were to come annually from an estate granted to the king in Kashmir. Deldan himself was obliged to accept Islam, which he did under the name of Aqibat Mahmud

Khan—by which name the Mughal and Kashmir authorities continued to address the kings of Ladakh; and one of his sons was sent to Kashmir, as a hostage and to be brought up a Muslim. The most substantial concession was that which gave Kashmir a monopoly of the purchase of raw pashmina, Ladakh's only product of any value, as well as of other kinds of wool.

Deldan's conversion has understandably been played down in Ladakh, and is not mentioned in the Chronicle. But it seems certain that in order to satisfy his new creditors he made at least a formal confession of faith, though no doubt as far as he personally was concerned it did not go beyond a form of words. However, though Islam continued the gradual advance from the west it had begun earlier, this further attempt to make Ladakh a Muslim country ruled by a Muslim dynasty was as unsuccessful as previous ones had been. The royal house, and the overwhelming majority of the people in the Indus valley, Ladakh's heartland, as well as points east, remained faithful to Buddhism. The Muslims found in those regions today are the descendants of immigrants, not of converts.

There still remained the Tibetans to be reckoned with. They had been repulsed, by no means annihilated, and had regrouped at Tashi-Gang, away up the Indus. Naturally when news of Deldan's acceptance of Islam reached Lhasa, it caused much consternation. The regent ruling Tibet after the death of the fifth Dalai Lama sent as emissary to Ladakh the supreme lama of the Drug-pa sect, who met the king at Tingmosgang, a royal residence near Khaltse, north of the present motor road. Deldan was in no position to dictate terms. By the Treaty of Tingmosgang (1684) the boundary between the two countries was fixed where we find it today, bisecting the Pang-Gong Lake, and thus Nyima-Gon's ancient province of Guge, reconquered by Sengge Namgyal, was lost for ever. Not exactly tribute, but presents for the religious establishment of Tibet were to go every three years from Ladakh; and the Namgyal family's bias in favour of the Drug-pa sect was to be balanced by encouragement to the Ge-lugs-pa. On the other hand, Ladakh got certain concessions in respect of the trade in tea; and while Kashmiri merchants were to be settled at Spituk for the purchase of the entire output of raw pashmina and coarse wool to send to Kashmir, this was to be drawn not only from Chang-Thang, the far south-eastern uplands of Ladakh

proper, but also from Rudok and other points east of the frontier,
to which none but Ladakhi merchants might be admitted. Ladakh
was to occupy a front-line position as between Buddhist and
non-Buddhist countries, and its king 'out of regard for the doc-
trine of Buddha must not allow an army from India to proceed to
an attack on Tibet.' (Future events were to show that Tibet possessed, in its climate, and in the fighting qualities of its people, much
more effective means of defence against attack from north-west
India than anything that the Ladakhis could offer).

　　These events, which put an end to Ladakh's independence in
the real sense—though the appearance of it lingered on for
another 150 years—demonstrate the extent to which the glories
of Sengge Namgyal's reign had been purchased at the expense of
the real interests of the country. Its failure to resist invasion by a
force whose numbers were far from overwhelming—about
5,000—is attributed to the economic weakness caused by Sengge's extravagant programmes of building monasteries, *mani* walls
and palaces, and of sending expensive religious missions to Tibet.
Impoverishment was completed by his closure of the Kashmir
trade route from 1639 to 1663, which must have played havoc
with the economy. In this weakened condition Ladakh was ready
to be toppled at a mere push; the tragedy is that the *casus belli* with
Tibet, its natural ally, with which it shared so much in terms of
race, language, religion and culture, was such an unnecessary
one, especially to be taken up at a time when the country did not
have the strength to withstand invasion. It is ironic that what
saved Ladakh from total collapse, with incalculable consequences, was Deldan's earlier unwilling and half-hearted acceptance
of Mughal suzerainty which alone, it may be supposed, enabled
him to appeal successfully to Kashmir for help.

　　From now on Ladakh was to occupy an ambivalent position
between Buddhist Tibet and Muslim Kashmir. In terms of religion and religious culture, the ties with Tibet remained para-
mount. The old institutional links between the monasteries of the
two countries remained as strong as ever; and the existing trade
ties were reinforced by the annual government caravan coming
from Lhasa, carrying mainly tea (from which it came to be popu-
larly known as the *cha-pa* caravan), and the triennial mission of
religious tribute going from Ladakh to Lhasa. As time went on, in
accordance with the commercial genius of all the Tibetan peoples,

this religious mission too, the *Lo-pchak* mission, became primarily an affair of trade: although it would be headed by a high lama, its management was in the hands of Ladakhi Muslim merchants.

Politically, the evidence of decline is clear. Although neither of the two suzerain powers—as Tibet and Kashmir had in effect become—interfered in its internal affairs, except Tibet on one occasion, freedom of action outside its boundaries was severely restricted, and we read no more in the Chronicle of the wars of conquest by which the earlier kings sought glory and the extension of their power. Ladakh's only extra-territorial activity seems to have been on the Baltistan border, where a series of skirmishes took place arising, it seems, out of a marriage alliance between the Ladakhi royal house and the rulers of the Balti principality of Khapalu, so that in any quarrel between Khapalu and the other Balti states, Ladakh felt obliged to intervene. These encounters are recorded almost exclusively in Ladakhi sources and, according to them, resulted in an unbroken run of successes for Ladakhi arms and Ladakhi diplomacy. Relations with Tibet were extended after the establishment of a form of Chinese suzerainty over that country about 1720, to an exchange of courtesies with the Chinese Emperor in Peking; and until Chinese control was established over Sinkiang in 1758–9, the Ladakhi government appears to have held a kind of watching brief for the Chinese over the movements of the Dsungar Mongols in the Yarkand area.

Perhaps the most interesting event of the eighteenth century is the visit of the Jesuit priest, Ippolito Desideri, in 1715. Desideri and his companion Father Emanuel Freyre came to Ladakh in search of traces of Andrade's mission of ninety years earlier. Failing in this quest, they proceeded to Lhasa where Desideri stayed for five years. His *Relazione*, while mainly concerned with Tibet and with Buddhism, contains the earliest general account of Ladakh by a western observer, and is thus a valuable supplement to the Ladakhi and Tibetan sources which are the basis of our knowledge.[8]

Otherwise, the century is a melancholy story of family intrigues, disputed succession, assassination and madness. Things deteriorated so greatly in the 1750s that the Dalai Lama sent an emissary, an incarnate lama of the highest standing, to call a council of the various factions in order to settle their differences.

[8]See Appendix I, The Jesuits in Western Tibet.

Unfortunately, by establishing and persuading all concerned to agree to the principle of primogeniture, the Tibetan paved the way for a thoroughly undeserving king in the person of Tshewang Namgyal II, in whom the symptoms of mental unsoundness already present in his father, developed into downright madness. The pity of it was that the father, Phuntsog Namgyal, was a younger brother who had ascended the throne by cheating his elder half-brother in some way, and persuading him to become a non-celibate monk at Hemis. This prince, known as Gyalras Rinpoche, or Precious Prince, had a distinguished ecclesiastical career in Ladakh and Tibet, which showed him to be a man of ability and energy, and much the same could be said of his son after him. Although probably no amount of ability and energy on the part of its rulers could have saved Ladakh from the fate that was about to overtake it, had a more vigorous branch continued to rule the dynasty might have escaped the undignified collapse it was to suffer shortly.

Nevertheless, though Tshe-wang's insane excesses caused some kind of revolt against him on more than one occasion, the dynasty itself continued to command the loyalty of the people; and Tshe-wang's elder son, Tshe-stang, installed as king at a tender age on the deposition of his father, gave promise of great mental and physical ability, which might have restored the prestige of his family. He is praised in the Chronicle for his solicitude for the people's welfare. He replaced arbitrary taxation by a system 'that henceforth taxes should be raised only in accordance with income, great or little proportionately.' Popular tradition however remembers him better for his prowess on the polo ground. Unfortunately, he died of smallpox at the early age of 23; his brother Tshe-spal who succeeded him as the last king of independent Ladakh, was an indolent and ineffective ruler, who left affairs almost entirely in the hands of his ministers. And so Ladakh and its ruling house fell into the decline that made an expansionist power south of the Himalaya turn a covetous glance on them with a fair degree of confidence that no effective resistance to invasion would be offered.

V
A Change of Direction

While recent research has done much to reconstruct the history of old Ladakh, the story still remains tantalizingly incomplete, and subject to conjecture. It is a drama over which the shadows of time and change have lengthened, obliterating much and leaving the motives of the players often obscure. Only occasionally a shaft of light illuminates some tiny corner of the action, as when Mirza Haidar, the invader from Kashgar, includes in his memoirs accounts of repeated expeditions to Ladakh, or Bernier, in an unconsidered aside, drops the hint from which we can infer Sengge Namgyal's trade embargo against Kashmir. Not until the nineteenth century, when the combination of European imperialism and scientific curiosity began to mesh the world together as never before, do the shadows begin to lift; and it is not perhaps surprising that it should have been an Englishman who rang up the curtain on this remote corner of trans-Himalaya: William Moorcroft, who with his companion George Trebeck, stayed from 1820 to 1822. Moorcroft was a veterinary surgeon— the first Englishman to qualify as such—and had come to Ladakh in the course of a journey to central Asia in search of horses for the East India Company's military stud, of which he was the superintendent. He and Trebeck were kept at Leh for those years waiting for permission, not eventually granted, to proceed to Yarkand. They made good use of the delay, travelling all over the country, and enquiring into every aspect of Ladakhi life. Their *Travels* provide what is still one of the best accounts of Ladakh, many of their observations holding good even today. Another European visitor whose work indirectly helped in bringing about knowledge and understanding of Ladakh, was Alexander Csoma de Koros, a Hungarian whose three-year stay overlapped with Moorcroft's, and who spent over a year in a monastery in Zanskar. The object of his journey was to seek the origins of the Magyar tongue, which is not related to the Indo-Aryan group of languages. He failed to establish its relationship with Tibetan, but as a result of his studies he is regarded as the founder of modern Tibetology.

Politically speaking, the emergence of Ladakh took place twelve years after Moorcroft's visit, when the awakening was a rude one that he had foreseen and tried to prevent. When Kashmir passed under the rule of the Sikhs in 1819 the Ladakhi king, Tshe-spal Namgyal, calculated that his advantage lay rather with the more distant British Government ('the legitimate representative of the dynasty of Timur', in Moorcroft's quaint phrase) than with Ranjit Singh's expansionist empire. He made an offer of allegiance to the East India Company's Government, a move not only encouraged but actively canvassed by Moorcroft, who even made himself responsible for forwarding the offer to Calcutta. He explains his motives thus:

On the one hand I averted from an amiable and harmless people the oppressive weight of Sikh exaction and insolence, and, on the other, I secured for my country an influence over a state, which, lying on the British frontier, offered a central mart for the extension of her commerce to Turkistan and China, and a strong outwork against an enemy from the north, should such a foe ever occur in the autocrat of the Russias. (*Travels*, Vol. I, pp. 420–1).

In this reasoning, we see the classic impulse of early British imperialism, the expansion of trade, combined with political motives that later came to dominate imperial strategy under the wry designation of the Great Game. But the days of the Game were half a century in the future; at this point, its hands tied by a treaty of 1809 with Ranjit Singh, giving him a free hand north of the Sutlej, the Company's Government turned the offer down. It is difficult not to agree with Moorcroft—who seems however to have been unaware of the terms of the 1809 treaty, and the constraints they imposed on the British Government in its relations with the Sikh Durbar—in regretting this, particularly in view of Ladakh's impending political extinction.

For, confined by the 1809 treaty to the area north of the Sutlej, and prevented by British relations with the Sindhis and the Afghans from extending its power south-west and north-west, there was only one direction in which the Sikh empire could expand—north-east over the Himalaya. The attraction of

Ladakh's bleak mountainous terrain lay in its position athwart important trade routes, and in particular in its monopoly, guaranteed by the Treaty of Tingmosgang, of the trade in pashmina—including that produced in western Tibet. This had been an issue with the Sikh Durbar since 1819, when Kashmir was added to Ranjit Singh's empire. The ensuing famine had driven many Kashmiri shawl weavers to seek their livelihood on the plains, particularly in the towns of Amritsar, Nurpur and Ludhiana; in order to supply the growing demand from these places, a certain proportion of western Tibet's pashmina had started being diverted down the Sutlej, through Spiti and Kinnaur to the plains, bypassing Kashmir altogether and thus further impoverishing its traditional industry. The development of this trade in smuggled wool was encouraged by the British, through whose territory it must pass. They repaired the tracks used by tne traders in Kinnaur, and offered the nomadic goatherds of western Tibet higher prices than those fixed by the Ladakhi and Kashmiri monopolists.

Both Ranjit Singh's own Government, and that of his most powerful vassal, the Dogra Gulab Singh, Raja of Jammu, were alive to the importance of this trade. The establishment of the shawl industry in Amritsar and Nurpur, both towns within the Sikh empire, was a development that suited Ranjit, who also undertook to rehabilitate the traditional industry in Kashmir. Gulab Singh attempted to open a pashmina route to the plains via Kishtwar, one of the hill districts he ruled over; this elicited complaints to Ranjit from the Sikh governor of Kashmir.

But Gulab Singh's ambitions went further than merely diversion of a part of this lucrative trade to his own territories. Ultimately he aimed at getting control over the entire pashmina-producing area—in the name of his overlord Ranjit Singh, of course, but effectively for himself. Thus it was that he conceived and planned the invasion of Ladakh. Before embarking on the enterprise, he gave notice of his intentions to the British authorities, and received *carte blanche* to go ahead. Although in the course of the next few years the Ladakhi king sent repeated appeals to the British agents at various places on their northwestern border, along with renewed offers of allegiance, there seemed to be nothing in them to tempt the British to break their treaty obligations to Ranjit.

The Dogra commander-in-chief, Zorawar Singh, accordingly invaded Ladakh in the summer of 1834, taking the route through Kishtwar and Zanskar. Ladakh would seem to be ideal terrain for defence, and particularly for guerrilla operations; given minimal competence on the part of Ladakhi military leadership, the invasion might have been fairly easily repulsed. But let alone competence, leadership of any kind was lacking; for, effectively, Ladakh had no army. The only preparation for defence in time of trouble was that a matchlock was supplied to every household, with a supply of powder; when the call to arms came, it was to be answered by one man from each house, armed with this primitive weapon, and carrying on his back bedding for the cold winter nights, and enough provisions—mostly in the form of *tsampa*, parched barley flour—to last him a month. Thus we have a picture not of an army in any real sense of the word nor even of a militia, but rather a rabble of untrained conscripts. With dash and imagination perhaps they could have been turned into a guerrilla force, harassing the flanks and rear of the invading army; it is conceivable that they might in that case have inflicted such damage to the morale, if not to the physical strength of the Dogras, that the latter would have been glad to retreat from this barren and hostile land. But the commanders of this unmilitary force suffered from the same limitations as the rank and file—and the most damaging of these was lack of experience, for during the century and half since the Tibetan–Mongol invasion, military operations had been confined to minor skirmishes on the Balti frontier which can have constituted no sort of preparation for the challenge they now faced.

So the Dogras were allowed to advance, without meeting any real opposition, till they reached Sankhu, above Kargil on the Suru river, where a hastily raised defending force gave battle to the invaders. It was defeated, enabling Zorawar to proceed as far as Pashkyum. Now winter was beginning to set in, and the Dogra general felt inclined to beat a strategic retreat. On the other hand, he had to have something to show his master for his four months' campaign; so he opened negotiations with the Ladakhi court, offering to withdraw on payment of an indemnity of 15,000 rupees. The Chronicle records that while the king and his ministers were on the whole inclined to take advantage of this offer, the queen showed more spirit (or a less realistic assessment of Zorawar's intentions), and as a result of her intervention, the Dogra envoys went back empty-handed. Again we see the lack of any vestige of military instinct with which the Ladakhis might have successfully followed up the queen's political initiative. Zorawar prudently withdrew to Kartse, near Sankhu, to see the winter through; he was allowed to entrench himself, and the Ladakhis made no call on their most powerful ally—winter's numbing cold. They postponed an attack till early April, when heavy falls of snow hampered them as much as their enemies; were defeated with grievous loss; and found themselves harried and in retreat, with the Dogras at their heels, almost all the way to Leh. So complete was the failure of the Ladakhi 'army' to defend the country, that when the Dogras reached the Indus, they found envoys from the villages upstream—Saspol, Alchi, Likir and Nyemo—bringing presents and prepared to do homage to Zorawar. At Basgo, the king himself came to meet the invader; and now he had to agree to terms very much worse than those rejected at the queen's instance a few months earlier. He was to pay an immediate indemnity of 50,000 rupees, and an annual tribute of 20,000 rupees, and henceforward to consider himself Ranjit Singh's vassal. There the situation might have rested if the Ladakhis, instigated it is said by the Sikh governor of Kashmir—jealous of the growing power of the Dogras—had not revolted repeatedly against Dogra domination. As a result of this, first Tshe-spal was deposed, and replaced by one of his ministers; later he was restored; but he died before long, to be succeeded as vassal king by his grandson, Jigmet Namgyal, a boy of only eight or nine.

Meanwhile Zorawar was extending his conquests. Adding to his army a contingent raised from the Ladakhi levies, he invaded Baltistan, which he speedily subdued. This was followed by an even more ambitious scheme. The occupation of Ladakh had not had the desired effect of plugging the leakage of pashmina to the plains. On the contrary, the disturbed conditions resulting from it had disrupted traditional patterns of commerce, to the extent that an important wool mart had developed at Rampur on the Sutlej, bypassing Ladakh altogether, where the value of pashmina coming direct from western Tibet and passed on to weavers on the plains rose from Rs 35,630 in 1837 to Rs 94,807 in 1840. To add the western provinces of Tibet including the great mercantile centre of Gartok to the Dogra dominion would be to ensure once and for all control of the whole pashmina trade from its very source. A more limited but equally desirable objective was the prospect of plunder held out by the fabled wealth of the Tibetan monasteries. The formal justification for invasion was Ladakh's ancient claim to the kingdom of Guge—indeed to the whole of western Tibet up to the Mayum Pass, east of Lake Manasarowar.

The time seemed opportune for the Dogras to make a forward move. Following Ranjit Singh's death in 1839, the Government of the Sikh empire was in disarray and in no position to control its powerful vassal. The British, who feared a link-up between the Dogras and the Gurkhas of Nepal, were too deeply involved in the invasion of Afghanistan to do anything but watch anxiously; while the Chinese, Tibet's nominal suzerains, were having their problems thousands of kilometres away to the east, as the opium war with the British dragged its squalid course. Accordingly, Gulab Singh—unaware perhaps of the kind of terrain he would be committing his troops to—ordered Zorawar to invade Tibet. As in Baltistan, Zorawar added to the nucleus of Dogra veterans in his army contingents from among the recently subdued peoples, Ladakhis and Baltis. He set off from the Indus valley in May 1841, dividing his army into three forces so as to cover the maximum number of important monasteries, with their treasures, as well as the major forts. At the onset of winter, enriched with spoils from the *gompas* of Hanle and Tashi-Gang, as well as several in Guge, he was well into Tibetan territory, in control of the sacred lakes Manasarowar and Rakas Tal, and the neighbouring Mount Kailash, and with a garrison installed at the strategically important fort of Taklakot.

The objects of the raid seemed to have been achieved, for the whole of western Tibet, from the Mayum Pass to the Ladakh border, was in Dogra hands. The leakage of pashmina to the Indian plains had largely been plugged: in 1841, the value of sales at Rampur had dropped to Rs 17,766, less than one-fifth of the previous year's total. Winter was approaching, and it might have seemed prudent to retreat while the going was good. On the other hand, a long-term solution to the pashmina problem would depend on conquest and permanent control, or at the very least on an agreement imposed on the Tibetans from a position of strength: to retreat now would be to lose the major advantage so far gained. It was important then to hold ground; in addition Zorawar probably underestimated the difficulties of the enterprise. Tibet must have seemed to him as easy a nut to crack as Ladakh had been. He might well have felt himself back in 1834, marching unmolested through a country peopled by unwarlike peasants, and meeting with only token resistance before the whole land would submit to the might of his sword. That year, his first experience of a Himalayan winter, he had dug in for the cold weather, and seen it out without coming to any harm. He failed to take into account firstly that he was much further from base, and secondly that he was at 4,500 metres, an altitude where conditions would be incomparably more severe than the 2,700 at Kar-tse, where he had spent the winter of 1834. Thirdly, and this is where his calculations were most grievously in error, he discounted the fact that Tibet did not stand alone and friendless as Ladakh had done. It had a powerful protector in the shape of the Chinese empire which, whatever its problems with the British on its eastern seaboard, was by no means going to sit back and watch the loss of several provinces of a country over which it claimed suzerainty. The result of a pitched battle between a well-supplied Tibetan force of 10,000, fighting on their home ground, and the much smaller Dogra army, far from their base and demoralized by the intense cold, was a foregone conclusion. In spite of the enormous odds, the Dogras fought bravely, holding the enemy at bay for three days; but their spirit did not survive the death of Zorawar; defeat turned into rout; and only the merest handful of those who fled in disarray from the field survived the bitter weather to make their way through the desolate tangle of the winter mountains and arrive back in India to tell the tale.

This brought to an end both the dream of a greater Dogra empire, and the flamboyant career of their most famous commander, Zorawar Singh. Zorawar surely possessed a modicum of military talent; but this has tended to be assessed with reference to his actual success, rather than to the quality of the opposition he encountered. It would have taken more than the feeble resistance offered by the Ladakhi levies to constitute any real test of his military ability. The invasion of Tibet showed faulty judgment, both military and political, by which the risks of the enterprise were totally underestimated; his failure in this, the most testing campaign of his career, must cast some doubt on the military genius which has been attributed to him.

Zorawar Singh's death raised hopes among the Ladakhis of regaining their independence; about 2,500 of the matchlock-men blockaded the Dogra garrison at Leh in the early months of 1842, and proclaimed Jigmet Namgyal their only sovereign. They were reinforced from Baltistan, and soon by a detachment from the Tibetan army that had turned back the invasion. However, it now became clear that the conquest of Ladakh had not been a one-man affair—the Dogras after all were considerable fighters, trained and hardened in Ranjit Singh's expansionist wars. Upon news of the approach of an enemy force of 7,000 men, well equipped and armed with cannon, the matchlock-men deemed it prudent to slip away to their villages, while the Tibetans fled east to where the rest of their army was waiting beyond the Chang-La, taking the young king with them. They were pursued, and a battle was fought near Tang-tse on the western side of the Pang-Gong Lake, in which the Dogras redeemed the honour of their nation and avenged Zorawar's death.

With this restoration of the *status quo* of 1840, both sides were happy to put an end to hostilities. The terms of peace between the Dogras and the Tibetans were embodied in the Treaty of Leh, concluded on 17 September 1842. The Tibetans, recognizing the Dogras as legitimate rulers of Ladakh, ratified the border 'as fixed from ancient times', while the Dogras abandoned all claim to western Tibet. The young king, Jigmet Namgyal, and his family were given the right to reside peacefully in Ladakh, provided they indulged in no intrigue against the Dogras. Later they were given the *jagir* of Stok, a village nestling at the base of the Zanskar range across the Indus from Leh. The Namgyal family remain *jagirdars* of Stok to this day, though the Ladakhis still honour them for the ancient dynasty they represent, and give the head of the family the courtesy title of Gyalpo or Raja. The nominal king was permitted, if he wished, to continue to send the triennial *Lo-pchak* mission of religious tribute to Lhasa, on the explicit understanding that this had no political connotation. As regards trade, the Dogras won their main objective with the Tibetans undertaking to 'allow the annual export of wool, shawls[1] and tea by way of Ladakh according to old-established custom'.

[1] By 'wool' must be meant coarse wool (from the *huniya* sheep—see below, p. 105), while 'shawls' means shawl-wool or pashmina. There was no manufacture of shawls in Tibet.

Both Ladakhi traders in Tibet, and Tibetan traders in Ladakh could take advantage of the privilege of free porterage—i.e. obligatory labour from the villages *en route*—and accommodation. Later, this treaty, concluded between the Dogra and Tibetan officials on the spot, without plenipotentiary powers, was ratified by the Sikh governor of Kashmir, representing the Sikh Durbar, and the Chinese *ambans,* Residents at Lhasa, in the name of the Chinese emperor.

Thus Ladakh became an integral part of the Dogra dominions. For administrative purposes it was bracketed with Baltistan, Leh, Kargil and Baltistan being the three *tehsils* of the Ladakh *wazarat,* or district. When the state of Jammu and Kashmir came into being, with Gulab Singh's purchase of Kashmir from the British at the close of the first Sikh War in 1846, Ladakh was part of the new entity—as it has remained in independent India.

The Dogra wars brought Ladakh into violent collision with the outside world; never again was it able to retreat into the traditional system of limited relationships in which it had lived till then. The ambivalence of its position between Tibet and Hindustan, which had enabled it to maintain an illusion of independence in the wake of the war of the 1680s, was at an end, and Ladakh was subject to an uncongenial outside power. On the whole, however, Dogra rule does not seem to have been unduly oppressive, and at a non-political level relations with Tibet and central Asia continued much as before. The religious life of the country was still directed from Lhasa, and the caravans still crossed and recrossed Ladakh with their loads of wool, tea and luxury items. Their centre was at Leh, which continued to be the home of a colony of Kashmiri and Yarkandi merchants, and latterly of a group from Hoshiarpur in the Punjab.

From this time, Ladakh and its neighbouring countries gradually began to figure on the map of the world, in which till then the regions north of the Himalaya had been mostly a blank, filled up only speculatively, if at all. This was due to the efforts of a handful of surveyors and explorers, of whom the first to attempt a systematic account of Ladakh, Alexander Cunningham, was deputed as early as the mid-1840's to survey and demarcate the boundaries between Ladakh and Tibet, and Ladakh and Spiti in British India.[2] A steady trickle of explorers, sportsmen and even

---

[2]Cunningham later became the first Director-General of the Archaeological Survey of India.

enterprising tourists reached Ladakh in the succeeding decades, and several of them published books recounting their experiences. A longer stay was made by Frederic Drew who, attached in 1862 to the Geological Service of the Maharaja of Jammu and Kashmir's Government, travelled the whole state, including the farthest plateaux of Ladakh, prospecting for minerals; and who completed his ten years in the Maharaja's service with a year's term as Governor of Ladakh. His account of the country and its people is one of the most accurate and sympathetic that appeared in the nineteenth century. He was succeeded as Governor by an improbable character reported in the Ladakh Chronicle as Corporal Johnson; whether actually a corporal or not, Johnson was a central Asian explorer of repute, the first and for many years the only European in modern times to reach Khotan, one of the most important trading cities on the fabled Silk Route.

In 1885 Leh became the headquarters of a mission of the Moravian church; and it was the mission which, in the years following, initiated the processes of change in a modest way. As well as a new religion, the missionaries introduced such useful skills as knitting and baking, and also the cultivation of exotic vegetables like potatoes, spinach, cauliflower, radish and tomato; the system of storing and preserving root vegetables in semi-underground chambers, so that they are available for the greater part of the winter, is also credited to them. Soon after their arrival, the missionaries were asked to take over the small western-style dispensary maintained by the Maharaja's Government at Leh; and a succession of doctors expanded its activities by work that can fairly be described as devoted. They built it up into a hospital for in- and out-patients, and travelled widely, bringing medical aid to the poorest and remotest villages.[3] The first radio in Ladakh belonged to the mission, in the 1940s; men now in middle age remember how the battery, which it took two men to lift, used to be carried down to Choglamsar, where the near approach of the mountains to the river causes the wind to blow up the Indus with great force, to be charged by a windmill; and what a big event it

---

[3]The fame of the missionaries' medical work was such that it is said that a cataract case made a seven-weeks' journey from Tibet for treatment; he returned home with his sight restored. An account of some of this work is given in A. Reeve Heber and Kathleen Heber; *Himalayan Tibet and Ladakh* (London, 1923, reprinted New Delhi, 1976).

was when the recharged battery returned to town; and how there would be a rush to the mission that evening to listen to the war news.

The cumulative effect of all these things must have been to create the sense of a world outside Ladakh: not merely a physical world, the idea of which had been made familiar to the Ladakhis long since by the carvan trade; but a world of new values, and achievements in the material sphere hitherto undreamt of. As a result, ambitious boys of good family began to go out to seek an education, and to discover the modern world. They seem, many of them, to have taken with relative ease and a minimum of cultural disorientation to the material culture of this century. The first Ladakhi to go overseas to study, Sonam Narboo, qualified at Sheffield University as a civil engineer in the 1930s. Later, he was instrumental in reducing the sixteen days taken to travel to school in Srinagar to a mere two; for he was the engineer in charge of the construction, first of the Leh airfield, and then of the Kargil–Leh highway. Other boys went to the universities of Lucknow and Banaras; now young Ladakhis, girls as well as boys, are graduating from universities all over north India.

But the change would probably have remained gradual—at least until Ladakh was brought within the scope of India's major effort in economic development in the last ten years—if it had not been for the catastrophic events of the period since 1947. In addition to their wider impact, these have had the unfortunate, in some aspects tragic, effect of disrupting Ladakh's centuries-old pattern of commercial, cultural and religious relations.

In 1948, in the wake of Partition, Ladakh found itself a battlefield, fought over by India and Pakistan. The struggle for Ladakh was one episode in the larger battle for Jammu and Kashmir; after 400 years central Ladakh again faced invasion from the forces of Islam. The raiders, mostly Gilgit Scouts from the far north-west of the Maharaja's dominions, pushed up the Indus valley during the early summer of 1948, and took Skardo and Kargil. In central Ladakh they reached the village of Taru, about eight kilometres west of Phiyang, and only a matter of twenty or so from Leh. The town's defences at that time consisted of a platoon of the State Force, a volunteer detachment from the 2nd Dogras, who had braved winter conditions to struggle across the Zoji-La the previous March, and a battalion of the local militia,

which had been hastily raised in response to the threat from
downriver, and was largely organized by the head of the old *Kalon*
family—hereditary prime ministers of the Namgyal *raj*—and by
Sonam Narboo, the engineer in charge of the construction of the
airfield which was to enable larger numbers of Indian troops to
fly in. A few of the raiders managed to reach Leh by an arduous
march through the mountains of the Ladakh range behind Taru
and Phiyang, dropping down on the city from the north; but not
in sufficient numbers to constitute any real threat. Summer
brought not only the arrival of troops by air, but also a battalion of
Gurkhas who marched up over the ridges and passes from Manali. Supplies were also sent up by this route. The raiders were
pushed back from the vicinity of Leh, and a few months later the
capture of the Zoji-La by tanks—an extraordinary feat—enabled
Indian troops to re-take Kargil, and secure the route to central
Ladakh. Thus Ladakh as we know it today was saved for Jammu
and Kashmir, and so for India. But Baltistan was on the other side
of the cease-fire line, abruptly snapping the friendly relationship
that had grown up, ancient animosities forgotten, during the
period when Ladakh and Baltistan were linked together under
Dogra rule.

One terrible concomitant of Partition was avoided in Ladakh:
there were no riots or massacres on the basis of religion. During
the period of confrontation between the raiders and the Indian
forces, just down the Indus, the situation in Leh is reported to
have been tense almost to breaking point. But the tradition of
goodwill between the Buddhist majority and their Muslim neighbours stood the strain—stiffened by the initiative of Sonam Narboo who, the seniormost representative of Government on the
spot, stood firm against any threat of violence against the Muslims. If such violence had occurred, shattering at a blow the
centuries-old feelings of mutual tolerance and esteem between
the Muslims and Buddhists of central Ladakh, it would have been
a tragedy that hardly bears thinking of.

The events of 1948 led to the constitutional and administrative
situation in which Ladakh finds itself today—as part of one of the
constituent states of the Republic of India. One consequence of
this was its involvement in the Indo-Pakistan wars of 1965 and
1971, in which once more it found itself in the front line. On these
occasions however it was Kargil and its environs, rather than

central Ladakh, that bore the brunt. Both times operations were confined to the area of the cease-fire line, which in 1948 had been left so close to Kargil town that its main bazaar was actually overlooked by a Pakistani picket. This picket was taken by the Indians in 1965, but was handed back the following year under the terms of the Tashkent agreement. In 1971 it was retaken, and the line of actual control pushed back to a distance of about twelve kilometres from Kargil town, where it still runs.

As far as Ladakh's internal situation was concerned, the two Indo-Pakistan wars were but episodes—incidents in a conflict of interests outside itself, which simply happened to take place within its borders. It was otherwise with the Sino-Indian war of 1962. In the course of this, the Chinese advanced to Chushul on the western margin of the Pang-Gong Lake. As in 1948, the first weight of the attack was taken by the Ladakh Militia, now a properly organized force; units of the regular army, even by then a considerable presence in Ladakh, also fought with gallantry and devotion.

The result of this war was to bring Ladakh for the first time into the consciousness of the Indian public, which suddenly became aware of it as a strategically important area on the northern frontier. The loss of the Aksai Chin plateau, a piece of Indian territory measured in thousands of square kilometres and the circumstances leading to this loss, had a profound effect on Indian attitudes and policies. However, it must be admitted that the Aksai Chin, a barren and uninhabitable waste, nowhere less than 4,500 metres above sea level, though of strategic importance to China as providing a link between Sinkiang and Tibet, had no material value for Ladakh or for India, and its loss has been of no practical effect. The main consequences for Ladakh of China's threat to India's north-west borders (as opposed to its policies in Tibet and central Asia) were the construction of the motor-road between Srinagar and Leh, and the beginning of the military build-up which today even the most unobservant visitor cannot fail to notice, and which has led to considerable modifications— on the whole beneficial—to Ladakh's life and economy.

But not even the war fought on its northern and eastern borders, or the loss of the Aksai Chin, had such deep and far-reaching effects on Ladakh as the policies of communist China in central Asia, and its occupation of Tibet. In 1949 the frontier

between central Asia and Ladakh was closed, putting an end to
the trade, perhaps of a thousand years' standing, across the
Karakoram, and depriving Ladakh of its traditional economic
base as the central mart on a network of important trade routes.
The following year Chinese forces marched into Tibet, and
throughout the fifties, in spite of resistance from guerrilla forces
in the eastern province of Kham, which gradually spread to
central and southern Tibet, the Chinese tightened their stranglehold till they were effectively in complete occupation of the country. During those years, the ages-old system of contacts between
the *gompas* of Ladakh and Tibet did not break down completely,
though it must have become progressively attenuated; but in the
wake of the 1962 war the frontier was closed. For reasons entirely
external and irrelevant to the logic of its own development,
Ladakh was deprived of its ancient reliance on the elders of its
faith in central Tibet. For seven centuries Ladakh had looked to
Lhasa for guidance in all its religious activity, and as much of its
cultural activity as was dependent on religon; now for the first
time the Ladakhi Buddhists were on their own.

Of the events since Partition, the four wars fought on its soil are
in a sense those that have touched Ladakh least. It is the abrupt
severance of its ancient ties with central Asia and Tibet that has
really shaken it to the foundations of its history and traditions.
Nevertheless, the economic set-back caused by the cessation of the
caravan trade has been recouped, and in good measure, largely as
a result of three new factors in the situation: the large-scale
military presence; the recent opening-up of Ladakh to Indian
and foreign tourists; and the extension to Ladakh of India's
ambitious programme of economic development. Ladakhis today
are at least as prosperous as at any time during the heyday of the
caravan trade, and much more so than the people in most districts
of Gangetic or peninsular India.

The religious situation is not so happy. The cutting-off of the
ancient relationship with Tibet, indeed the eclipse of the old
religion there, has dealt Ladakhi Buddhism in general, and the
gompas in particular, a blow from which in the long run they may
not recover. Many of the head lamas, or *kushoks*, who are incarnations, were recurrently 'discovered' in Tibet, and it remains to be
seen how the present generation will be replaced: whether the

search for the children reincarnating these hallowed souls will be successful among the relatively small population of Buddhist Ladakh—a little over 50,000—or among the Tibetan refugees.

A fundamentally more critical problem is that no tradition of letters or scholarship developed in Ladakh's *gompas*, aspiring lamas being sent in the old days to complete their novitiate in the mother-houses of their respective orders in central Tibet. Theology, dogma and scriptural exegesis remained the jealously guarded preserve of the Tibetan pontiffs, whose monopoly of learning forbade the setting up of religious colleges in Ladakh. It is true that now the Dalai Lama and other senior lamas from Tibet have made at least a temporary home in India, and that Ladakh enjoys the occasional blessing of His Holiness's physical presence. But the institutional base which existed in Lhasa for the training of monks from the periphery of the religious empire has been destroyed, and it is believed that, since this source of traditional wisdom was cut off, standards of learning in Ladakh's *gompas* have plummeted. It is particularly unfortunate that this should have happened at precisely the time when traditional beliefs and practices are being exposed to pressure from the modern world—as must inevitably happen with the opening up of Ladakh—and when the ancient ties with the centres of the faith in Tibet might have helped in withstanding such pressures. All this is not to say that Buddhism is dying on its feet, either inside or outside the *gompas*—yet. Nor is the possibility of a revival, on the basis of indigenous talent, independent of Tibetan authority, inconceivable. But at present all seems to point to a gradual but probably accelerating decline in corporate wisdom and individual fervour.

However, considering the fate of Buddism in Tibet itself, it seems almost ungrateful to providence to cavil about the circumstances leading to its decline in Ladakh. Given China's will to domination over all the lands to which it has the faintest shadow of a historical claim, one can only be thankful that Ladakh's history never involved it in political dependence on Tibet; and feel that things have turned out, if not for the best, then at any rate for the least bad. The modern world is hardly tender to small non-aggressive nationalities, which may find their best chance of protection and self-fulfilment under the umbrella of a more or less benevolent larger state, as Ladakh does in India. The present

system of administration under the Government of Jammu and
Kashmir is far from perfect no doubt; in fact in 1981 and 1982 the
State Government's inept handling of reasonable grievances provoked an agitation leading to violence. Whatever changes the
future may bring, however, Ladakh's status as an integral part of
the Indian Union is not in question. In this lies the only realistic
hope of fulfilling to a fair extent the legitimate aspirations of the
Ladakhi people.

VI
Hazardous Trails

Ladakh might seem isolated, tucked away in the midst of mountain ranges among the world's most formidable; nevertheless in the old days it was situated squarely between some of the great mercantile towns of south and central Asia, and there is evidence that traders may have been using the Ladakh route as early as the ninth century A.D. Close to the old Indus bridge at Khaltse are the ruins of an ancient fortified customs-house, identified as such by an inscription referring to the 'lord of the trade in the lower valley'—a high-sounding title for a prosaic customs-officer. Willy-nilly, the *kafilas* had to toil up Ladakh's high passes, traverse its dusty valleys, in order to effect the perennial exchange of the silks and spices of Hindustan, the shawls and saffron of Kashmir, the opium grown in the Himalayan foothills, with the tea of China, the tobacco and minerals of central Asia, and above all the 'shawl-wool'—pashmina—of Ladakh's own south-eastern plateaux of Chang-Thang, and the Tibetan province of Rudok, further east. These were the staples of the trade; undoubtedly the most important of them was the raw pashmina that went (as it still does, in much reduced quantities) to Kashmir, to be worked into shawls famous the world over for their softness and warmth.

The importance of the pashmina trade was such as to have a decisive effect on Ladakh's political destiny. This fact first received formal expression in the Treaty of Tingmosgang (1684), at the end of the Ladakh–Tibet war. By this settlement, a double monopoly of pashmina was established: only Ladakhi traders might enter the pashmina-producing areas of Ladakh itself and western Tibet, to buy the raw wool from the nomadic herdsmen; and they in their turn might sell it to none but Kashmiri merchants settled at Leh (initially at Spituk) for the purpose. It was in order to lay hands on this highly lucrative trade that Gulab Singh undertook the conquest of Ladakh, and later attempted to invade Tibet. Although the latter enterprise failed, in the long run its object—to prevent the leakage of pashmina direct to the plains via Spiti and Kinnaur—was achieved. The Punjab shawl industry developed along different lines, using coarser wools, and the manufacture of 'cashmere' shawls remained the monopoly of Kashmir.

The trade in pashmina was subject to risks and hardships that could only have been justified by expectation of the highest profits. Desideri, in the early eighteenth century, tells us something about its logistics:

The merchants of Kascimir keep a large number of agents in Second Thibet [Ladakh] who collect the wool during the year, paying a most miserable price; and in May, June, July and August, thousands and thousands of men go from Kascimir to Lhe, otherwise called Lhata, the capital of Second Thibet, and carry back infinite number of loads of wool; this is spun in Kascimir to marvellously fine thread from which is woven the thin, very delicate Kascimir cloth, renowned all over India. (*Account of Tibet*, p. 73.)

Desideri, who crossed the Zoji-La in May, must himself have witnessed the outward journey of the porters. His description of the road is horrifying; 'jhoola' bridges gave him vertigo, and the road, never more than a track, had in places been swept away by landslides or avalanches, so that he could only proceed if his guide went ahead and cut steps with an axe.

In some places there was really no road at all, only large boulders and rocks covered the ground, over which we had to climb like goats with great trouble and difficulty. As no animal can travel over such bad roads, the whole journey from Kascimir to Lhata, which takes forty days, must be done on foot. (*Account of Tibet*, p. 77.)

This included the porters with their loads of pashmina, and Desideri adds that many of them, falling, 'lose their lives or are crippled for ever'—a grim comment on a trade on which so many were totally dependent, from the Chang-Thang nomads to the Srinagar shawl-weavers. The road remained in the same state until the 1830s when Zorawar Singh, alive to the military importance of good communications, improved the track and built *pukka* bridges.

Apart from pashmina, by far the greater part of the trade from

India across Ladakh was with Yarkand, in Chinese-ruled central Asia, an entrepôt of such importance that it could be regarded as the gateway to 'the whole of Central Asia, from China to the Caspian Sea'. The words are Moorcroft's; and the establishment of commercial relations with Yarkand through Leh was a cherished, though subsidiary, aim of Moorcroft's journey. He lambasted the Company's Government for its 'misplaced squeamishness and unnecessary timidity' in neglecting the opportunity his presence afforded to do this, thus leaving the whole vast area wide open for economic penetration by Russia. On his own responsibility, acting 'on behalf of the British merchants of Calcutta', he even concluded a commercial agreement with the Ladakhi authorities, who granted the former freedom to trade with and through Ladakh at moderate duties, and permission to establish a permanent 'factory' or office at Leh. Moorcroft envisaged from this a flood of British goods swamping the markets of central Asia's illimitable expanses; little did he realize that it was not only the East India Company's apathy that was against the expansion of trade on such a vast scale, but also the incredible severity of the Karakoram route, something of which he seems to have had no realistic conception.

Yarkand was a major trading centre on the Silk Route, and Moorcroft was undoubtedly correct in his estimate of its importance as a point of distribution all over central Asia, and even into Russia and metropolitan China, for the goods which came from India through Leh and over the Karakoram. A major commodity of this trade in the nineteenth century was opium, despite repeated Chinese Imperial edicts against its use, in the wake of the Opium War with Great Britain. Cunningham, reporting on conditions in 1847, tells us that 'the drug produced in our hill states is of a superior quality, and as it is much prized by the Chinese, the land trade in opium is yearly increasing.' From Yarkand in exchange came tobacco and *charas* (hashish); according to Cunningham these were mostly consumed in Ladakh and not reexported. Other staples of the trade coming from India were spices, of which the most valuable was saffron, brocades, fine and coarse textiles, and coloured leather—to which, if Moorcroft had had his way, would have been added a whole range of British manufactured goods, altering the entire complexion of the trade relationship. Already the balance of the trade was in India's favour, for the value of imports from Yarkand—tobacco and *charas*, some tea, a small amount of pashmina, sugar candy made from Indian molasses—was not sufficient to pay for what went north over the Karakoram, and the Yarkandi merchants had to meet their obligations by the export of silver bullion into Ladakh.

Fifty years after Moorcroft, the Government of India did briefly sit up and take notice of the possibilities of the Yarkand trade. The Chinese had been temporarily expelled from their central Asian province of East Turkestan (now Sinkiang), and the *de facto* ruler was an adventurer from Khokand called Yakub Beg. Two missions, both led by Douglas Forsythe, were sent across Ladakh to Yarkand and Kashgar, with instructions to woo Yakub by offers of commercial privilege and diplomatic support, the object being to make of East Turkestan a friendly buffer against the advancing might of Russia. The first mission, in 1870, was a fiasco, provoking the very reaction on the part of Russia that it was designed to circumvent—a threat against Yakub Beg's independence. The second Forsythe mission, three years later, was a much more impressive affair, whose aim was to show the Russians that the Government of India by no means accepted that East Turkestan fell within their sphere of influence. It was organized on a lavish scale, its permanent staff amounting to 350 persons, while there were never less than 500 pack animals. This cumbersome *kafila* made its way across Ladakh and over the Karakoram without a hitch, thanks to the efforts of W.H. ('Corporal') Johnson, who threw all the resources of the district administration behind it, stockpiling supplies of food, fodder and fuel at the halting stages, and even laying on local pack animals to spare those belonging to the mission. Ladakh's economy is said to have taken four years to recover from the unprecedented demands made on it.

Alas, in spite of all its pomp and show (Yakub was presented with a personal letter from Queen Victoria, housed in a casket of yellow quartz, embellished with gold and onyx, and borne in state by a kilted corporal of the Gordon Highlanders), the mission turned out to be a damp squib. Yakub gave it a friendly reception, and a treaty was concluded which purported to establish free trade between India and East Turkestan, subject only to a nominal duty of 2½ percent, while British commercial agents were to be installed at the principal cities, and an ambassador received at

Kashgar. But when the following year Robert Shaw, British Joint Commissioner at Leh, and ambassador designate, travelled to Kashgar to present his credentials and get the treaty ratified, he was rebuffed and had to be recalled, having failed on both counts. In 1877 Yakub Beg, on whom the British had staked their bet, was assassinated and by the end of the 1870s the Chinese were back, this time for good. With the possibility of a Russian takeover at India's back door thus eliminated, official British interest in the Yarkand trade also died. In truth, apart from a few enthusiasts in the Moorcroft tradition, no one had ever considered it as of potential value *per se*, but rather as an element in the strategic problem, a move in the Great Game.

The only tangible result of the episode was the establishment of The Central Asian Trading Company, by Robert Shaw, foremost of the enthusiasts. His agent, a Scot called Andrew Dalgliesh, settled in Yarkand, married a Yarkandi wife, and when the company failed, set up in business on his own. For fourteen years he was actively engaged in the Leh–Yarkand trade, himself regularly struggling across the fearsome passes of the Karakoram with the carvans. It was on one of these expeditions that he met his death, not from cold or exposure, but (an unncessary additional hazard, it might seem, on this most punishing of mountain routes) from the knife of an assassin. Dalgliesh's caravan—a small one, the staff consisting only of two servants and seven pony-men besides himself—fell in with another small party on the very crest of the Karakoram Pass, where they halted for the night. A member of the other party, an Afghan called Daud Mohammad, lured Dalgliesh out of the tent, attacked him with a sword and hacked him to death. The motive for the murder remains a mystery. Daud Mohammed was arrested for it two years later in Samarkand, but died in prison—by his own hand, according to the Russian authorities—before he could be brought to trial, or throw any light on his action. A memorial to Dalgliesh was erected on the spot where he was murdered; his body was brought to Leh, and buried just behind the British Joint Commissioner's bungalow. Thus the first and only Briton to engage in the trade across the Karakoram met an untimely and mysterious end, though his body was not left to add to the bones that whitened along the Yarkand trail.

The last caravan crossed the Karakoram in 1949, but faint

echoes of the Yarkand trade linger on in Leh. Several leading Muslim families trace their descent to Yarkandi merchants settled there; and in their houses, or—more accessible to the visitor—in the antique shops of Leh bazaar, may be found copper jars and cooking pots of exquisite workmanship, and other artefacts in the great tradition of Islamic design, which have surely come across the Karakoram from central Asia. The great dish of Ladakhi *haute cuisine* (which otherwise shows traces of Chinese influence, derived from the Tibetan connection, and relies largely on noodles and meat-filled dumplings) is Yarkandi *pulau*, rice richly cooked with meat and spices—a creation again in the great Islamic tradition.

The Lhasa trade was largely organized round two official missions, both of them originating like Kashmir's pashmina monopoly in the Treaty of Tingmosgang. The first of these, going from Leh to Lhasa, was known as the *Lo-pchak* mission—*Lo-pchak* means the Salutation of the New Year, and this was a mission of religious tribute from the kings of Ladakh to the supreme religious authorities at Lhasa. It went every three years, carrying gold, saffron and textiles as an offering to the Dalai Lama, as well as gifts for other important lamas. An annual trade mission also came from Lhasa to Ladakh, organized by the Tibetan Government, and carrying mainly tea—a minimum of 200 animal-loads was stipulated by the Treaty; for this reason it came to be known as the *Cha-pa* caravan. The tea was carried in the easily portable form of 'bricks' of dampened and compressed tea-leaves. As anyone who has lived in Ladakh may guess, the greater part of the *Cha-pa*'s 200 animal-loads of tea was not re-exported, but kept for consumption within the country. Cunningham in the 1840s adds that 'there is good reason for believing that a considerable quantity of Chinese tea is smuggled into Ladakh.'

Obviously, neither of these Government enterprises would return to its starting-point empty-handed; indeed it was stipulated that the *Lo-pchak* mission could take back 200 animal-loads of goods; as time went by, the importance of this mission gradually became more commercial than religious. After the loss of Ladakh's independence, its management was entrusted by the titular king to professional traders, often Muslims; for many years it was controlled by the family concern of Haji Nazir Ali Shah, a prominent merchant who figures in the accounts of

European visitors around the turn of the century. Sven Hedin's description of the old merchant (1906) tells us something about the organization of trade, and also gives a picture of the lifestyle of Ladakh's merchant princes.

In a large room on the first floor, with a large window looking over the Indus valley, the old man sat by the wall, on soft cushions, with his sons and grandsons around him. All about stood chests full of silver and gold dust, turquoise and coral, materials and goods which would be sold in Tibet. There is something impressively patriarchal about Hajji Nazer Shah's commercial house, which is managed entirely by himself and his large family. This consists of about a hundred members, and the various branches of the house in Lhasa, Shigatse, Gartok, Yarkand and Srinagar are all under the control of his sons, or their sons. Three hundred years ago the family migrated from Kashmir to Ladak...

The real source of their wealth is the so-called Lo-pçhak mission, of which they possess a monopoly... [This] has been a source of great profit to them especially as several hundred baggage animals are provided for the mission gratis, for the journey from Leh to Lhasa...

The mission had left eight months before under the charge of one of the Hajji's sons. Another son, Gulam Razul, was to repair in September to Gartok, where he is the most important man in the fair...

The old Hajji [was a devout Muslim; in addition] he had more than enough of the good things of this world, for his extensive business connections brought him in yearly a net profit of 25,000 rupees, and his name was known and respected throughout the interior of Asia (*Transhimalaya*, Vol. I, pp. 55–6).

But not all the traffic was over such tremendous distances as to Lhasa or Yarkand. Jane Duncan, an intrepid and perceptive visitor in 1904, reports a barter trade between the inhabitants of 'Lower Ladakh'—the Indus valley below Saspol—and Baltistan, and the nomads of Chang-Thang. The former carried great quantities of dried apricots up to the barren plateaux, and exchanged them with the nomads for salt, which they then carried down to Leh, to sell for cash with which to pay the Maharaja's taxes. The nomads also carried salt which they panned from the brackish lakes direct to Zanskar and Kargil, where they traded it for butter and *tsampa*. This kind of barter trade extended into western Tibet, where apricots, cereals and cotton cloth brought up from the valleys were exchanged for pashmina and coarse wool; *toosh*, the Tibetan antelope's winter growth of under-wool, in demand for the manufacture of shawls even softer and finer than those made of pashmina; and livestock in the form of sheep, goats and yak.

Much of this local trade was conducted on sheep-back, the *huniya* sheep of Chang-Thang having a load-bearing capacity of about fourteen kilograms. The same was true of some of the long-distance trade, which otherwise made use of mules, ponies, yak (in Chang-Thang and on the Tibet routes) and, unexpectedly, camels The principal pack-animal on the caravan routes of central Asia, the shaggy two-humped Bactrian camel, can well be imagined traversing with measured tread the deserts of Turkestan and Mongolia. But the use of camels was not confined to the undulating ground of the dusty steppes; laden with merchandise, and panting in the rarefied air of 5,000 metres and above, they were urged over the steep and icy passes of the Karakoram into Ladakh. It adds a touch of the exotic to Leh bazaar in the old days, to imagine their stately forms pacing along it. Before the Karakoram route was closed in 1949, a few camels were acquired by certain big landholders in Nubra and central Ladakh. A small population of them survives in Nubra, where they continue to prove their worth as pack animals. They are reproducing, and from sixteen in the early 1950s their numbers had grown to 35 by 1980. With the construction of more roads fit for wheeled traffic their usefulness will decline, and eventually no doubt they will be bred no longer. Meanwhile they exist as a relic of the Yarkand trade, and probably the only specimens of their breed in India.

Apart from pashmina, coarse wool, salt and small amounts of borax and sulphur extracted from deposits on the Chang-Thang plateaux, the only home product exported by Ladakh, then as now, was dried apricots. But the trade in foreign commodities was more than enough to make of Leh one of the major entrepots of central Asia, and its bazaars housed a community of merchants drawn from many of the great trading cities of a wide area: Yarkand, Khotan, Kashgar, Gartok and Lhasa; Srinagar, Amritsar, Ludhiana and latterly Hoshiarpur. (A community of Hoshiarpuri merchants still controls a fair amount of the business in Leh bazaar.) The Ladakh Government, in the days of its independence, derived most of its revenue from the trade carried on across its territories, both directly from the levying of import and export duties, and indirectly from the fact that the carrying trade for the whole of the way between Yarkand and Srinagar, the most important of the routes, was entirely in the hands of the Ladakhis. According to Cunningham, the most important trader in Ladakh was the king himself.

As for the actual routes, seven important ones converged on Leh. All of them crossed passes of at least 4,000 metres, and one, the main 'highway' from Yarkand, rose a giddy 5,575 metres over the Karakoram Pass. The only way of bypassing this was to take the Aksai Chin route, whose barrenness and average altitude of over 4,500 metres made it however quite impracticable. There were in fact two Karakoram routes, for use in winter and summer. Many traders considered winter, despite the bitter cold, to be the more favourable season for travel through the mountains, because streams and rivers which in summer were raging torrents impossible to negotiate, were at low ebb and frozen solid. The winter route accordingly tended to follow river valleys, while the summer one attacked the mighty ranges headon, crossing no fewer than four major passes, in addition to the Karakoram Pass. This though the highest was not the most formidable; that distinction was reserved for the glacier-imperilled Saser-La, between the Shayok and Nubra valleys. The most important of the other routes was from Srinagar—the pashmina trail—roughly along the line of today's motor road. Two tracks came in from the Punjab: one, via Jammu, Kishtwar and Zanskar, which was the way chosen by Zorawar Singh; and one, via Mandi, Kulu, the Rohtang Pass, Lahul, the Bara-Lacha, Lunga-Lacha and Thung-Lung Passes, to Upshi on the Indus, and thence down the river to Leh. Moorcroft and Trebeck came this way in 1820. The north-western route came in from Skardo in Baltistan, up the Shayok, over the Hanu Pass, and up the Indus. (The apparently direct route up the river from Skardo was impassable at most seasons.) Two trails came in from the east: one from Lhasa, via Lake Manasarowar and Gartok, and down the Indus; the other from a more north-easterly direction from the interior of Tibet, via Rudok, Chushul and the Chang-La. This was the route by which the Tibetan–Mongol army invaded Ladakh in 1680.

These were routes, by no stretch of the imagination roads; their nature can be gathered from the stage-by-stage descriptions given in the *Gazetteer of Kashmir and Ladak* published under Government auspices in 1890. Here are a few extracts:

Camping ground on left bank of a tributary of the Shyok... No fuel or forage procurable. Road very narrow and difficult, and risky from stone avalanches. Follow up course of stream and cross it repeatedly by narrow fords; it flows in a raging torrent, rolling over great boulders in a tight winding gorge...

To the Dipsang Plain (17,800 feet), about 18 miles broad. Cross this bleak barren undulating plateau, from which the world around subsides, the highest hilltops only appearing above the horizon. Soil soft and spongy, gravel and clay mixed, and where water-logged, soggy. Breathing distressed...

Camping ground right bank Yarkand river. No wood or grass and no water from end of October to end of April...

A few stone enclosures in which travellers rest for the night at foot of the Suget Pass; cold usually intense; no grass or fuel; water scarce. Proceed north over an elevated, arid, stony plateau, a desert, gradually descending. Breathing oppressed on this march. The whole region a bleak, desolate and inhospitable waste. (*Gazetter of Kashmir and Ladakh*, pp. 970–1.)

All these extracts relate to the Leh–Yarkand route, over the Karakoram Pass, where travellers' tales had it that the trail was marked by the scattered bones of men and animals left to whiten along the way. This was surely the most difficult of the routes; but it was also the most frequented by caravans. It is hard even to imagine what the organization and execution of a trading expedition across such terrain, routinely undertaken by the merchants and their Ladakhi agents, must have involved. The purchase of food, fodder and fuel, where available en route, and the stock-piling on the backs of precious pack-animals for the stages where nothing would be found; the paraphernalia of tents, bedding, cooking-pots, nose-bags, apart from the bales of merchandise that were the *raison d'être* of the whole operation; the daily chore of making and breaking camps; the monotonous effort and sheer physical hardship of it all, to say nothing of the very real risk of death: considering all these things, and considering too that the articles of this trade were, on the whole, some of the least essential that man has turned to his own use; considering the profits that must have been expected to make such expenditure of money and human enterprise anything like worthwhile—then we cannot but reflect that, if trade sometimes follows the flag, yet at others it has its own momentum, and will push its way over all but insuperable obstacles, through the seemingly inaccessible places of the world, where few would willingly follow.

Ladakh Present

VII
The Daily Round

The loose suzerainty claimed rather than exercised by the Mughal Empire from the seventeenth century onwards, developed via the Dogra conquest and the establishment of the Jammu and Kashmir state into the situation in which Ladakh finds itself today, as an integral part of the Indian Union. Till 1979 it was a single district; in June of that year it was bifurcated into the two districts of Leh and Kargil. The boundary between them runs north-west along the line of the Zanskar Range, so that the Zanskar Valley is included in Kargil district, as well as Dras, and Purig, the area within striking distance of Kargil town. A little beyond the Fatu-La the boundary turns north to cross the Indus, so that most of the Sodh Ilaqa, the area along the river below Khaltse where the *brokpa*, the Buddhist Dards live, also falls in Kargil. Leh district includes the Indus valley above Khaltse, Nubra, and the south-east plateaux of Chang-Thang, up to the margins of the Pang-Gong Lake. The total area of the two districts is about 98,000 square kilometres; and its population is now probably a little above 135,000 (132,299 by the 1981 census), giving a population density of about 1·35 per square kilometre.

But this in a sense is an unrealistic way of looking at it, considering that the greater part of the region is uninhabited, most of the population being clustered together in small enclaves where cultivation is possible. For a start, a considerable area (37,500 square kilometres, according to the 1971 census) in the north-eastern corner, the plains of Aksai Chin and Lingzi-Thang, is under the illegal occupation of the Chinese. However, these high-altitude plateaux are a desert, incapable of supporting human life; their loss does not affect the real issue, which is the area of cultivable land. Of the 60,500 square kilometres that remain when the Aksai Chin is left out of account, a mere 210 square kilometres are

under crops, vegetables or fruit; thus the pressure of the population on the cultivated area is very great—about 630 per square
kilometre. This of course includes the population of the two
towns, and the nomadic population of Chang-Thang, who do not
live directly off the land. But the townsman and the nomad have
to eat; ultimately their food too comes from the earth.

As in every other region of India, Ladakh's population has
grown during the present century, rising from 63,519 by the
census of 1901, to 132,299 in 1981, an increase of 103 percent.
Assuming that the amount of cultivable land today is roughly the
same as that available in 1901, this means that at that date each
square kilometre had to support about 300 persons; while by
1941 with the population registering almost exactly 76,000, the
pressure on the fields had gone up to nearly 350 per square
kilometre. There are Ladakhis with a clear recollection of conditions before 1947–8 (when the present phase of Ladakh's history
may be said to have begun), who are emphatic in their assertion
that apart from small quantities of rice, which is regarded as a
luxury article, there was no import of foodgrains up to that date.
But the figures given above cast some doubt on the correctness of
this; indeed the early writers state categorically that Ladakh is not
self-sufficient in food. Moorcroft in the early 1820s tells us that
the Ladakhis 'rear an inadequate supply of food', and that grain is
imported from Kashmir, the Punjab and the provinces south of
the Himalaya; and Cunningham, including Lahul and Spiti in his
calculations, gives figures to prove the impossibility of Ladakh
producing enough food to sustain its inhabitants. He states that
the total annual value of the grain imported was a little less than
250,000 rupees, and adds that 'this sum was defrayed entirely by
the profits of the carrying trade, of which the Ladakhis have an
entire monopoly between Yarkand and Kashmir.' It seems likely
that over the centuries a complicated and delicate economic balance evolved, based ultimately on the caravan traffic, the only
possible source of the profits necessary to buy food for a population which, even then, pressed heavily on the fields.

Various factors have contributed to keeping the population
relatively low. There were social constraints: according to Cunningham's estimate in 1847, something like seven percent of the
population of both sexes chose the religious life and became
monks or nuns, remaining celibate. The relative prosperity of

Ladakh, compared to neighbouring Baltistan where because of Islam polygamy was practised, was accounted for by nineteenth century travellers as the effect of polyandry, which surely made the number of children born less than in a monogamous or polygamous society. But there was in addition a high rate of infant mortality, showing that in the past the harshness of the environment acted as a check on the population, so that it at no time outstripped the resources necessary to provide every individual with the means of survival. Obviously these necessities are much greater for a Ladakhi than for a peasant in, for instance, north Bihar. Thus what seems like a modest degree of prosperity actually represents, as much as the poverty of the plains, the threshold of survival. The only difference is that this threshold is much higher in Ladakh.

To a great extent, and with exceptions in the towns of Leh and Kargil, the economic and everyday life of the Ladakhis continues in the early 1980s much as it must have done for the last millennium or so. To describe it briefly is no easy matter, for there are great differences between the different regions of the two districts. In Leh and Kargil, for instance, there exists a small class of families, mostly representatives of the old aristocracy, who are wealthy by any standards. They made their fortunes in the distant and not-so-distant past, by the time-honoured and universal methods of Government service at the highest levels; ownership of land; trade—in this case participation in the caravan traffic which was the only thing that raised Ladakh above the level of a subsistence economy; and most recently, as contractors to Government in the large-scale programme of public works that has been going on ever since the construction of the Srinagar–Leh highway in the early 1960s. The life led by these families is comfortable, but not ostentatious; many of them are now using their capital to invest in Ladakh's most recent source of profit, the tourist trade.

The ordinary people of the countryside, peasants and herdsmen, live scattered over an area of 60,000 square kilometres, at altitudes from 2,750 metres to 4,500 metres above sea level. Such a range of altitude naturally implies tremendous climatic and environmental variations, which in turn impose great differences on the people's way of life. To take extremes—there is little in common between the Sham Ilaqa and Sodh Ilaqa, the lower regions down the Indus, at a level of 2,750 metres or even less, where the length of the summer permits of double cropping and autumn sees a rich harvest of fruit, and the bleak upland plateaux of Chang-Thang, where there is no cultivation worth speaking of, and the nomads herd their flocks of sheep and pashmina goats at the entire mercy of the weather which is hard enough at the best of times. The other desperately poor region is Dras which, with its heavy snowfall and long winter, can harvest only one crop; it has the added problem of a severe shortage of firewood for winter fuel. Although it is on the main road into Ladakh, few benefits accrue to it from the traffic across it, for unless there is a blockage on the road the tourists and truck-drivers stop at Dras only long enough to refresh themselves with a cup of tea. Indeed, historically, Dras has been impoverished by its position on the road to Kashmir. Its inhabitants were subject to a system of forced labour for porterage for which they got no recompense, the profits of their labour going to their joint suzerains, the king of Ladakh, and the *malik*—lord—of the neighbouring Kashmir area of Sonamarg.

Zanskar, while it shares some of the characteristics of Dras—a long hard winter with heavy snowfall—is relatively better off. There is some willow plantation that provides a supply of winter fuel, and enough cultivation and livestock to have made it a surplus area. Zanskar butter is still exported to Leh, and grain to Chang-Thang, where it is bartered for salt. Purig, comprising Kargil town and its immediate neighbourhood, the Suru valley, and the Mulbekh, Bodh Kharbu and Chigtan areas, occupies a middle place in terms of the relative prosperity of the different regions. The climate is extreme, but the amount of winter snow manageable; around the villages of Sankhu and Mulbekh the soil is productive and the people fairly well off. Some of the best of Ladakh's apricots are grown around Kargil.

For the last three centuries, Leh has held an unchallenged position as the commercial as well as the administrative capital of Ladakh. The prosperity that the caravan trade brought to the town spilled over into its hinterland, compensating for the limitations imposed on agriculture by the length and severity of winter. Nubra is one of the relatively kindly areas, comparable to the Sham Ilaqa, being situated at a slightly lower altitude than other regions, so that double-cropping is possible; in addition it has large tracts under hypophae, a low woody shrub which makes excellent firewood.

In regions where cultivation is possible, it is broadly true to say that agriculture is the main occupation. Below 3,000 metres wheat is grown, while elsewhere the staple crop is naked barley, known in Ladakhi as *grim*. In the Sham Ilaqa and the Sodh Ilaqa—say from Nyemo downriver to where the Indus leaves Ladakh—and in parts of Purig, cultivation of grain is supplemented by fruit-growing; these are the homes of the apricot, the only cash crop and, apart from pashmina, the only product exported from Ladakh in any quantity. Wherever apricots grow, apples can also; and in the Sodh Ilaqa there are even mulberries, a particularly sweet variety of melon, and grapes from which the *brokpa* make a perfectly palatable white wine.

The Ladakhi farmer, conscious of the limitations under which he has to work, is an extremely careful husbandman. Wherever the availability of firewood makes him independent of animal dung for fuel, he makes a point of keeping his animals to graze among the stubble for as long as possible after the harvest, so as to take advantage of the natural manure they give; his system of sanitation is geared to the same end. Ladakhis use dry closets built a few feet above the ground, in which the refuse, falling through a hole, is collected in a lower chamber, from which it is removed periodically and taken out to the fields. After the harvest, the fields are ploughed once before the earth hardens so much in the grip of winter as to become unworkable. As soon as the streams unfreeze in the spring, they are watered, then ploughed, manured and ploughed again. Sowing may be done broadcast, or in the furrow, and is followed by a period of intense activity, for weeding and watering have to be done regularly. The water is snow-melt, taken from mountain streams, and conducted to the crops by a system of channels and sub-channels, the flow being regulated simply by large clods of earth placed across them. Weeding starts about three weeks after the seed has been sown; as well as directly benefiting the growing grain, it supplements the supply of fodder available for the livestock. The work of weeding and watering is done mostly by women—a custom carried over, perhaps, from the days when a majority of the able-bodied men left their homes in summer to go with the caravans as porters and pony-drivers.

The results by any standards other than those of modern mechanized and scientific agriculture, are excellent. In 1821 Moorcroft who knew about such things, was full of praise for the crops he saw. 'In no other country have I seen an equal surface in barley as regularly covered with plant, and never plants with better heads.' This he attributed partly to the extremes of temperature to which the plants were exposed in this harsh climate, combined with the dry atmosphere and the irrigation with very cold water; but partly also to the care taken in preparing the fields and looking after the growing plants. Talking of a particularly fine crop near Bodh Kharbu, he declared, 'It was the finest crop I ever beheld; and a spirited English farmer would have thought himself sufficiently repaid for a ride of many miles by a sight of it.' This was high praise from a man of post agricultural-revolution England, whose profession as a veterinary surgeon must earlier have taken him riding long distances among the fields and farms of rural England. Conditions in Ladakh have not changed greatly between Moorcroft's time and ours.

In the villages, as well as in Chang-Thang where the nomads lead a pastoral life, almost every family keeps some livestock, if no more than a goat or two. The plough is drawn by the *dzo*, a hybrid between the male yak and the common cow. For the purpose of breeding these—for the female *dzo*, the *dzomo*, though not sterile, does not produce viable offspring—each farmer must keep one or two cows; while several combine in the ownership of a yak, known as *gon-yak* or *yul-yak* which, rather like the Brahmini bull of the Indian plains, wanders free to perform his duty of impregnating the cows.

In Chang-Thang, where there is virtually no agriculture, animal husbandry is a way of life, and the people's whole existence revolves round the migration of their flocks in search of pasture. The chief source of the nomads' livelihood is the pashmina goat; their two other animals are the yak and the *huniya* sheep. From the yak come the hair out of which their tents are woven, milk and butter (though not in great quantities), meat, when an animal has to be slaughtered, and above all power, for it is primarily a carrying animal. The *huniya* sheep is also a pack animal which provides in addition coarse wool and ultimately meat. But, whether in Chang-Thang or in the primarily agricultural areas of Ladakh, meat-production is the least of the purposes of livestock-rearing. Even the Buddhist inhabitants of this cold and harsh climate are not above sacrificing merit to bodily considerations, and eating meat when occasion offers. Nevertheless they are keenly aware that the real value of their animals lies in the produce they give recurrently, milk, wool and power; they have more sense than to deplete the sources of these by indiscriminate slaughter. Meat is rather a by-product of the necessary process of culling animals from the flocks, which takes place before the winter, so as to avoid wasting scarce fodder on animals which have outlived their usefulness. This system has the incidental advantages of providing a supply of meat at the season when the climate gives natural refrigeration, enabling it to be kept for many weeks or even months; and of providing a source of protein when the weather puts the greatest strain on the human body.

Otherwise, the diet of the people seems poor enough, though it or something like it has provided nourishment to the populations of the Tibetan plateau for millennia. The staple ingredient is *tsampa*, parched barley flour; this is mixed to a kind of gruel either with butter-tea, or with *chang*, a mildly alcoholic drink, best described as fermented barley-water, and drunk by all the Tibetan peoples. It is probably true to say that everyone has enough to eat—they could not survive otherwise in this climate—but there is little enough margin.

Nevertheless, the Ladakhis are a sturdy people. Over generations, their physique has developed in response to the harsh environment. In particular, to cope with the rarefied air they have to breathe, they show unusual strength of the heart and lungs, which few outsiders even after years of acclimatization, will be able to match. Where a plainsman may pant, or need to stop for breath, the Ladakhi will forge ahead, showing no signs of distress. Like all the hill peoples of India, the Ladakhis can shift loads that seem incredible to the pampered products of a sophisticated civilization. This too has been a way of adapting to life in a land where there were no roads fit for wheels (and where, as a result, the use of the wheel for transport is unknown), and so the only way of carrying goods from one place to another for a man too poor to own pack animals was on his back. Frederic Drew was impressed by the stamina of his porters:

I have had women employed to carry my baggage, according to the custom of the country, who have done twenty-three or twenty-four miles with sixty pounds on their back, and have come in at the end singing cheerfully.[1]

Similarly, by the standards of most outsiders, the Ladakhis are impervious to cold. These adaptations vary in degree according to the varying conditions within Ladakh itself. The nomadic herdsman from Chang-Thang, used to an altitude of 4,500 metres, will feel intolerably oppressed by the summer's heat in Leh, and the thickness of the atmosphere. In thirty degrees of frost on a winter night, he may prefer to sleep under the stars, rather than in the stuffy warmth of the *ribo*, the yak-hair tent which is his home.

These qualities must have been acquired by generations of natural selection, and if, as is believed, there is a high rate of infant mortality even now, this shows that the process continues, ensuring that only the sturdiest survive. One result of this is that at the other end of the scale, longevity is greater in Ladakh than in other places where conditions are easier, the census figures (1961) showing that over 10 percent of the population were over 55 years of age, while the figure for other districts in Jammu and Kashmir varied from 5.5 to 8 percent. No doubt there are particular health problems, which have been identified by the local administration as part of the fact-finding process which is a *sine qua non* of its efforts to improve the condition of the people. These relate largely to maternal and child welfare, and nutrition in general. Many children seem to have caries, an uncommon ailment in the plains, perhaps because the fluoride content of the water is low. Chronic diseases found mostly in limited areas are leprosy in the Sodh Ilaqa, and tuberculosis around Kargil and in the Dras and Sankhu belts. The fact that tuberculosis is almost absent in Buddhist Ladakh, being found only in parts of the Kargil district, may be partly explained by the seclusion of women in the Muslim areas, who spend much of their time cooped up in the close interiors of their houses. In Buddhist Ladakh, by contrast, men and women alike spend as much time as possible out of doors, even in winter, gratefully savouring the sun's warmth. As in every rural society, the Ladakhis have an indigenous system of medicine based on herbs and other natural substances. Its practitioners who are called *amchis* undergo a long and rigorous course of training.

[1]Frederic Drew *The Jummoo and Kashmir Territories*, p. 248.

There are a surprising number of literate people in Buddhist Ladakh, even in the villages. This was noticed by Drew a hundred years ago, and it remains true today. It is probably due to the fact that there is a *gompa* in almost every sizeable village, and in the old days it was usual for at least one child of every family to be dedicated to religion as a lama. After his novitiate, he would probably spend as much time in the village as in the *gompa*. But the tradition of literacy extended also to lay people, and may have something to do with months of enforced idleness in winter. Drew remarked approvingly that the literate Ladakhi had a distinct edge over his counterpart in Kashmir or elsewhere in India, in the matter of reading and comprehending a map.

The impact of modern education outside the towns of Leh and Kargil and their immediate neighbourhoods has nevertheless been small. There is good reason for this. Even now, to people whose main occupation is farming, the connection between any intellectual attainment beyond that of mere literacy, and the prospect of economic betterment may not be obvious; on the contrary, sending children to school is counter-productive, because for the hours they are in school they are not free to help with the real work of the family, in the fields or with the flocks. This is a particular problem in Chang-Thang. The difficulties of organizing a system of schooling appropriate to a nomadic society anywhere are here redoubled by the extreme harshness of the environment.

However, attitudes are changing, though only gradually. In Leh, for example, there is a shortage of educated Ladakhis to man Government offices, particularly at the higher levels, with the result that there is a large non-Ladakhi element—mostly Kashmiri and Dogri—in the local administration. It is not difficult for people to understand that education is at the same time the way to fulfil the aspirations of Ladakhis in general for a greater say in their own affairs, and the way for individuals to achieve better jobs and higher status for themselves. This awareness is now beginning to filter down to the villages.

Technology in Ladakh is of the simplest. The absence of any kind of wheeled transport in the traditional scheme of things comes as a surprise at first, for one thinks of ignorance of the wheel as the hall-mark of a society still at a primitive level of culture. But one soon realizes that the reason for it lies, like so much else, in the environment—in the rugged mountainous terrain which makes the wheel utterly impractical as a means of transport. It is far more sensible to use sturdy pack animals, or even to heave a load on one's own back, than to try to invest the same amount of energy in propelling a cart up a steep and stony incline, or in holding it back on the downward slope. This does not mean that the use of the wheel for other purposes is unknown, where energy really can be saved. Most obvious of these is the prayer-wheel; of a more workaday application is the mill-wheel—not as in Europe a ponderous affair set vertically and needing the strong current of a large volume of water to turn it, but rather a circular set of paddles set horizontally and operated by a fairly modest flow, its axis prolonged to turn the nether millstone. Although this type of water-mill is current elsewhere in the area of Tibetan influence—Michel Peissel describes it in Mustang—it is believed to have reached Ladakh from Baltistan; the Baltis, though of a Tibetan stock similar to the Ladakhis, have been credited with superior engineering skills. Really primitive—in Ladakh as almost everywhere in India, the plains and the hills alike—is the plough, simply an iron-shod piece of wood, guided through the earth by the farmer's grasp on its handle, and drawn by the docile *dzo*. Other agricultural tools—the hoe and the spade—are equally simple. As for the manufacture of homespun cloth, the spindle is often no more than a sturdy twig, about 20 centimetres long and the thickness of a child's finger, worn smooth by years of use, and dangling free, or with its spin supported in a tiny saucer. The looms are equally unsophisticated. Outside the Government-sponsored weaving centres, the flying shuttle is unknown even now, and the thread of the weft is passed laboriously from hand to hand—a procedure which necessarily limits the cloth to narrow widths.

Construction methods have the same simplicity; anything that is built is built entirely by hand. Houses are made of stones collected from the ground, or of hand-formed sun-dried bricks; the only plaster used is mud which, in a climate as dry as Ladakh's, serves the purpose admirably. The roof-beams are of timber—usually poplar—the interstices being filled with neatly-laid bundles of willow twigs, and the whole covered with earth, well beaten down. J eh palace, built 350 years ago, and the *gompas*, are constructed according to exactly the methods in use today.

The fields have been prepared for cultivation in the first inst-

ance by clearing the ground of the stones with which it is everywhere encumbered; these stones have provided the material for
the dry-stone walls that divide the fields from each other, and also
buttress the 'steps' where sloping land has had to be terraced.
Moorcroft also describes a system whereby walls are constructed
along the mountainsides towards their base, and left for years to
trap the alluvium brought down by the melting snows, thus laying
the foundations for future cultivation.

But the most impressive technological feat achieved in old
Ladakh is undoubtedly the amazing system of irrigation, found
mostly in the western regions. Water is conducted, often for
kilometres, along channels high on the slopes of steep-sided valleys to a patch of land flat enough for cultivation, or to a slope
gentle enough for the construction of terraced fields. Given the
limitations of technique, anonymous and unsung engineers have
performed what are not far short of miracles; again it is the Baltis
rather than the Ladakhis who are believed to have had the skills
necessary to work them.

In every part of Ladakh except Chang-Thang, winter is relatively an idle season. Once the harvest is gathered in and the last
ploughing done, there is no more work in the fields until spring
comes and they have to be prepared for sowing. Of course animals have to be looked after in winter as in summer; but in the
villages they stay close to their quarters, which are usually on the
ground floor of the dwelling-houses, so tending them is mainly a
matter of giving them their fodder, no more. The main work of
this season is weaving, which is done on primitive looms often set
up on the sunny rooftops. Apart from these, even the new kinds
of economic activity brought by the processes of 'development'
and 'modernization' come largely to a halt in winter. No construction of a modern or traditional kind can be accomplished, as the
intense cold induces cracks in every kind of cementing agent,
whether mud-plaster or lime-mortar. In the old days there was a
tradition of migrant labour in the Kargil region: the able-bodied
men would go out in winter to Kashmir or Baltistan where their
robust physique and their willingness to endure cold and other
hardships made them much in demand as unskilled labourers.
But increased prosperity, largely derived from the work available
during the six months' construction season on various projects of
the public works programme, or on the continuous process of

road maintenance, has nearly put an end to this. In the Buddhist areas, winter is punctuated and given colour by the annual festivals of the various *gompas*, which take place at intervals during the cold season, only the one at Hemis falling in summer. People come from far and near to attend these traditional religious ceremonies around which gathers much of the atmosphere of a *tamasha*.

Thus there emerges the picture of a hardy people, intelligent yet unsophisticated, living a life that varies according to the conditions in different regions, but that has hardly as yet been touched by the winds of change and modernization. In Nubra and the Sham Ilaqa as in Chang-Thang, the rhythm of life is dictated by the cycle of the seasons: ploughing, seed-time and harvest; the rearing of animals, birth and death among the flocks, and their wanderings in search of pasture. It is a life lived close to nature, modified by only the simplest of technological devices, where a most delicate balance operates between man, his physical environment, and the rhythm of the seasons.

VIII
Change

The balance with the natural environment which is the basic characteristic of Ladakhi life is today threatened by the forces of change and so-called progress which no ancient society, brought face to face with the modern world, can hope to escape. Not least of these is the deliberate application of the techniques of economic development by a number of Government agencies. This is a sensitive area, fraught with danger. So delicate is the existing balance that any tampering with it in the name of development may do more harm than good. The Ladakhis have over the centuries evolved methods of meeting the challenges posed by their inhospitable environment—methods which have stood the test of time. It is the developer's job to understand these, and build upon them. Government's success in preserving ancient social and work patterns as it plans to improve material conditions, will be a test of its commitment to the real interests of Ladakh and its people.

Basic to Government's development policies is the improvement of communications. In the past, the simple needs of far-flung populations could be met either locally, or in the form of loads carried in on the backs of animals or men. Consequently wheels, and the roads necessary for wheeled transport, were irrelevant. In the old days too, rivers proved formidable obstacles, often swirling through deep chasms, almost always rushing too impetuously over their stony beds to make fording safe or easy. Travellers' tales of the last century are full of exciting accounts of river-crossings by rope-bridges swaying precariously over the foaming torrent beneath. But today, things are different. The administration is committed to policies—whether it be in health, education, agriculture or animal husbandry—involving imports of material and manpower that make it imperative to have roads

adequate for truck and jeep traffic. Thus nearly half the development budget of the two districts is devoted to road- and bridge-
building. The impact on the communities so opened up remains
to be seen.

The tapping of potential sources of power is another aspect of
development on which Government is laying stress, with the
construction of hydro-electric projects, particularly in the immediate neighbourhoods of Leh and Kargil towns. A more promising approach may be the exploitation of solar energy. This is
being tried less by official agencies than by groups interested in
appropriate technologies, and the search for new and unconven-
tional sources of energy. Experimental systems introduced in the
villages of Sabu and Skara near Leh, and the SOS Tibetan Children's Village at Choglamsar, have shown that for an outlay that is
not excessive houses may be heated in winter exclusively by solar
power.

Ladakh is basically a rural economy, and any effective drive
towards material progress must be largely directed towards agriculture. The main constraint here is the extreme shortage of
water for irrigation, and hence of cultivable land. As the population increases, this may become a serious problem. Here there is
no doubt that Government can play a most useful role, planning
and executing large-scale irrigation schemes which are beyond
the resources of private enterprise. The virtual absence of rainfall
makes Ladakhi agriculture totally dependent on irrigation; but
all those sources that lie within the scope of traditional technology
have already been tapped. Most of the schemes already completed by Government have been devoted to setting up model and
experimental farms directly under the district administrations—
like the Khumbathang farm up the Suru from Kargil. Major
projects under construction are the Kharbathang Canal, which
will tap the Wakha River between Mulbekh and Pashkyum, to
bring water to the barren plateau opposite Kargil; and the High
Martselang Project, planned to irrigate the whole of the gently-
sloping alluvial tract, some forty kilometres in length, on the left
bank of the Indus opposite Leh. The land made available for
cultivation by these two schemes is to be leased or sold to the local
farmers, not used directly by any Government agency.

Apart from irrigation, efforts are being made to improve the
yields of traditional agriculture by the introduction of high-

yielding varieties of foodgrains, and the use of chemical fertilizers. Although this latter programme has met with a fair degree of acceptance by the farmers, which proves it to be compatible with traditional methods, the administration seems unaware of its potential dangers, and its known tendency to backfire after a few years. Difficulties of access to the villages of the interior will for the present limit its application to those areas which are within easy reach of main roads, and fortunately give the opportunity for its long-term effects in Ladakhi conditions to be assessed before it is introduced more widely. The harsh climate has also limited the success of the high-yielding varieties programme. Again, the decision to introduce any new strain of wheat or barley should be made taking into consideration the farmer's traditional methods. If it involves any kind of disruptive change in old-established patterns of co-operative labour, the increased yield may be purchased at too high a cost.

Work is also going forward on the development of fodder production, an important matter in a land where animals have to be stall-fed for six months of the year. There is an old local tradition of growing lucerne, going back to the days when thousands of pack animals regularly traversed Ladakh in the trade caravans. It is called *ol* in Ladakhi, and several varieties exist, of which the one known as Yarkandi *ol* is preferred, because it is perennial for a period of up to twenty-five years, thus requiring a minimum of labour. The Agriculture Department is encouraging the cultivation of Yarkandi *ol*; Government plots for the multiplication of its seed have been established, and already enough is being produced for distribution to interested farmers.

The presence of the army has given an impetus to fruit- and vegetable-production, particularly in and around Leh; the Leh vegetable-growers' co-operative does business with the Army to the tune of about seven lakh rupees annually; while in 1980 the Army contracted for forty quintals of dried apricots. Apricots, being Ladakh's only cash crop, offer enormous possibilities. In the last four or five years, the district administrations have devoted a lot of attention to this area, experimenting with new strains, and new methods of grafting, as well as with improved methods of drying the fruit. These efforts have been accompanied by a vigorous advertising and marketing campaign outside Ladakh, which has been encouragingly successful. Even allowing for transport costs, Ladakhi apricots can be sold in the bazaars of Delhi and Calcutta for half the price of those imported from Afghanistan. At the same time, the farmer is now receiving double the price he could expect in 1976.

Ladakh is virtually without trees, except around the oases of cultivation, and the possibilities open to the Forest Department are strictly limited. When the amount of arable land is less than can support the population, the question of sparing irrigation for the development of forests hardly arises. Certainly, there can be no grandiose schemes of ecological rehabilitation through afforestation (as is being done in certain more recently denuded areas of the Outer Himalaya, where rainfall is relatively abundant) but more modest aims of providing limited amounts of fodder for the omnivorous goat, timber for building, and fuel. Firewood is imported from Kashmir, where there is no shortage of timber, for use in the towns; but the villages will continue to rely on local sources for fuel, and if firewood is not available, they will have to continue to use animal dung, which could more profitably serve to fertilize the fields. So far, only Government has done much in the way of plantation along roads and river-banks, and wherever the administration owns a patch of irrigated land. Efforts are concentrated mostly on the traditionally grown trees, poplar and willow, both of which are multiplied from cuttings, and to both of which traditional methods of pollarding, peculiar to Ladakh, are applied, so that they produce repeated crops of fuel- and timber-wood, as well as of leaves for fodder. The Department has also taken up a programme of planting hypophae, which makes an excellent fuel. The pencil cedar, a handsome tree considered sacred by the Buddhists, was common in the days of Moorcroft and Drew in the Dras and Kargil areas and the lower Indus valley about Khaltse; it has now largely disappeared. Nurseries have been established for it and for exotic varieties like pine and acacia from which cuttings are supplied to the villagers.

Since the ratio of domestic animals to humans in Ladakh is three to one, animal husbandry offers a lot of scope to the 'developer'. Apart from increasing fodder production, the administration's efforts have mostly been directed towards improving, where appropriate, the local breeds of livestock. But this is a matter to be approached with care, and Ladakh itself provides a cautionary tale in the fate of the Purig sheep. This little animal made a great impression on Moorcroft and Cunningham for though small, it gave a good quantity of wool—two clips a year— and its meat was particularly delicious. It gave two lambs a year and its great advantage was that it could be kept at practically no expense, as it was happy to eat almost anything—leaves, grass, straw, household refuse like vegetable parings and spent tea-leaves; Moorcroft even saw one nibble a bone. But this little prodigy seems to exist no more—possibly because of well-intentioned but ill-conceived attempts to 'upgrade' it; more likely because of interbreeding between the local animals and the sheep of the Gujars and Bhakarwals, nomadic tribes who bring their flocks up from the Kashmir valley and the plains to the high pastures of Dras and Kargil in summer.

The animals actually existing in Ladakh are mostly well adapted to their environment, and it would be rash to assume that the introduction of exotic blood would in every instance improve upon the result of centuries of natural selection. A case in point is the *huniya* sheep, which constitutes a good part of the wealth of the Chang-Thang nomads. This big-boned animal lives comfortably at 4,500 metres thriving on the scanty grasses and desert plants, the only nourishment it can find at that altitude. It gives a large quantity of rather coarse wool, which not only is of value to the nomads for their own clothing, but whose long staple makes it a useful raw material for the carpet industry. Until Chang-Thang is opened up by motorable roads, its value as a pack animal will endure. In short, it is an animal ideally suited to its environment. It is pleasant that this fact has been unequivocally recognized by the district authorities, so that plans to send merinos to Chang-Thang to 'upgrade' the *huniya* stock have been abandoned. On the contrary, the *huniya* has been recognized as an original stock which can be used to upgrade the sheep population of other highland areas outside Ladakh, and there is a project to send selected *huniya* rams to Doda and Udhampur, the hill districts north of Jammu, for this purpose.[1]

Pashmina, Ladakh's only export apart from dried apricots, is the *raison d'être* of the Chang-Thang herdsmen and of their nomadic way of life. This valuable product, since the seventeenth century the basis of the multi-crore shawl industry of Srinagar,

This project was first suggested by Alexander Cunningham in 1854.

has had a decisive impact on Ladakh's history, and probably
provides the explanation why successive rulers of Kashmir, from
Shah Jahan onwards, were so anxious to establish their suzerainty
over it. In 1684, an institutional guarantee that pashmina from
Ladakh and western Tibet would find its way exclusively to Kashmiri looms was obtained by the Treaty of Tingmosgang. Despite
the efforts of the East India Company to break this monopoly in
the early nineteenth century, the provision holds good to this day
in the form of the Jammu and Kashmir Government's Pashmina
Control Order. The unfortunate effect of this has been to keep
the price of pashmina artificially low, thus frustrating attempts to
improve the lot of the herdspeople. There is probably no immediate danger of the rearing of the pashmina goat becoming so
uneconomic as to force the nomads to abandon their ancient
vocation, but even the possibility is a nightmare, for apart from
the disappearance of a unique lifestyle in Chang-Thang, it would
spell disaster for thousands engaged in Srinagar's shawl industry.
Accordingly, proposals have been made for the lifting of a signifi-
cant proportion of each year's pashmina by Government agencies
at an economic price, and the establishment of shawl-weaving as a
cottage industry in Ladakh. The amount of wool available to the
Tibet Baqals, the caucus of Srinagar merchants who enjoy a
monopoly of the wholesale trade in pashmina, will thus become
less, and the price it can command automatically rise.

Other means of helping the herdspeople of Chang-Thang are
the construction of kidding-sheds, to bring down the painfully
high mortality among the kids, born in the coldest months of
winter; and the establishment of fodder-banks, to keep the
animals alive in those winters—say one out of five or six—during
which there is enough snow to cover the scanty pasturage on
which they browse in winter as well as summer. These two programmes have been implemented only since 1979, but already they
have led to a dramatic fall in mortality, and increase in the number of goats.

Although the yield of the Chang-Thang goat is very low—
hardly 500 grams of raw pashmina annually—there is so far no
programme to 'upgrade' the breed by the introduction of exotic
stock; for its pashmina is finer than that of the central Asian and
Mongolian goats, which yield a larger quantity, and the soft and

delicate fabric it produces is at a premium. Experiments in selec-
tive breeding are being conducted, though at the most optimistic
they can produce results only in the very long run.

Although pashmina is Ladakh's most important product, little
or nothing is known about the nomadic lifestyle of the Chang-
Thang herdspeople, or about their system of rearing these valuable animals. That there is a system is certain; the herdspeople's
wanderings are not done at random; but as yet it is unstudied, as is
the amazing variety of Chang-Thang's grasses, maintaining a
tenacious hold on life in a hostile environment, which provide
nourishment for the pashmina goat and the nomad's other livestock, the yak and the *huniya* sheep. Are the nomads aware of the
danger of overgrazing these fragile pastures, and damaging them
irrevocably? We do not know; though there is a strong presump-
tion that communities living in such close touch with the earth,
will have derived from the experience of generations a lively
ecological awareness. Until the social and environmental bases of
life and work in Chang-Thang have been thoroughly studied, the
administration will be wise to limit its efforts at 'development' to
such obvious aids as kidding sheds and fodder banks.

As for the ordinary goats, sheep and cows of the villages, they
possess no remarkable qualities, so there is no theoretical objection to improving them by the introduction of exotic blood.
Cross-bred merino rams are being successfully introduced to
increase the wool-yield of the local sheep, and cross-bred Jersey
bulls for increased milk-yields. The success of this latter scheme is
limited by the farmer's unwillingness to put more than half his
cows to the Jersey bull, reserving half for the yak, with a view to
the production of *dzos* to yoke to the plough. A programme which
should benefit the poorest families is to take cross-bred billy-goats
of the Alpine and Sannen breeds to the villages, to improve the
local breed. There is hardly a household which does not own a
goat or two; and yet the only milk available for children is from
the mothers, who often suckle their babies for three or four years.
All these programmes depend on experiments to establish the
ideal percentage of exotic blood in the animals to be released as
breeding-stock, and that combination of genes which gives the
highest yield—whether of wool or milk—as well as the com-
pletest resistance to Ladakh's climatic conditions.

The Government's health and education programmes will surely be potent agents of change, but whether for better or worse will depend on how they are handled, and the aims and motives of those operating them. Recent years have seen a certain re-thinking about the health service, which is at present organized on a pyramidal pattern, with dispensaries in the villages providing outdoor treatment for minor ailments. Serious complaints are referred to the hospitals in the two towns. This system, developed in the heavily-populated districts of the plains, is totally inappropriate for Ladakh where a man might have to walk thirty kilometres to reach the nearest dispensary, and still be four days' march from the road-head for the hospital where alone a serious case can be treated. Consequently the average village doctor, waiting in his dispensary for patients to beat a path to his door tends to see cases of minor ailments only; often it is only when the serious cases have reached an advanced stage, at which treatment may be difficult or impossible, that they make the effort to come to him. Clearly, this does little to raise the level either of health among the villagers or morale among doctors. A suggested solution is the creation of a mobile medical service in which the doctor will go to the patients, rather than wait for them to come to him. More hopefully, programmes of preventive medicine have been initiated to combat chronic diseases like tuberculosis and leprosy; also programmes of maternal and child welfare. Such emphasis on prophylactic rather than merely curative medicine is to be welcomed, though it is important to ensure that modern methods do not altogether undercut the traditional system, an important base of Ladakhi society.

An urgent need is the development of an appropriate philosophy of education to ensure that the school curriculum is relevant to Ladakh, and also to help preserve its endangered heritage of music and oral literature. One cannot wish Ladakh to be cut off from the world as it actually exists, but the world-view presented to its children must be a balanced one, showing in true perspective the failures as well as the achievements of the material culture that is encroaching so rapidly on their lives. At the same time, a local orientation should inculcate pride in Ladakh's traditional culture, and in a society which, striking a happy balance between individual and community rights and duties, has recently been described as showing a striking similarity to 'Gandhi's Utopia, the ideal he believed had existed only in the agrarian villages of ancient India.'[2]

Unfortunately, there is no evidence that the Education Department which is largely manned by outsiders at the higher levels, is applying its mind seriously to evolving an education adapted to Ladakh's peculiar conditions. Rather there seems to be an unthinking adoption of the stereotype applied elsewhere in India (where it may be no more appropriate than in Ladakh), essentially a low-grade version of the western model. It would be a tragedy if the widespread diffusion of this type of valueless pedagogy should result—as it has in the plains—in the creation of a semi-educated proletariat, whose skills scarcely extend beyond basic literacy, and who are both incapable of thinking for themselves, and divorced from their cultural roots. It is probably too much to expect Government to appreciate the damage that can be done by inappropriate educational policies. The initiative in evolving a type of education peculiarly suited to Ladakh's needs may have to come from the Ladakhis themselves.

There is one development which, though hardly initiated by the administration, is likely to bring more change to parts of Ladakh than all its efforts in the fields of agriculture, animal husbandry, road- and bridge-building, health and education put together: the arrival of the tourist industry. The presence of outsiders is indeed no new thing for Ladakh, and every citizen of Leh over the age of forty remembers the days of the caravan trade, when the routes to central Asia and Tibet were open, goods came over the Karakoram Pass, and the bazaar was home to a colony of foreign merchants, their agents coming and going with the *kafilas*. In a sense, then, the arrival of the tourists is the continuation of an ancient tradition; but there is this grave difference that, coming from an unfamiliar world as they do, and as the merchants of the old days did not, they pose a new kind of threat to existing values—or rather, they pose in an immediate form the threat inherent in the whole process of change and modernization.

There can be no doubt that the purely economic aspect of the tourist influx has been a blessing. Particularly remarkable is the

[2]Helena Norberg-Hodge, 'Ladakh: Development Without Destruction', *The Himalaya: Aspects of Change*, ed. J. S. Lall (New Delhi, 1981) p. 282.

eagerness and self-confidence shown by the local people in making the considerable investments necessary to exploit this new source of profit. This is true even of the man of modest means who has built a room or two on to his house to accommodate paying guests during the season; the more prosperous have built hotels, three or four of which even if they fall short of 'five-star' standards of luxury, can welcome all but the most exacting of foreign tourists without a blush. When considering what such investment involves, it must be remembered that apart from the actual stones and mud of which the walls are made, every physical component has been carried in from outside, over the Zoji-La, and for Leh, over the two other passes as well.

The initial investment made, the returns are sure. A people who have little other marketable surplus are enabled to sell their services: an 'invisible export', in which moreover transport costs are paid by the consumer. It is not only the proprietors of hotels and guest-houses who stand to profit; employment is created in a whole range of tourist-related services, and shopkeepers benefit too. The relatively small scale on which tourist facilities have developed means that the newly-generated income is dispersed, bringing to quite poor people profits which must make a considerable difference to their lives.

Unfortunately, this pattern has always been distorted by the influence of neighbouring Kashmir, with its long-developed expertise in exploiting tourists to the utmost. Since almost all the Ladakh tourists come through Srinagar, a certain amount of the profit tends to be siphoned off by agencies there. A graver development is the recent arrival in Ladakh of a few giant hotel chains, whose presence may well attract a wealthier class of visitor, but will surely prevent much of the resultant profit from percolating down into the local economy. It is sad for those who love Ladakh to see its special qualities being exploited for outsiders' gain.

A side effect of the tourist boom is the way in which it has spurred on the authorities to make improvements to the region's somewhat sparse amenities, from which the local people benefit too. Road transport has been developed, so that now every day during the summer ten or twelve buses are plying between Srinagar and Leh; scheduled air services from Delhi via Chandigarh and Srinagar have been introduced; and the two towns, Leh and Kargil, have been considerably spruced up. Otherwise, Government and the district authorities have taken only a limited part in the provision of tourist amenities, preferring to let private enterprise get on with it, and confining themselves to a regulatory role.

While the benefits brought to the local people by the tourist trade are material and tangible, the negative side of it is more subtle, though familiar enough from other parts of the world where the uncontrolled influx of outsiders has had the effect of destroying the special qualities that appealed to them in the first place. A recent paper on Nepal has described tourism as 'the goose that lays golden eggs, but also fouls its own nest '[3] The self-consciousness that must creep into local attitudes, as people feel themselves under the scrutiny of uncomprehending outsiders, cannot be healthy. Even more disturbing is the inevitable commercialization of values among a people whose relationships with each other are based a good deal less on the cash nexus than those of more complex societies. Tourists represent a quite different equation, and thus bring a new element into the attitudes of the local people. Emphasis on purely material gain may debase relationships, as a proportion of those coming in contact with the visitors learn that it is possible to make a fast buck by taking more in the way of money, and giving less in the way of goods and services in return. Thus the canker at the heart of the modern world creeps into a land which has so far escaped it: the man who has learnt to get what he can out of the tourist is not likely to be over-scrupulous in his dealings with his own people. This process does not yet seem to have gone very far among the Ladakhis, but it is not likely that they will be able to resist it indefinitely.

So far, there has been one saving grace, by which Ladakh has been spared saturation exposure to the corruption of values inherent in the modern economic system. The tourist season lasts only from May to November, the Zoji-La being closed for the remaining months. Although this means that the investment in tourist facilities gives returns for only half the year, it also gives the Ladakhis the opportunity to turn in on themselves, draw strength from their cultural and religious roots and slip back into more normal modes of living and relating to one another. Now even this respite from confrontation with the modern world is

[3]D. D. Bhatt, 'The Nepal Himalaya and Change' in Lall (ed.), *The Himalaya.*

threatened. Air services from Srinagar and Delhi via Chandigarh have at a stroke breached Ladakh's winter defences; it is unlikely that the giant hotel chains that have started operating in Leh and Kargil intend their investment to give returns for only six months a year. Serious students and devotees of Buddhism will be grateful for the opportunity to get to Ladakh at the season when all the *gompas* except Hemis have their annual festivals; those less committed however may doubt whether the intense cold of Ladakh's winter is worth the attraction of what to them will be little more than a *tamasha*. Very likely, the main effect of the air service (apart from adding to the mobility of the Ladakhis themselves) will be, not so much to attract hordes of visitors in the depth of winter, as to lengthen the tourist season by giving access in April and May, when winter has already begun to recede, but the road has not yet opened.

Tourism undoubtedly has enormous potential as an earner of foreign exchange and a generator of revenue; and Indian Government policy has always regarded it in this light only, giving no thought to its effect on the places thus exposed to outside influences. As long as this attitude persists the tourist trade will remain a threat to Ladakh's ancient culture and values. And yet, there could be a different approach, like the one adopted by Ladakh's historical ally, Bhutan. Bhutan must be one of the few countries in the world where tourists are not welcomed indiscriminately, but given entry permits only if they can prove an informed interest in some particular aspect of its history, culture or physical features. The revenue-earning potential of the industry is taken care of by the stipulation that a minimum daily expenditure—$130 in 1981—be incurred. As a recent newspaper report put it, 'This is a conscious decision to abjure earnings to protect a unique way of life. Bhutan shudders at the thought of becoming another stop on the hippie's hash trail like Kathmandu.'[4] It will certainly be hard to impose such restrictions in Ladakh now, after so much local investment in the tourist industry has been made. But if a system similar to the Bhutanese one is not adopted, and Ladakh placed on the far side of a kind of cultural 'inner line' (analogous to the political one which keeps visitors a safe distance from the China and Pakistan borders), there is a real danger that in a few years its culture will be eroded, and a way of life that has given contentment to its people for centuries disappear for ever.

[4]Sunanda K. Datta-Ray in *The Statesman*, 21 July 1981.

The problem of tourism raises a basic issue: how far is it possible, even desirable, to keep Ladakh—or for that matter, any 'traditional' society—isolated from the modern world, with all its material achievements and its social and spiritual failures? There is no escape from the century in which we live; probably the best the Ladakhis or anyone else can hope for is to be given the chance to accept it on their terms, not its own. This is what Bhutan is aiming at; it is cautious and discriminating in the welcome it offers not only to tourists, but also to all forms of aid from abroad.

Ladakh does not have the same degree of control over its own affairs as independent and relatively prosperous Bhutan. Hence it behoves the authorities responsible for its destiny to apply their minds to its particular situation and problems, and to avoid the unthinking introduction of stereotypes of 'development' worked out in totally different contexts, which may in Ladakh prove not only inappropriate but positively disruptive. One precaution they must take is to ensure that the local people are consulted at every step. The possibility of going disastrously wrong can be minimized only if the villager, the person whose life will be affected by any change, is put fully in the picture regarding the implications of the new options being made available to him, and due weight is given to his perception of their likely effect on his pattern of life and work.

It can even be argued that Ladakh should be exempted from the whole process of purposive economic development. Here is a society free from grinding poverty; its way of life is based on laboriously evolved techniques, admirably adapted to the environment, which have proved their worth over centuries. This is a viable society: why change it? The short answer is that change is going to come, like it or not. In a hundred ways the modern world impinges. A villager from Chigtan learns to drive a car. The daughter of a well-to-do Leh family has her education in the convent at Srinagar. A doctor's wife, planning to have a new *goncha* made, chooses not *pattu* as the material, but polyester. A Chang-Thang shepherd on a trip to Leh to trade salt and butter for barley-flour is amazed at the variety of human types he sees as he rubs shoulders in the bazaar with visitors from Kanpur and Kyoto, Adelaide and Aberdeen. Such an all-pervasive challenge cannot leave society unchanged. This is the real justification for the Government-inspired development programme: if change has to come, let it be controlled to some extent, and let it benefit the people who most need help—the poor of the villages. Certain kinds of development seem to represent an absolute improvement, which hardly needs justification. The most obstinate traditionalist should not grudge the village people a supply of pure drinking water, or a system of medical care geared to the prevention as much as to the cure of disease. Nor, when it comes to modifying existing techniques, can objection be taken to the aim in view: to increase the return the owner of land or flocks can get from his property and the labour he puts into it, and so furnish him with a margin, something to fall back on when times are hard. The viability of society as a whole must be a matter of small consolation to the individual who is feeling the pinch: to the herdsman, for instance, who has lost four-fifths of his precious stock of pashmina goats because after five years there has been snow in Chang-Thang.

The main thrust of the development programme is being directed towards improving conditions in the villages, where the majority of Ladakhis have their homes and where, particularly in the remote interior among the crumpled masses of the mountains, there is little likelihood of change for the better unless a conscious effort is made. Everything points to the importance of this. Whether change is controlled or not, the exposure of Ladakh to the outside world is going to result in increasing prosperity in the towns, Leh and Kargil. It is here that the tourists chiefly congregate; here that the administrative offices generate employment at many levels; here that the military have their headquarters; here that there are the only bazaars worthy of the name; here that construction booms; here, in short, that there are opportunities. Comparable conditions all over the world have had the consequence of a rush from the village to the town, and the degradation of life in both. While the scale of the problem in Ladakh is such that urban blight does not seem to be an immediate danger, there is a real fear of the depopulation of the villages. By increasing the returns to the farmer and adding to his material comforts, this trend might be avoided.

While this is a universal problem, the situation in Ladakh has certain unusual features. For a start, the village is still largely cut off from the world outside, and the glamour of the big city limited to whatever Leh and Kargil have to offer. Secondly, and in contrast to the rest of India, Ladakh is relatively under-populated, so that efforts to develop rural life may well have positive results, and increased production do more than merely keep pace with a spiralling population. These considerations give grounds for hope that greater prosperity among the farmers might prevent the drain of talent from country to town, and thus help to preserve and enhance the qualities the Ladakhi village undoubtedly has as the setting for a simple yet satisfying life.

At the root of the Ladakhi social system is a tradition of co-operation, with the competitive spirit noticeably absent. Good relations with your neighbour, implying willingness to go out of your way to help him in the confidence that he will do no less for you, are at least as important as material profit. To give an example, although water for irrigation is in such short supply, disputes over the sharing of it are rare. Negotiations between the farmers are carried on in a friendly spirit, with mutual appreciation of the other man's needs and compulsions. This is in marked contrast to Kashmir, for instance, where, particularly in years of relative drought, water disputes needing the intervention of the authorities and occasionally leading to violence are common. The great fear regarding any programme that ignores the quality of life and thinks exclusively in terms of material development is that it may vitiate this attitude of mutual trust and dependence. A high-yielding variety of barley, if it required more water than the local strains, more than was available to everyone in an equitable system of sharing, would surely lead to a crisis in relationships among the villagers, which would be too high a price to pay for the increase in production. The planner in Ladakh must learn to think in human as well as in economic terms, or face the possibility of disaster as one change leads to another in an unpredictable chain reaction.

The risk is being taken, the challenge accepted, though with how sensitive an awareness of considerations beyond the purely economic, there may be some doubt. Only if it builds on a sure foundation—the wisdom of generations with its instinctive understanding of the importance of maintaining a balance between man and nature—can development fulfil its purpose of helping a people rooted in the past to face the inescapable challenge of the twentieth century.

IX
Polyandry and Polo

The Ladakhis are the result of a long blending of different races, of which the two most important were the Dards and the Tibetans. Although the Baltis, down the Indus to the north-west, are classified as a Tibetan race, it is noticeable that the further west you go in Ladakh, the less the people's appearance seems to betray any large-scale infusion of Tibetan stock. The people of Purig seem to be basically non-Tibetan, with some admixture of Tibetan genes; while in Dras, and the Da-Hanu area down the Indus from Khaltse, there are pockets of more or less pure Dard population, betrayed as such not only by their appearance, but also by their language. This belongs to the same sub-family of the Aryan group of languages as Kashmiri; but the Kashmiris being in contact with a wider world than the Dards, their speech has acquired a grace and polish that Dardish lacks, as well as a much wider vocabulary derived largely from Sanskrit and Persian. The 'standard' form of Dardish, known as Shina, is that spoken around Gilgit, the original Dard homeland; elsewhere the language has split up into forms said to be no longer mutually comprehensible. That spoken at Dras now has a strong admixture of Kashmiri words and idioms, while the speech of the Da-Hanu people has been influenced by their Ladakhi neighbours, and contains many Tibetan-derived expressions. The Dras Dards at some point embraced Islam, and so lost their original cultural identity; of much greater interest, from an anthropological point of view, are the Da-Hanu Dards, who have kept their ancient religion—Buddhism diluted with remnants of the Bon-chos—and much of what may be assumed to be their ancient way of life. They are known as *brokpa*, people of the pastures; and among the most striking of their customs is a dread, and almost complete avoidance, of washing. For ceremonial purification they burn the fragrant twigs of the pencil cedar. The riddle is how they have managed to remain almost unchanged over the centuries, although settled on one of the main lines of communication between Ladakh and Baltistan.

What is presumably a remnant of the original Dard population exists in almost every village of central and eastern Ladakh, in the shape of a group known as the Mons—a Tibetan word used generally to refer to the non-Tibetan populations living or originating south of the Himalaya. Distinguished by their non-Tibetan features, they are for the most part carpenters, blacksmiths and musicians; all the professional musicians, the players of *surna* and *daman*,[1] are Mons; and in particular contexts the word Mon has come to have the secondary meaning of musician. Although there is no caste in Buddhism, nevertheless the Mons, as a distinct group, are regarded as being of inferior status, in a way which cannot fail to call to mind the disabilities suffered by the lower castes of Hindus.

In central and eastern Ladakh, the great majority of the people bear on their features the imprint of their Tibetan origins, until in Chang-Thang an almost pure Tibetan population is found. In Leh and its neighbourhood, the Tibetan look is often seen in combination with some reminder of Indo-Iranian blood—wavy hair, for instance, or a prominent nose, or a heavy beard; and a few faces look pure Indo-Iranian. Among the Muslims of Leh town there are communities that even now pride themselves on their descent from foreign merchants settled there during the great days of the caravan trade. They came from Srinagar, and from the great trading cities of central Asia—Yarkand, Khotan and Kashgar. Nineteenth-century writers on Ladakh show a properly strait-laced disapproval of the willingness of Ladakhi women to enter into unions with these settlers; today we should be more tolerant, particularly in view of the presumed imbalance between the numbers of men and women consequent on the system of polyandry. In any case it seems to show an admirable lack of sectarian spirit on the part of the girls themselves, and presumably their families too. Certainly, these communities are today among the most influential and respectable citizens of Leh, and possibly the best-looking too.

[1]See below, p. 140.

Nineteenth-century travellers were unanimous in their praise for the character of the Ladakhis, who are described as a simple, cheerful, non-aggressive people, and, in Drew's words 'much given to truth-telling'. Most would agree that this assessment is as true today as it was when it was written. Even now the crime rate is extraordinarily low—crimes of violence are practically non-existent, and few people bother to lock their doors at night. No doubt personality differences between individuals are as great here as anywhere else; but as a rule today's visitor should find no difficulty in his dealings with the local people.

The Ladakhi character seems to be naturally democratic. Apart from a condescending attitude towards the Mons, and one or two other hereditary occupational groups such as blacksmiths, there is nothing like a caste system among the Buddhists. Class distinctions there are, and respect, even deference, is paid to members of aristocratic families on the basis of their birth alone; but this falls very far short of either servility on the one hand, or arrogance on the other. A man of the humbler classes stands up straight and looks his social superiors in the eye. This basic humanity in the sense of real appreciation of a man's worth irrespective of his position in terms of class, is palpable in the main bazaar at Leh, where most often the 'sahibs' are indistinguishable in dress and appearance from the rest; when they are recognized, they are usually seen in easy and unconstrained conversation with 'ordinary' men.

This is surely related to the complete emancipation of women in Buddhist society, something that strikes the traveller all the more forcibly because his approach to Ladakh has been through Muslim areas where women are kept in social seclusion, though not, among the peasants, restrained from working in the fields. The cheerfulness shown by people of all sorts and conditions in central Ladakh may well be due partly to the fact that one half of the population is not kept in a state of perpetual subjection by the other. In Buddhist Ladakh, wherever there are men to be seen, there are women too; and one of the most charming features of Leh bazaar is the group of ladies who sit at the right-angled turn with their baskets of freshly-gathered vegetables, spinning and chatting with one another and with the passers-by as they sell their produce. The emancipated position enjoyed by women, as well as various other indications, leads one to conclude that among the

Buddhist peoples of Tibetan origin sex is not the bogey it appears to be in most other societies—to an exaggerated extent in some Asian ones. As Michel Peissel puts it in his book on Mustang, 'sex is not smothered in inhibiting taboos'. People are accepted as individuals, primarily as human beings rather than as members of this or the other sex; consequently women, not being hedged about with a spurious sanctity, have remarkable dignity and self-respect. These attitudes have communicated themselves to many of the Muslims of the Leh area among whom, apart from a few families of very high status, there is no seclusion of women. Among the Kargil Muslims, strictly traditionalist attitudes prevail, on this as on most other subjects.

At the same time, there is no question of women being dominant, any more than men; and the Buddhist custom of fraternal polyandry by no means indicated a matriarchal or matrilineal system. Rather it went hand in hand with inheritance by primogeniture, and so operated to prevent the subdivision of property. The mechanics of the system were simple. Of a number of brothers, the eldest was accepted as the heir to the property, and usually at least one of the others was dedicated to religion as a lama. Any remaining brothers were free either to go and make their own way in the world, or to remain in the family home—in which case there was a clear understanding that they occupied a position subservient to the eldest brother. This involved them in marriage to his wife; if they wanted to marry on their own account they had to leave and set up a separate home, without being entitled to a share in any part of the family property. Within the polyandrous marriage, the paternity of the children was regarded as irrelevant: all the children were accepted as being of the eldest brother, whom they addressed as 'big father'; the younger brothers would be 'little fathers'. In a family in which there were no sons, an exactly reverse system operated. The eldest daughter, the heiress, married a husband, known as *magpa*, who enjoyed no rights over her property; his only role was to work for his wife's interests, and to help her to produce heirs. Her sisters were given the same rights in the *magpa* as were the younger brothers in a polyandrous marriage. It might be thought that either way this kind of marriage would lead to every sort of personal jealousy and rivalry; but all authorities testify that it has gone hand in hand among the various peoples of Tibetan stock with a complete lack of personal possessiveness, both among the different spouses, and as regards their children.

The origin of the system is obscure. Cunningham relates it to the joint marriage of the Pandava princes to the princess Draupadi in Hindu mythology; but it seems more likely that it evolved in response to conditions on the Tibetan plateaux, where cultivable land was scarce, and most holdings must always have been small. It surely contributed to social stability by preventing the fragmentation of such holdings into uneconomic units, and by helping to keep the population within limits. The riddle of what became of the surplus women is one that has not been satisfactorily answered. Certainly fewer women than men entered the religious life; and yet there is nothing to indicate, in Drew's words, that 'there were many old maids'. In the Leh area a certain number of girls who might not otherwise have found husbands were no doubt mopped up by marriage to merchants from outside, and this may partly account for their willingness to enter into such marriages. Polyandry is now illegal in India, and therefore also in Ladakh; but polyandrous marriages are still contracted in remote villages in the interior.

Another unusual feature of the Tibetan family system, closely related to polyandry, was a custom known as *khang-bu*, or 'little house'. When the eldest son had reached years of discretion, and had married and produced an heir, the parents retired gracefully to a small house adjoining the main property, taking one or two animals with them, and retaining only as much land as they needed to support themselves. All the responsibilities of managing the property devolved on the eldest son, who was now recognized as the legal owner; the parents had no more claim on it. If there were 'two fathers' alive—or even more—they would all share their retirement in the little house. This system is surely analogous to the practice of the Tibetan dynasties, in which the heir-apparent would be associated with the work of government in the old king's lifetime, the latter sometimes abdicating in his favour. The premium put on youth and vigour in preference to age and experience is one of the most attractive things about Tibetan social thinking. It does not seem to indicate any lack of respect for age, whose wisdom after all remains available to energetic, though inexperienced, youth.

It is interesting to compare some aspects of Ladakhi life today with accounts of a hundred years ago, of which the most detailed and reliable is that by Drew. Many of Drew's observations hold good today; the differences we notice point to a distinct increase in prosperity since he wrote. For example, he says that, while tea is a favourite beverage, most people are too poor to be able to afford to drink it every day. Today, there may be a few households in the poorer regions where tea, liberally laced with butter, is not a daily drink; but generally speaking tea is no longer considered a luxury, but a necessity of life. Again, according to Drew,

All [Ladakhis] have a rooted objection to washing. I was told that there was a custom of bathing once a year, but I could never get any satisfactory corroboration of the report. Their clothes, worn next to them, are never washed, but are affectionately kept around them until they fall to pieces. [2]

Here too things have changed. It is true that during the long cold months of winter there is little inclination to take a bath, and even among outsiders staying in Ladakh it is probably only a few orthodox Hindus, for whom bathing is ritual necessity, who will take regular and frequent baths. But even in winter most Ladakhis (with the exception of the Da-Hanu Dards, and possibly of the Chang-Thang nomads) make an effort to keep themselves acceptably clean; while in summer bathing is commonplace, and every stream is the scene of vigorous laundry work, particularly during the early weeks with a winter's grime to be washed out of heavy woollen clothes. Clearly, a hundred years ago cleanliness was a luxury few could afford; the fact that it is no longer so is a pointer to an improved standard of living. Another such pointer may be deduced from Drew's description of the people's clothes. The *goncha*, he says, the enveloping woollen coat worn, with differences in style, by both sexes, is their sole garment—nothing is worn underneath. Nowadays the *goncha*—which men in cosmopolitan Leh often discard in summer in favour of western-style dress—usually conceals, not only a full set of warm underclothing, but shirt, trousers and sweater as well; the women's *goncha* too is worn over a complete set of clothes.

The *goncha* continues to be the national dress of Ladakh; and a

[2] *The Jummoo and Kashmir Territories*, p. 248.

good deal of the charm of the villages, and of Leh itself, is derived from the unselfconsciously picturesque appearance of the people. The *goncha* is a supremely practical dress for a climate of severe cold; and the men's version is a distinctly stylish garment. It is, in effect, a double-breasted calf-length coat; it is cut wide, and the extra material pulled to the back to form two pleats, which are secured by a brightly-coloured cummerbund. It is fastened on the right shoulder and down the right side with brass buttons and loops, and the edges of the stand-up collar are piped with silver brocade. The *gonchas* of the poorer people are made from coarse homespun woollen cloth, usually dyed to a dark shade of maroon. (The Kargil people more often wear the natural undyed, unbleached cloth.) The well-to-do will use a variety of material for their *gonchas*, even, for summer wear, lightweight synthetics. For formal occasions, there can be few more elegant garments than a *goncha* in black velvet, the silver gleam of the piping at the border and collar, and a cummerbund of shocking pink.

The women's *goncha* has less style about it. It has a full skirt, gathered into a great number of small pleats, and it too is fastened with a bright cummerbund. Older women, particularly from the villages, add a goatskin tied around the shoulders, wool inside. This may be replaced by a multicoloured embroidered or brocade mantle, with long silk fringes. The outfit is completed either by a hat, or by the *perak*, the traditional headdress. This is a long strip of leather, reaching from the forehead half-way down the back; it is covered with cloth, to which are stitched, graded in order of size, rows of turquoises. The Ladakhi woman actually carried—and often still carries—her dowry on her head; the prospective suitor need have no doubt as to the value of what his bride will bring with her. The *perak* is worn over a foundation which protrudes on both sides in two stiff wide flaps; although the ears are not covered, the fashion is said to derive from the request of a queen of Ladakh for a headdress which would protect her from the draughts that gave her earache. The hat seems to be a comparatively new fasion, for nothing like it is described in the nineteenth-century accounts. It is rather the shape of a top-hat, but smaller so that it sits more perched on the head. The brim is cut away over the forehead, leaving something like two horns on the two sides. It is usually covered with brocade, or black velvet embroidered in silver thread; a red lining shows at the upturned brim. From the occasional sight of such a hat much lower in the crown than usual, and giving much of the appearance of a cap with ear-flaps, it may be deduced that the hat is a stylized development of such a cap. It is worn by women, and by men of the older generation—the women's straight, the men's at an angle.

In spite of the somewhat bunchy cut of her *goncha*, the well-to-do Ladakhi lady in full fig has a striking and opulent appearance. Her *goncha* for formal occasions is often in heavy figured Chinese silk—a reminder of the caravan trade through which, in the old days, such luxury goods were imported from great distances. Its usually sober hue is an appropriate background not only for her brightly coloured brocade mantle, but also for the heavy strings of jewellery—baroque pearls, turquoises, coral and amber—that adorn her neck and ears.

Among the more fashion-conscious of the younger generation of women in and around Leh, the *goncha* is often replaced by the *chuba*, the more streamlined and elegant Tibetan gown. This is sleeveless, and can be worn over different types of blouse. It has a cross-over front, and is pulled to the back in two deep pleats from waist-level. The striped apron worn with it by the Tibetan women is discarded by the Ladakhi borrowers of this pleasing and comfortable dress.

In their architecture, as in their dress, the Ladakhis show a natural aesthetic sense. The villages blend into the landscape; and their houses, so satisfactorily adapted to the environment, delight the eye. They are built of sun-dried bricks or local granite, and are plastered with dried mud. In a climate where no more than 13 centimetres of moisture are precipitated annually, cement is a dispensable luxury. Without cement, and without the mechanized methods of modern construction, the building of a Ladakhi house is a fairly simple affair—and above all it is a noiseless one. Today, with something in the region of 10,000 visitors (more than the whole population of the town) coming every year and spending money, Leh has something of the aspect of a boom town, and a great amount of new construction is going on. But it is a boom town on its own terms. Here, construction does not imply the mechanized thumping, crashing, clashing and general soul-shattering racket that assault the ears and fray the nerves in any modern city. In Ladakh the only mechanization may be the use of a three-tonne truck to bring the construction materials to the nearest road-head—for the town centre is already fully built up, so new houses are being built on the outskirts, in the midst of fields, often approached only by a footpath. From the road-head, labourers carry loads of stone and bricks on their backs to the site, lightening the task with rhythmical antiphonal work-chants. The actual construction is done by hand, and is not highly skilled work. Apart from a carpenter, who should be able to execute the fairly simple decorative work applied to the lintels of doors and windows, and a mason, whose sole qualification need be to know the difference between a straight and a crooked line, there is no need for any skilled labour at all.

Apart from the introduction of electricity in the towns, the main departure from tradition in the houses of even the well-to-do today is the extensive use of glass. This has clearly made all the difference between comfort, and a mere toleration of discomfort. It must surely be a recent innovation, for until the motor road was built, the import of glass was obviously not an enterprise worth attempting. Now, in the towns and those villages which are easily accessible by road, not only do many of the houses have their windows glazed in the usual way, but every reasonably prosperous home has a 'glass room'—a room one or two of whose outside walls, facing south or west, are glass from top to bottom. The value of such a room is incalculable. Winter in Ladakh is cold— for two or three months bitterly cold—but it is a bracing cold with clear skies and bright sunshine for most of the time. The sun is so strong that if the cold air is screened off, even in deepest winter it will heat a glass room to a very comfortable temperature, no other form of heating being needed during the day. It is not a very sophisticated way of using solar energy, but it is certainly effective.

Inside as well as out, Ladakhi houses give evidence of innate good taste, not yet corrupted by contact with a more vulgar civilization. Before the introduction of glass, and even now in the villages, the centre of the Ladakhi home was the one room which in the nature of things would always be warm—the kitchen. The kitchen of an old-style Ladakhi house is a delightful room. It is large, and usually rather dark, since the number of windows is kept to a minimum in the interests of warmth. Around the walls are shelves of polished wood bearing an array of pots and utensils—ranging from beautifully worked antique copper pots, the relics of the Yarkand trade, to the more utilitarian items usual today: aluminium steamers in several tiers for cooking *mok-mok*— meat-filled dumplings; handleless saucepans, Indian style; and the ubiquitous pressure-cooker. Ready to hand is the *gur-gur*, the cylindrical wooden brass-bound churn used for mixing butter-tea. In the centre is a free-standing stove of baked earth or iron, sometimes decorated. It burns wood, and its chimney-pipe goes out by a hole in the ceiling. In the villages, instead of the wood-burning stove, there will be an open hearth burning cakes of dried animal-dung. The bellows is an important fixture. The facilities for cutting vegetables and washing dishes—the more messy but indispensable parts of kitchen work—are tucked away unobtrusively somewhere. One wall is left free of kitchen para-phernalia for low carpet-covered divans and low tables—*chog-tse*—where family and guests may sit. It is as homely and dignified an arrangement as one could wish; and though clearly evolved in response to climatic and other limitations, it has the great addi-tional merit of allowing the cook to do her work without being segregated from the rest of the life of the house: perhaps yet another expression of the emancipated way of life of the Buddh-ist woman. In the old days, and even now in the villages, the kitchen served as sleeping quarters for the whole family in the cold months of winter.

Regrettably, few modern houses adopt this old-fashioned arrangement—largely because the use of glass gives a room that is warm for most of the day, even in winter; also because increased prosperity, in the towns at least, has led to the use of heating devices in rooms other than the kitchen. Usually this is a form of the *bokhari*, the cylindrical free-standing stove used in Kashmir, where it burns wood; here it is adapted to give a fiercer heat by burning hard coke or kerosene oil. Nowadays, in the houses of the well-to-do, guests are usually received in the glass-room. This may, as a concession to modernity, have a few chairs, but its basic furnishing consists of divans and *chogtse*, the low wooden tables which are often elaborately carved and painted. There is no separate dining-room, and if a meal is being served, it is brought to the guests where they sit, and arranged on the *chogtse*.

Thus the kitchen, in such a house, has lost its position as the focal point of family life, and with that all its old attractiveness. The introduction of alternatives to wood or dried dung as cooking fuels leads in the same direction. The gas cylinder may reach Leh in a year or two; and after the completion of the first stage of the Stakna hydro-electric project which is expected to give an ample supply of power to Leh and its neighbourhood, cooking on electricity will become possible. In the meantime, what has been almost universally adopted is the primus stove which, though troublesome to use, is at least cleaner and simpler than either a wood-burning stove or an open hearth; it has the great advantage of giving the high heat necessary for cooking in very low temperatures, and in particular for making efficient use of that now indispensable article, the pressure-cooker.

The Ladakhi language is a dialect of Tibetan, and will be unfamiliar to most visitors; but most of the people with whom the traveller comes in contact have a sufficient grasp of Hindustani—some of the Leh Muslims indeed speak a very chaste Urdu—and in Leh itself many of them have at least a smattering of English. The overseas visitor will find no more difficulty about language in Ladakh than anywhere else in India. The presence of outsiders, whether from India or overseas, still has enough novelty to excite curiosity, particularly among children, and of course more so the further they move away from Leh. But such interest, naïvely expressed, has nothing in the least offensive about it; and if met in the same courteous spirit in which it is extended, may result in genuine, if ephemeral, friendships. The all-purpose greeting is 'Jooley', and people are delighted when it is reciprocated. In Muslim areas 'Salaam Aleikum' is more appropriate, with the reply 'Waleikum Salaam'.

The sociable nature of the Ladakhis is perhaps stimulated by the climate of their land: by the long winters when agricultural work comes to a standstill, and the people, with little to do, must keep themselves occupied as best they may. In most villages, during the long winter evenings, there are story-telling sessions, when the villagers gather to listen to stories drawn from their rich folklore, told by that one among them whose gifts have made him the acknowledged tale-teller of their group.

Every family event is the pretext for a celebration, with song and dance, at which great quantities of *chang* are consumed by men and women alike. The dances are slow, grave and graceful, and every Ladakhi Buddhist learns them from childhood. The

steps contain subtleties not immediately apparent to the uninitiated. The spectators appraise and criticize the dancers' performance by uncompromising standards. A flick of the wrist or point-
ing of the toe may make or mar a person's reputation as a dan-
cer—or alternatively, may betray that he comes from a different
region, whose style of dancing, it goes without saying, leaves
much to be desired. These are social dances, and all take part,
participation being governed by a strict code of etiquette. At a
wedding, for instance, groups will come out from among the
guests—a group from the bride's family, then one from the
groom's; a group of youngsters, followed by representatives of
the older generation, and so on. The privilege of leading the
dance is given to the senior member of whichever group is dancing; in the dances not confined to particular family groups, the
invitation to lead the dance is given to the senior member of the
best family present—'best' in terms of social status. In the old
days it could be a matter of mortal insult, generating all manner of
family quarrels and even the instigation of civil suits, if a man or
woman felt slighted by not having been invited to take the lead to
which he felt himself entitled. This is one of the ways in which
class feeling gains expression; but it is not obvious to the outside
observer, whose attention is focussed on the slowly changing
patterns of the hand- and foot-movements of the dancers. Group
by group they come out, the men and women sometimes separately, sometimes together, dance their dance, and then go back to
their seats. It gives a feeling of timelessness; the continuity of
tradition is palpable; and for a moment of tranquillity there is the
illusion that the Ladakhi way of life is immutable and secure.

Apart from *chang*, the characteristic beverage of Ladakh is
gur-gur tea, the butter tea consumed in one form or another by all
the Tibetan peoples. In central Ladakh (though not in the Kargil
area) it is made with fresh, not rancid butter. This is added with
salt and milk to a well-boiled infusion of tea to which a little
bicarbonate of soda has been added. The mixture is then churned
in a churn or *gur-gur* (the word is onomatopoeic) till all the
ingredients are well blended. *Gur-gur* tea is made in bulk, can be
kept hot (traditionally in a decorative copper pot on a charcoal
brazier; nowadays more often in a prosaic thermos), and is drunk
in enormous quantities by the Ladakhis, thirty or forty coffee-size
cups a day being quite a normal quota. It is both warming and

nourishing, particularly when mixed with *tsampa*—altogether a comforting drink in a cold climate. To an outsider it tastes more like a bland soup than tea as he knows it.

For the guest in a Ladakhi house, whether he is alone or whether it is a party, there is a fixed etiquette for drinking either *chang* or *gur-gur* tea. Most probably he is sitting on a carpet-covered divan, only a fraction above floor-level, with a *chogtse* in front of him. A glass or small cup is placed on the *chogtse*, and filled up. A tea-cup will be covered with a lid of chased metal to keep it hot. Etiquette demands that the host should never let the guest's cup be less than full. Conversely, it is polite on the guest's part to refrain from drinking until the host is ready to give him a refill. Accordingly, he does not touch his drink until the attendant returns with the jug and urges him on. Only then may he turn his attention to his cup or glass, sipping tentatively or draining it down, as he pleases. It is as well for the visitor who is hoping for an entrée into Ladakhi homes to acquire a taste for these two beverages. *Gur-gur* tea may present a little difficulty, though if he thinks of it as soup rather than tea, and if he has no aversion to the taste of melted butter, he should be able to do all right. But the richness given it by the butter may make it difficult for him to stomach an amount which will satisfy the hospitable instincts of his host. *Chang* should present no problems at all. It is in effect fermented barley water; it has a pleasant sourish taste. While it may be drunk without great enthusiasm at first, most visitors find it grows on them.

The traditional summer pastimes of the Ladakhis are archery and polo; and recently in the Leh area football has become very popular. Championships are organized, and fans are as ardent and vociferous in support of their chosen teams as their counterparts anywhere else in the world. The standard of play is comparable to that of amateur football anywhere; no allowances have to be made for the altitude.

The same cannot be said of archery; and as far as the Leh area is concerned, the so-called archery festivals seem to be little more than excuses for a summer party. Boldly patterned *shamianas* shelter a crowd decked out in its Sunday best, the men sober yet stylish in their smartest *gonchas*, the women colourful with their brocade mantles and heavy strings of jewellery. As important as the shooting itself are the interludes of dancing and miscellaneous entertainment, and *chang* flows freely. There is nothing to show that, apart from these 'festivals', archery is taken at all seriously as a sport, and the flight of the arrows tends to be erratic. Nevertheless, as with the dance, a strict etiquette prevails. The competing teams must be captained by someone from an aristocratic family, preferably the senior member present. Whenever he or any other person of high social status takes the bow, the music which accompanies the shooting swells in volume and increases in tempo to do him honour.

In Kargil archery has fewer extraneous accompaniments. The rather austere form of Islam followed there frowns on such frivolous activities as music and dancing, and the question of drinking *chang* does not arise; so an archery festival is actually what its name implies, and the standard is much higher.

Polo is indigenous to central Asia and parts of the Himalaya, but its precise origins are lost in the obscurity of time. The Iranians have claimed it for their own, and so have the Chinese, and it was being played by the princes of Byzantium in the twelfth century. It seems to have been the early Muslim rulers who first introduced it into India, and it was popular at Akbar's court; but it died out, except among the ruling families of some Rajput states, and was unknown to the British during the early days of their rule. It survived however on India's far eastern border, and in the western Himalaya where it had been played from time immemorial independently of its existence in mediaeval India. The sportsmen of the *Raj* first played polo in Calcutta about 1860, having discovered it in Manipur. It had already been described by travellers in the western Himalaya like Moorcroft, Vigne and Cunningham thirty or forty years earlier, and it was played by British visitors to Kashmir in 1863. From there it reached the Punjab, at about the same time as it also arrived from the direction of Calcutta; by the early 1870s it was being played in England. The British modified and 'improved' the game (as their nineteenth-century ethos dictated they must): invented their own rules, introduced the chukker system out of consideration for the horses, and generally tidied it up. The game of international polo was born.

But in Ladakh, and other remote areas of the Himalaya and the Karakoram like Hunza, Nagar, Chitral, Gilgit and Baltistan, peo-

ple continued to play polo as they had always done. In 1935, Peter
Fleming saw in Hunza a game practically identical with what in
Ladakh today is known as Balti-style polo. The feature that struck
him most was that a player was allowed to catch the ball, after
which he need only ride between the posts with it to score a goal;
'but', Fleming adds, 'since he may legitimately be thwarted by any
method short of a knife-thrust, this is not as easy as it sounds.'[3] In
Ladakh the player is permitted to throw the ball between the
posts, and a goal is awarded. There are no chukkers, but each half
ends when either team has scored nine goals; the only foul is to cut
across the path of another player's horse, which is obviously
dangerous. Otherwise there are no rules, least of all any regulat-
ing the size of the ground or the number of players. The size of
the field is determined by how big a patch of level ground may be
spared from cultivation in this rugged terrain of steep mountains
and narrow valleys; and the strength of the team by the availability of good players. A traveller lucky enough to see polo played in
one of the villages of the interior may still see something like the
game Cunningham described at Mulbekh, when twenty players
on each side pursued the ball up and down a field 360 metres long
and 75 broad.

The skill of the Ladakhi players permits of at least one practice
that has had to be edited out of international polo. It is well
described by the Hebers, in *Himalayan Tibet and Ladakh* their
record of Ladakh early this century. They have just shown us a
goal scored by 'a pig-tailed Ladakhi'; after each goal, ends are
changed, so the late scorer is now playing towards the opposite
goal:

Now watch him carefully, for he will show you a pretty piece of play. He
has dismounted, picked up the ball, and, remounting, takes both it and
his stick in his right hand, then gallops down the field as hard as he can.
Reaching the half-way, approximately, he throws up the ball, and, with
the stick, which is still in the same hand, he hits the ball full and straight
into the enemies' goal. To do this at such a pace needs good horsemanship and a wonderfully steady eye and aim.

Although this manoeuvre does not always lead to the immediate
scoring of another goal, it occasionally does so, and it remains the

[3]Peter Fleming, *News from Tartary*, p. 369.
    [4]A. Reeve Heber and Kathleen M. Heber, *Himalayan Tibet and Ladakh*, pp.
154–5.

accepted way of resuming play after a goal. That such skill was beyond the command of English players was admitted by the Hebers in their description of a match between a local team and an English one composed of Dr Heber himself, the British Joint Commissioner, and two visitors up for the shooting. Not one of them was capable of throwing the ball and hitting it at a gallop, so they had to adopt the expedient of having two players ride to the half-way point, the first of whom dropped the ball for his companion to hit. With this concession, the English team won by one goal; but obviously this result did not reflect the relative skills of the two sides.

Polo was introduced to Central Ladakh from Baltistan, where Drew, in *The Jummoo and Kashmir Territories*, testified to its popularity in the late nineteenth century:

The people are passionately fond of the game; those of rank look on the playing of it as one of the chief objects for which they were sent into the world; but not to them is the pursuit confined; all who can get a pony to mount join in it, and the poorest enter thoroughly into the spirit of it; the children from an early age get their eye and hand in accord by practising it on foot—playing indeed the ordinary hockey of our country. It is not surprising that such an active pursuit of the game should produce good players. I have met with young men of most admirable skill.[5]

Some authorities say that polo was brought to Ladakh by Sengge Namgyal whose mother was a Balti princess, early in the seventeenth century, and that it was Sengge who laid out the first royal polo ground, in the Mur-tse garden below Leh (now the site of the Defence Ministry's Field Research Laboratory). Others aver that it was brought by the colony of Baltis settled at Chushot, a village just across the Indus, a few kilometres up-river from Leh. Indeed, these two accounts may not be incompatible. The date of the Chushot settlement has not been established, but it may well have been as early as Sengge Namgyal's reign; and considering the Baltis' almost fanatical devotion to polo, it may not be too improbable to imagine the half-Balti Sengge bringing and settling a colony of his mother's compatriots for the express purpose of playing polo and popularizing it in Ladakh. The Chushot Baltis, though in most respects fully assimilated to the Ladakhi way of life, have retained both their religion—they are Shia Muslims to a

---

[5]Drew, *The Jummoo and Kashmir Territories*, pp. 380–1.

man—and a clear consciousness of their own identity. They still have all the old Balti enthusiasm for polo, and it is they alone who have kept the game alive in the Leh area during the last 150 years, since the loss of Ladakh's independence led to the withdrawal of royal patronage. Chushot is the only village in central Ladakh with its own polo ground, the Leh ground not having been laid out till 1885. Till then, polo in Leh was played up and down the main bazaar; perhaps this is the reason why, planned in an age when there was no wheeled traffic, it was made so wide.

Even now, many of the finest players in and around Leh are Baltis from Chushot. This does not mean that today there is any lack of enthusiasm among the Leh Buddhists for the game—quite the contrary; interest is universal, and there are a fair number of Buddhists among the front-rank players. But strangely enough, although horses and horsemanship were part of the way of life in old Tibet, polo never caught on in Buddhist Ladakh; its distribution in the western Himalaya is more or less co-extensive with the penetration of Islam. Apart from the Leh area, polo is played only in parts of Ladakh that have a Muslim population, such as Dras and Chigtan in the Kargil district, and the Turtuk-Bogdang region of Nubra, down the Shayok river to the north-west.

Languishing till recently in and around Leh, polo has revived in the last few years, as a result of positive steps taken by the district administration to encourage it. Regular exhibition and tournament matches are held, and the standard of play has improved dramatically—less as regards individual skill, which left little to be desired, than as regards teamwork and tactics. As played today, it is a slightly modified form of the original game, but still it makes few concessions to international polo. Usually there are six players on each side, and play lasts for an hour with a ten-minute break in the middle. There are no chukkers, but the hardy Zanskari ponies scarcely seem to suffer, even at the altitude of 3,500 metres, and at the end of play are going as strongly as at the start, though the game is sometimes very fast. The presence of the army gives a sharpened interest to the game, and the army players, who often include some of all-India standing, sportingly adopt the local style of play—though they draw the line at chucking the ball. Undoubtedly the most exciting matches are those in which a local team takes on the army. Partisanship is intense on both sides, and freely expressed; and when the local team wins, the crowd goes wild.

The Leh polo ground provides a spectacular setting. It is a little above the town, and from the grandstand spectators look over a vista of flat roofs to green fields and bare hills beyond. To the right, on its rocky spur, is the square-hewn bulk of Sengge Nam-gyal's palace, and crowning the peak behind it the temple and ruined fort of Namgyal Tsemo. On the other side the ground falls away to the Indus, beyond which rise the steep flanks of the Zanskar range, dominated by the graceful peak of Stok Kangri. Here matches are played in the late afternoon when the sun, slanting across the ground, casts shadows that seem almost three-dimensional against the golden clouds of dust raised by the drumming hooves. There is no barrier to keep the crowds who throng to every match off the field; when the ball goes out, it is simply picked up and thrown back by someone from the mass of onlookers. Often the spectators are forced to retreat, swaying back against the press behind, when the mêlée of men and horses, intent on the ball, spills over the line, and right among them. At the start and finish of play and to celebrate every goal players of *surna* and *daman*[5] strike up special polo music, which adds a final touch of excitement to an occasion whose atmosphere is unique.

It all adds up to something as different from international polo as a *goncha* from a three-piece suit. And there is one other striking difference. Balti-style polo as played in Ladakh is not a rich man's game. The Chushotis and others who make up the local teams are for the most part small farmers, or school masters, or shopkeepers, or are employed in the various departments of the district administration as office messengers, drivers or syces. A few of the better off have their own horses, some of them very fine animals indeed; others ride departmental horses, or those belonging to the recently formed Polo Promotion Committee. These players are unassuming men, without pretensions of any kind; but after a victory they walk as tall as kings, for polo is one of the things they live for.

[6]See below, p. 140.

X
The Native Genius

The overwhelming influence of Tibet on Ladakh's religious culture can both be deduced from a reading of Ladakhi history, and observed in practice. Ladakh is part of the great Tibetan plateau, and is separated from Tibet's cultural and political centre at Lhasa only by a matter of distance, some 1,500 kilometres, and not by any formidable physical barrier, such as the Great Himalaya which cuts it off from India. The population of central and eastern Ladakh is of preponderantly Tibetan racial stock, and the Ladakhi language is a dialect of Tibetan. Nevertheless, the barrier of very distance—implying something like four months' march in the old days—might perhaps have been enough to separate this far-flung outpost of the Tibetan people from their cousins in central Tibet, and to allow them to develop their own distinctive form of the parent culture. However, things were not allowed to take their natural course—partly perhaps because of a unifying and centralizing tendency in the organization of Buddhism itself, and partly because of the deliberate policy of a line of kings which appears never to have forgotten, even with the passage of centuries, that it was an offshoot of the ancient Tibetan dynasty.

In the earlier centuries, the second of these factors was perhaps predominant. For as long as Buddhism remained a living religion in India, the land of its origin, both central and western Tibet continued to look in that direction for inspiration as to the fountainhead of their faith. When that fountain dried up as it did about the twelfth century, central Tibet and Lhasa in particular took its place, and adopted a kind of pontifical authority. This development was certainly fostered by the kings of the first Ladakhi dynasty, with what motivation or under what compulsion we can hardly guess. The early-established system of novices being sent to monasteries in central Tibet for training lasted till 1962, and must have been the most effective of the various channels through which Tibet's religious culture was transmitted to Ladakh. From the fifteenth century onwards, two of the monastic orders of central Tibet started setting up monasteries in Ladakh too—the Ge-lugs-pa and the Drug-pa, the latter often under the patronage of the Namgyal kings. Thus firm institutional links between Ladakh and Tibet were forged, which chimed in well with the predispositions of the dynasty, and which seem to indicate that Vajrayana Buddhism, no less perhaps than Roman Catholicism, had developed a highly structured organization with authority radiating out from the centre to the peripheries.

The authority claimed by the Tibetan pontiffs in the chief monasteries of the different orders seems not to have been confined to doctrinal matters, but to have extended to the smallest details of ritual and iconography. Thus, to the extent that cultural forms were dependent on religion, it constituted a cultural as well as a religious stranglehold. With the exception of whatever paintings and images remain in the earliest monasteries—those of Rin-chen-zang-po's time, of which Alchi is the prime example—all the works of art in the *gompas* of Ladakh reflect the Tibetan style, and this is as true of work being done today as it is of past centuries. Religious painting is a living tradition, in the sense that it is carried on even today; but it is carried on strictly within the bounds laid down by an iconography that has ceased to develop. Every gesture of the figures represented, every detail of the background, every choice of colour, has a symbolic meaning, and there is no room for individual interpretation. There is a sameness about the murals in almost all the *gompas*, whether they depict the divine beings in their terrible or their benign aspect. The eye becomes surfeited with ravening jaws, flaming tresses, skull headdresses, trampled and bleeding foes; with plump white clouds, five-pointed crowns, delicate hand-gestures, the multiplicity of limbs and heads. The *thangkas* too—devotional paintings on cloth, a kind of Buddhist icon—repeat the same motifs endlessly. The various styles of painting that an art historian can trace down the centuries have either been abandoned—like the presumed Kashmiri style so amazingly exemplified at Alchi—or absorbed into a single style, from which no departure is permissible, and of which the largest component is the Tibetan tradition.

When one thinks of some of the detail among the earlier wall-paintings—particularly the little scenes of secular life that appear now and then, especially at Alchi, also the court scene in which Tashi Namgyal's portrait appears in the *Gon-Khang* at Namgyal Tesmo—then the present state of religious art, which means in effect its state for the past two or three hundred years, seems by comparison to be lacking in richness, and hidebound by tradition. For this, the control over every aspect of religious life exercised by the incarnate lamas, the heads of the various monastic orders in central Tibet, must be held responsible. Four months' journey notwithstanding, there was a constant exchange of personnel between the monasteries of Tibet and Ladakh, Tibetan monks bringing the dogmas and traditions received at the centre of this religious empire, and Ladakhi ones travelling to the centre to absorb them. Local initiative was given no chance to develop local forms.

Thus in one sense Ladakh became and remained a cultural colony of Tibet. In another direction too historical circumstances conspired to inhibit the creativity of the Ladakhis. Ladakh's position at the centre of an important network of trade routes meant that, in the old days, whatever people's requirements beyond the basic necessities of life might be, they could be met by imports, and there was no demand for the development of indigenous industry. Carpets came from Yarkand and Tibet; decorative metalware—some of it very fine—from Yarkand and elsewhere in central Asia; brocades, silks and velvets from China; and fine shawls from Kashmir. The patronage of the rich was given to the merchants who could supply these items from outside, rather than to craftsmen who would thus have had an incentive to develop the skills necessary to manufacture them locally. In this way a vicious circle seems to have been established, with lack of demand leading to lack of incentive leading to lack of skill. Practically no tradition of artistic handicrafts developed; and this the visitor may find a disappointment.

Traditionally, every household spun and wove its own woollen cloth, and in the villages this continues even today. It is usual to see people, men and women alike, with a hank of raw wool round their wrist and a spindle dangling, abstractedly spinning as they walk, or chat, or sell vegetables, or pursue any kind of occupation that leaves the hands idle. In the winter sun, or the summer's shade, simple looms are set up, and the thread woven into the *pattu* which is universally the poor man's clothing. But there seems to be no aptitude for fine work. The woollen home-spun is coarse and rough, though certainly it fulfils the basic need for warmth. Ladakh's most famous product, the warm soft winter under-coat of the pashmina goat, what used to be known as 'shawl-wool', was never in the past entrusted to the local people for any kind of processing beyond the most basic preliminary cleaning, which involved merely picking out the admixture of coarse hairs belonging to the goat's shaggy outer coat. The fine pashmina shawls justified the name by which they were world-famous, 'cashmere', by being manufactured in Srinagar by the more nimble-fingered and artistic Kashmiris. Even now, when not all the raw pashmina leaves Ladakh with its potential value unrealized, the shawls manufactured in the Government-sponsored district weaving centre, while they have all the softness and warmth of genuine pashmina, entirely lack the fineness of 'cashmere'—pashmina as processed in Srinagar. They sell too at half the price, which is as it should be, since a great part of the value of a 'cashmere' shawl is derived from the minute and pains-taking labour of cleaning the raw wool, and the skill developed by generations of craftsmen in spinning and weaving it to an exquisite fineness.

Otherwise, the district handicrafts centre has been hard put to it to create many departments. It exists rather to train the local people in various useful skills—a praiseworthy end in itself—than to preserve any old-established tradition of crafts. It has a knitting and hosiery department, where training is given in both machine- and hand-knitting. Among the Ladakhis—in apparent contrast to the Tibetans—knitting is not an old-established skill. It was introduced less than a hundred years ago by the Moravian missionaries, and Ladakhi women knit European-style with the wool round the fingers of the left hand, not the right as in Britain and elsewhere in India—and among the Tibetans. In the past the village women were no doubt fully occupied with the work of spinning and weaving; nowadays they learn to knit in the Leh handicrafts centre, or in village welfare centres.

As well as knitting and hosiery, the handicrafts centre has a design department, whose products verge on the 'folksy', run-ning largely to clay models of women sporting *peraks*, and

panels with brightly-coloured Chinese-type dragons. Carpets are
manufactured according to the Tibetan technique; but a finer
product may be found at the Tibetan refugee camp at Choglamsar, up the Indus, eight kilometres from Leh. The embroidery
department uses crewel-work, a skill borrowed from Kashmir, to
produce cushion-covers with stylized flower-patterns, again *à la*
Kashmir, enclosed in Tibetan-style geometrical borders—an
attractive hybrid. Authentically Ladakhi are the low carved and
painted tables—*chogtse*—sold in the centre, but manufactured in
a workshop in the village of Likir. The *thangkas* produced in the
centre, and on sale, remain squarely within the limitations of
traditional religious art. Lastly, there is a metal-work department,
turning out the decorative tea-cup stands and lids in demand
locally for the decorous serving of *gur-gur* tea. The work is unre-
fined compared to the old exquisitely crafted pieces from central
Asia and Tibet available (at a price) in the bazaar, and even the
spurious but often attractive decorated copper pots and jugs
brought in from outside to be sold in the town's curio shops.

One village of Ladakh indeed has a tradition of craft in metalware: Chiling, about forty kilometres up the Zanskar river from
its confluence with the Indus at Nyemo, but reached—except
during deep winter when the solidly frozen waters of the river
form a pathway—only by a strenuous march over a mountain
pass from Alchi. Tradition has it that the people of this place are
descended from artisans brought from Nepal by order of Gyal
Katun, Sengge Namgyal's mother, to construct the gigantic Buddha-image at Shey (the Chronicle, as a matter of fact, attributes
this image to Sengge himself), and later settled at Chiling. The
shapely copper pots that they produce for serving *gur-gur* tea and
chang are certainly of a workmanship far superior to that produced by local craftsmen anywhere else in Ladakh.

We begin to discern the Ladakhi genius when we turn from
religious art, and the crafts requiring manual skill, to the arts of
the body and spirit: dance, music and literature. While at the
somewhat rarefied level of religious art and ritual the theocratic
control exercised from Lhasa inhibited the development of distinctively Ladakhi forms, the bonds between Ladakh and Tibet
were much looser at the popular level; and this is where we find
the Ladakhi achievement. Indeed, from its geographical situa-

tion at one extremity of the Tibetan plateau, Ladakh was exposed to cultural influences other than the Buddhist, particularly those derived from Islam; and developed some of the characteristics of a composite culture. Insofar as cultural forms evolve in accordance with environmental conditions, no doubt there is much in Ladakh to remind us of old Tibet. Leh palace and the *gompas*, for example, clearly belong to the same architectural tradition as the Potala; the houses of the two countries too are built to withstand the same climate—of the same sun-dried bricks, and on the same basic pattern. Similarly, the *goncha*, the men's version at least, is a variant of the Tibetan *chuba*. But in those fields where a people's creativity has a relatively free rein, not directly subject to environmental limitations, the Ladakhis possess a vigorous cultural identity all their own, and owing little to Tibet.

Take, for example, the dance. The religious dance-dramas performed in the *gompas* are in their entirety an import from Tibet, in which no local element intrudes. But the social dance of Ladakh is a different matter altogether. To the outsider, it may seem slow and monotonous, the variations between its different steps so small as to be of little account. It cannot hold its own as a 'performance' on a stage, particularly in comparison with a show of Tibetan dances, which, drawn from a much wider area, have a grace and vigour, as well as a wealth of different styles, which the Ladakhi dance comes nowhere near to rivalling. The beauty of the Ladakhi dance is that it is a living tradition, and even now, in the accelerating tempo of the modern world which is just beginning to reach Ladakh, it remains an important part of every Buddhist's training in the social graces. On a stage it looks artless and awkward; but as an integral part of a social function, whether a marriage or a village archery festival, it is perfectly appropriate. And it owes nothing to any outside influence.

With the music of Ladakh too, there is a clear division between the religious and the secular traditions. *Gompa* music, used in worship, and as an accompaniment to the dance-dramas, no doubt follows Tibetan forms wholesale. Its most characteristic instrument is a horn so long that as it is played it rests on the ground a good way in front of the player's feet, and in procession has to be supported at the bell end in a loop of cloth carried by an acolyte marching ahead. (For storage it closes up like a telescope).

It gives a deep note, almost a groan. Heard more continuously are the *geling*, a shawm with a circular projection covering the mouth just in front of the double reed; and drums, much the shape and size of warming pans, which are held upright above the drummer's head and beaten with sticks in the form of question marks. The sounds of all these are punctuated by the boom of the gong and the clash of cymbals.

Of secular music there are two main strains. The earlier one is derived from Tibet; its instruments are the flute, also an unusual kind of double flute, and the *damnyen*, an instrument of plucked strings akin to the Indian *sitar*. These are still played privately; but for public and ceremonial occasions they have been supplanted by the *surna* and *daman*: the *surna*, an oboe-like instrument related to the Indian *shehnai*, and *daman*, a pair of drums like the Indian *tabla*. These were introduced at the time of the Balti connection at the beginning of the seventeenth century: a band of musicians with their instruments came from Baltistan as part of the dowry of Gyal Katun, Sengge Namgyal's mother. They were settled at Phiyang; and they and their descendants enjoyed the title of *Khar-Mon*, the word *Mon* in this context indicating not a caste or ethnic group, but simply musician: musicians of the palace. Now indeed the professional musicians, Mons by caste, have taken up the *surna* and *daman* all over Ladakh; on these instruments is played the music that accompanies all important public occasions, and such ceremonial private occasions as marriages.

In the introduction of the *surna* and *daman* into central Tibet we find perhaps the only example of the fertilization of Tibetan culture from Ladakh. In Tibet their music was played only on very special occasions, like the entry of a new Dalai Lama into Lhasa, or the death anniversaries of Tson-ka-pa and the various Dalai Lamas, when it sounded over the city from the roof of the Potala. In Ladakh, on the other hand, no public or auspicious event, whether a polo match, an archery festival, a marriage, even the inauguration of the ploughing or harvesting season, is complete without its musical accompaniment. Of this music, the most immediately striking feature is the beat. The rhythms are amazingly intricate and, though emphatic and compelling, difficult for the uninstructed listener to follow. It seems paradoxical that the Ladakhi dance which, again to the ignorant observer, seems to be something in the nature of a dignified shuffle, should be based upon rhythms of such vigour.

Though the outsider may not find them easy to distinguish, the forms of Ladakhi music are many, each being appropriate to a particular occasion. The consummate form is called *Lha-rnga*, or music of the gods: it is played at the beginning of any auspicious occasion such as sowing, or the arrival of spring, and also when serving food to incarnate lamas, or to members of the aristocracy. It also accompanies the dance of the oracle at Shey, the ancient royal capital, at an immediately pre-harvest festival in celebration of the ripening of the crops. This is said to be the most complete *Lha-rnga* played, and to consist of 360 tunes; on other occasions a shorter form is played. In addition to the *Lha-rnga*, there are musical forms proper to every ceremonial occasion: a form for the arrival of dignitaries, and one for their departure; a form for exorcising evil spirits, or getting rid of evil men; special music for polo, rising *accelerando crescendo* when a goal is scored, and similarly for archery to celebrate a bull's-eye. There is music for ploughing and for harvest; and music for every different kind of dance.

In the old days, when the representatives of the Namgyal dynasty were kings in more than name, and held their royal state at Leh and Shey, indeed right up to the time when the old order finally passed away a mere thirty or forty years ago, the nobility of Ladakh would gather on the spacious roof of Leh palace on special occasions, to celebrate with song, music and dance the glories of the dynasty and of Ladakh's history. Such occasions were *Losar*, the New Year festival, and *Dosmoche*, the Leh winter festival. On the roof of Sengge Namgyal's palace, they sang of Sengge, and the splendour he gave to Leh by building it; they sang of other kings, of Tashi and Jamyang, Deldan and Tshestang. They sang of the *ketuk-chenmo* itself, the spacious roof, which gave its name to the whole festival, and all the beauties and wonders to be seen from it—lovely maidens, and mills that worked automatically, powered by water. And with the songs they danced an equal variety of dances, of which the principal one was the dance of *ketuk-chenmo*. The climax of the whole event was a dance known as *shondeol*, which was performed in the main bazaar by the ladies of certain noble families who had the privilege of dancing before the king. Naturally, for *ketuk-chenmo* and *shondeol* alike, the music could be provided only by the musicians of the palace, the *Khar-Mon*.

The *ketuk-chenmo*, the spacious roof of the palace, is still there;

and though the twentieth century impinges at many points, the prospect before the visitor today is essentially the same as that which the Namgyal kings and their courtiers saw, and celebrated in song. But the festival of *ketuk-chenmo* is today only a memory, recalling the vanished glories of the time when the palace was the centre of an independent kingdom. From another point of view, however, it does more than that. It reminds us that, in much the same way as there is no great divide between the aristocracy and the common people, so there has never been any gulf between aristocratic and popular culture (the gulf indeed was and is between religious and secular culture); and that the blend of dance, music and song that went into the *ketuk-chenmo* festival is the essence of Ladakh's popular culture. The cycle of *ketuk-chenmo* songs is also a pointer to the strength of an oral tradition which includes a body of unwritten poetry remaining to this day almost completely unstudied.

In the early years of the twentieth century, the Moravian missionaries Karl Marx and A. H. Francke laid the foundation of Ladakh studies, and Francke published versions of the Kesar Saga, the national epic, as well as collections of songs and proverbs. Since then, scholarly attention has concentrated on the fields of history and religious art, and the oral tradition has been neglected. One or two collections and a few translations into Urdu have recently been prepared though not yet published by Ladakhis of the new stamp, educated and with a conscious desire to study and record their heritage. A few tapes have been made by Master Hussain, a great folk singer; and the Leh station of Radio Kashmir does regular broadcasts. But all this barely scratches the surface of a body of oral literature whose richness is believed to be immense. The literary genius of the people, perhaps denied more formal expression on account of the stranglehold of the lamas at the religious level, overflowed in the creation of a tradition of popular verse to give expression to every mood, and to celebrate every occasion. Those in a position to know state that in the oral literature of Ladakh is to be found an insight into every phase of the people's life.

As the predominant feature of Ladakhi music is its beat, so the folk verse, while it does not have any fixed forms, or even metres, does have a strong sense of rhythm, derived from the music to which it is sung. The imagery is rich and powerful; much of it relates to the sun, and many songs begin with an invocation to it. Anyone who has lived in Ladakh can realize what the sun means, both materially and emotionally. Materially in that it provides the warmth that not only sustains life directly, but also by melting the snow on the heights provides almost the whole of the water that slakes the thirst of the earth, the crops and all living things (the snows, particularly the glaciers, are another important element in the imagery). Emotionally, because in this climate of extreme winter cold, and a short summer season, it is only the fact that the sun does shine, many more days than not, even in the depth of winter, that makes life not only bearable but on the whole happy. The number 'three' is also an often-repeated part of the imagery in almost all types of song.

Ladakhi songs can be classifed on the basis, not of form, for the forms are not rigidly defined, but of content. One or two are associated with particular groups, or regions, such as the *zhabro* songs of Chang-Thang, which have little literary merit, and are actually composed as a musical background for the vigorous foot-stamping dance of the same name. The words of the *zhabro* are usually suggestive, if not downright bawdy. Very different is the *ghazal*, the classical form of Urdu and Persian poetry, a variant of which developed in Baltistan and was imported from there into Ladakh, particularly during the hundred years or so of the Dogra *raj* when Ladakh and Baltistan were yoked together administratively, and there was constant intercourse between them. The tone of the *ghazal* is introspective, romantic and melancholy; and though it did become popular in Ladakh, it lacks the robustness of the indigenous forms developed by a people whose spirit is cheerful and outgoing rather than melancholy and introspective.

An accurate reflection of social life is provided by a class of satirical songs in which, for example, groups of young men and women bandy humorous insults in traditional couplets. Of marriage songs there are said to be 360, covering all the different episodes of a traditional marriage, which in the old days might take weeks. An endearing Ladakhi quality is the strong sense of local patriotism: to a Tikse man there is no place in the world to compare with Tikse; the native of Sabu will never fail to feel a lift in his heart when he returns to Sabu, from exile ten kilometres away in Leh. This quality too is reflected in the folk-verse, and almost every village has been celebrated in song by its local bards.

Perhaps the most vigorous and characteristic among Ladakhi songs are the work songs. Many of these are simple 'heave-ho' chants, designed to lighten the effort of labour by giving rhythm to a hard slog. But this is only the beginning. Each process of the agricultural cycle has its appropriate songs, their forms and rhythms suited to the particular work in hand. Thus a harvest song, describing the crop like shining gold, and the flashing sickle of steel cutting through it with the speed of the mountain cascade, is sung in chorus; while the winnower, sitting alone tossing the grain in the wind to separate the chaff, sings a solo, inviting the winds to blow, bearing a richness of crops up from the fertile plains of India, and varies his song with episodes of whistling. The ploughman sings in praise of the gallant *dzo*, with their shining horns, come from the land of the gods to help in opening the earth to receive the seed; while the women irrigating the fields invite the sun to shine and melt the snows for the water without which crops will wither and man and beast will die.

Away down the Indus, near where it enters Baltistan, the *brok-pa*, the Buddhist Dards, have retained much of the ancient Dard culture, which disappeared elsewhere when the Dards of Dras and of the original homeland Gilgit embraced Islam. Their dress, customs and way of life all differ as much from those of the Muslim Dards as from the Buddhists of Tibetan origin in central Ladakh; but the clearest expression of their individuality is in their songs. Apparently content to live under the rule of Ladakh's Tibetan dynasties, they have nevertheless preserved down the centuries the memory of their origins, harking back to them in the triennial Bono-na festival, whose hymns recall another way of life, and the migration from another country. One song traces the route by which their ancestors travelled from Gilgit, and gives honour to the gods for bringing them to their new home. Another is a stirring description of an ibex-hunt, and celebrates the skills of the hunter: how he climbs the mountainside, and imitates his quarry's call; his art in driving the herd this way and that, and isolating his chosen prey; and finally the kill. After the hunt come ceremonies of thanks to the gods. Other songs describe the life of a pastoral community: taking the flocks and herds to the mountain pastures, the preparation of curd from the milk; and the beauties and pleasures of such a life—the springing wool, the horns 'growing in screw-windings', and best of all the pleasure of killing and eating a fat he-goat.

Evidently the religion of the Dards retains—even more than that of the Ladakhi Buddhists—marked traces of the pre-Buddhist animistic religion, usually referred to as Bon-chos. The second song of the Bono-na series gives an account of the origin of the world, which is seen as consisting of three realms growing out of a lake. These are the White Jewel Hill, the Red Jewel Hill and the Blue Jewel Hill, each of which has a tree of the same colour, with a different kind of bird sitting on it. This is very similar to the cosmic system of the Kesar Saga, an epic also rooted in the pre-Buddhist past of Tibet, Mongolia and China, which has become the national epic of Ladakh, and the basis of much of its folklore.

In common with all the myths passed down by oral tradition, the details of the Kesar story differ widely, even as between the versions told in the different villages of Ladakh, let alone between those current in Ladakh, Tibet and Mongolia. In all, however, the common basis can be recognized. Essentially it is a collection of nature myths, and purports to tell the story of the creation of the world, and of its early days when it was peopled by wicked giants, and authentic, though endearingly fallible, heroes. To this extent it may be compared, even related, to the other great mythologies of the Eurasian land-mass. The Greek myths, for instance (though the intellectual and artistic achievements of the later Greeks have made it difficult for us to reconstruct them in their primitive form) show the hero-giant motif clearly, as does Indian mythology; and the Norse mythology, fragmentary though our knowledge of it is, has in additon to this elements to which parts of the Kesar myth seem to correspond more closely. In both, the world—or, in the Kesar story, the land of Ling, of which Kesar became king—is created from various parts of the body of a giant who has been killed by some hero or divine figure—an *ur*-god; and in both, the archetypal hero carries the war into the enemy's country, slaying the giants by his magic powers. For giants or devils remain a threat to the men of Ling, among whom one of the lord of heaven's sons, Dongrub, incarnated as Kesar, has come to rule as their king. After various adventures, he goes off to subdue the devil of the North. Arriving at the devil's castle, he finds only his enemy's daughter, Bamzabumskyid, at home; in the approved manner which has found its way into myths and fairy-tales ranging from Thor's visit to Jotunheim to England's Jack and the Beanstalk, she hides him and allays her father's suspicions concerning the presence of an intruder, thus enabling Kesar to fulfil his mission. However, she then gives Kesar a magic potion to drink, which makes him forget his wife Bruguma; he marries Bamzabumskyid and stays with her in the North. This, the abduction of Bruguma by the king of Hor, Kesar's return to remembrance and his rescue of Bruguma, have been interpreted—as have many of the lesser anecdotes in the saga—to be a myth of the departure of life and warmth from the earth in winter, and their return in spring. Other features of the saga call to mind India's Krishna legend—particularly Kesar's amorousness (not in the same league as Krishna's, admittedly) and his sense of mischief when, in the guise of a beggar boy, he not only passes all the tests necessary to win Bruguma's hand, but deliberately plays all sorts of tricks so as to shock and upset the aristocracy of Ling gathered for the marriage.

Although the Kesar saga must have had its origins well before the introduction of Buddhism into Tibet—a good two thousand years ago, most likely—its different versions have been updated at various times and places by the accretions inseparable from the process of oral transmission. Thus we hear of firearms, naïvely supposed to have been invented by Kesar as a gift to wild animals, who will be warned of danger by the report of the gun, as opposed to the arrow which kills silently. There is also mention of Muslims, not always complimentary; but this brings us to the curious fact that in some of the Muslim parts of Kargil district, the Kesar Saga is as popular as it is in Buddhist Ladakh. In fact, the best narrations of the Saga are said to be those given by the bards of the Muslim villages of Chigtan.

In Chigtan indeed, though it is separate and distinct from Ladakh's Buddhist heartland along the Indus valley above Khaltse, the composite culture is epitomized. Islam came to Chigtan about the second half of the sixteenth century. But, imposed from above by the rulers probably for political reasons, it took centuries to be wholeheartedly accepted by the people; and up to recent times so marked were the traces of Buddhism that Chigtan might be described as having been no more than half Islamized. The last lama to be custodian of the Chigtan *gompa* left or died more than a hundred years ago; and in 1909 Francke found the temple being looked after by two Muslims, the representatives, they told him, of the family of the former Buddhist custodians, who were punctilious in lighting the butter-lamps and attending to the images. They told Francke that the temple was still visited by Buddhist Dards from across the Indus.

At the social level too, the Chigtanis have had a tradition of rejecting the exclusiveness of Islam. In some villages intermarriage between Muslims and Buddhists has been common almost right up to the present; and in the same family one son might be brought up Muslim and another Buddhist, while occasionally composite names were found, like Ali Tsering. There were villages in which the dance was an integral part of social life, as in central Ladakh, and men and women participated together openly, heedless of the Aghas, the religious leaders of Kargil, and their disapproval of the innocent pleasures of dance and music. However polo, which flourishing in the Muslim areas of the western Himalaya may be thought of as a facet of Islamic culture, has been taken up eagerly. In Chigtan it is played with a verve and skill comparable only to those seen among the Chushot Baltis, and the Chigtan *shagaran* or polo-ground is the subject of a famous ballad.

It is in Chigtan that perhaps the greatest wealth of oral literature is to be found. This ranges from the primitive animistic concepts of the Kesar Saga—here so modified by the surroundings in which it is told that Kesar is represented, for instance, as starting a journey or any other undertaking with the Muslim invocation *bismillah*, 'thanks be to God'—to the romantic *ghazal* type of verse derived from one strain of Islamic culture. Indeed, not only in Chigtan, but in the whole of Ladakh, the glory of the popular culture lies in the oral literature; the pity is that it must remain so largely hidden from the rest of the world. As always, translations can convey but a poor and inadequate idea of the riches existing among a people who, if not highly gifted in the visual arts, have a literature which demonstrates outstanding endowments of tongue and mind.

The poems which follow have been collected by Akbar Ladakhi, himself a poet and one of the foremost authorities on Ladakh's

oral literature; the versions here are based on his literal translations. These poems, or others like them, would be part of the
mental equipment of any Ladakhi over the age of 30—an assessment by Akbar which at the same time demonstrates the all-
pervasiveness of the oral tradition in times gone by, and high-
lights its precarious position today, in face of the inroads being
made by the modern world. The first, a ballad, is one of the most
famous of all Ladakhi poems, and shows how the oral tradition
has preserved memories of Ladakh's history. 'The Hillock of
Wakha' is one of the best known of the many poems in praise of a
particular place. 'Taru, My Home', as perfect as a Shakespeare
sonnet, is not well known; Akbar collected it at Silmo, down the
Indus, many miles from Taru.

The Birth of Sengge Namgyal:
An Ode to Ali Mir

See the conjunction of the stars today!
Was there ever a day so blessed by every auspicious sign?
Read in the stars all the symbols of fame and good omen!
Over against the stars of good fortune, the Milky Way is dancing,
And to confirm the favourable signs, the moon is at the full.

Today the old king's name shall resound through the universe,
For see the lovely babe his grandson, born today.
See him in the arms of his mother,
This child whose name shall be famous in all the world.
See him in the arms of Zi-Zi[1] the queen,
This child whose name shall be famous in all the world.

In the four-pillared audience-chamber of the king,
Hundreds of kings are gathered together to celebrate the day.
In the audience-chamber of the Khan,
Thousands of wazirs are gathered to celebrate the day.

O grandfather! Yours is the victory!
Your golden sword is like lightning;
Your gun with the two barrels like the thunder-giving clouds.
O my grandfather! Yours is the victory!

[1]Zi-Zi was a title given to Muslim queens of Ladakh, of whom there were several
after Gyal Katun, Sengge Namgyal's mother.

The Hillock of Wakha

From the hillock of Wakha, my home,
The whole universe is spread out before me;
The depth of the sky, the abode of the gods—
From the hillock of Wakha my home.
I can see the courtyard too;
Behold it! a corner of heaven on earth.

We are the young men of Wakha; our strength
Is like a wall of steel.
But the strength of our maidens
Is subtle and soft, yet enduring,
Like a loose bundle of silken threads.
Ah! the art that there is in plaiting those threads into a ball;
No easy task to make a ball from loose silken threads.

Behold in the courtyard, we youths and maidens are disporting
    ourselves with water.
Who are those who presume to forbid us?
Why should we not rejoice with water?
Who knows how long this life will last?
Why should we not rejoice with water?
Who will live for ever in this world?

(Slightly edited)

Taru, My Home

On the heights of Taru, my home,
Up there on the heights a glacier is forming.

When the glacier forms on the heights,
It will give birth to a turquoise lake.

When the lake forms on the low lands,
And from the lake flows out bubbling water,
Bubbling dancing water,
It shows how blessed is Taru with good fortune.

This is the stream of Taru, my home;
Flowing impetuously, foaming and roaring.
But my love, if you pass by,
For you it will run gently and slow.

XI
Buddhists, Muslims and Christians

Of the three religions represented in Ladakh, the Christians form a tiny minority, not much more than 100 persons, almost all of them in and around Leh. Buddhists and Muslims are found in more or less equal numbers, with a preponderance of Buddhists in the north and east, and of Muslims to the south and west. Kargil town, Dras, the Suru Valley and Sankhu belt, Pashkyum and Shagkar-Chigtan are almost exclusively Muslim; Mulbekh and Bodh-Kharbu have mixed populations, with a distinct Buddhist majority in Mulbekh. Zanskar is basically a Buddhist area, the small Muslim community there being immigrants from the Jammu region who came in the wake of Zorawar Singh's invasion. The Indus valley from Khaltse upstream, and downstream on the right bank (where the *brokpa* practise their own variant of the religion) is almost uniformly Buddhist, and so are Chang-Thang and Nubra. The exceptions are a small but influential Muslim population in Leh itself and a few of the surrounding villages, and a few Muslims in the Turtuk-Bogdang area of Nubra, down the Shayok river to the north-west.

For centuries Ladakhi life and ways of thought have been moulded by Buddhism, the particular form followed in Tibet and Ladakh being the Vajrayana, the Vehicle of the Thunderbolt. Its external expressions are everywhere. At the approach to every village there are a number of *chorten*, the *stupas* of ancient Indian Buddhism, referring in their origin to the grave-mounds erected over the divided ashes of Gautam Buddha. The erection of these was accounted a work of piety, and the greatest number of them is found in and around the ancient royal residence at Shey, fourteen kilometres up the Indus from Leh. Those in or near the *gompas* often contain sacred objects: block-printed scriptures, or clay images, or offerings of ritual cakes; while inside the temples, made of beautifully worked metal and precious stones, they serve the purpose of reliquaries. When situated near the approach to a village, they are superstitiously supposed to bar the way to the entry of evil spirits. There are eight different types of *chorten*, the different shapes symbolizing different aspects of the Buddhist way. For example, the one with a tapering spire in thirteen sections or 'wheels' represents the progress of the soul towards enlightenment. Like every other religious structure, the *chorten* is to be circumambulated in a clockwise direction, symbolizing the unity of the soul's awakening with the movement of the planets: the unity of all things in the cosmic order. A Buddhist as a matter of instinct and reflex will never pass a *chorten* even casually without keeping it on his right; and he may undertake ritual circumambulation, which has the purpose of cleansing the soul, increasing merit, and ultimately bringing the soul nearer to enlightenment. Sometimes *chorten*-like structures fulfil the function of a gateway, the main building being raised off the ground to form an arch, under which a road passes. The inner walls of these are painted with religious motifs, and the small ceiling-space filled with a mandala.

Near the *chorten*, or isolated in the midst of the desert, are seen long, straight, apparently functionless walls. These are *mani* walls. One or two metres in height, and two to three metres broad, they vary in length from a few metres to about a kilometre. They are built of sand and rubble, and are faced with stones carrying inscriptions—a prayer or an invocation—engraved in the beautiful Tibetan script. Most often this is the *mantra, Om Mani Padme Hum*—'Hail the Jewel in the Lotus'—an invocation of secret tantric significance, particularly associated with the Bodhisattva of Compassion, Avalokiteswara. *Mani* walls, like *chorten*, are to be passed on the right; at a *mani* wall accordingly the footpath bifurcates, so that both going and coming the wayfarer may keep it on his right.

Prayer-flags printed with texts and invocations, and prayer wheels twirled in a clockwise direction similarly serve a symbolic purpose. The prayer-wheel, whether an enormous cylinder let into the wall of a monastery to be set in motion by the hands of the faithful as they pass, or set on paddle-floats to be kept in perpetual rotation by the action of running water, or on a handle spun by a gentle movement of the wrist, bears witness to the Buddha's conception of the law of all existence—*dharma*—symbolized by the endless motion of the wheel.

It may indeed be doubted whether the ordinary Ladakhi cherishes a deep appreciation of the inwardness of the beliefs connected with these common objects, highly charged with symbolism as they are. He spins a prayer-wheel, scrupulously keeps a *chorten* or *mani* wall on his right as he passes, without every time necessarily thinking of the cosmic turning of the Great Wheel of all existence. For, as with all the great religions of the world, and perhaps—because of its complexity—most of all, there has developed in Buddhism a deep split between popular practice and belief, and the higher teaching of theology. This split is surely emphasised by the fact that the person who takes his Buddhism seriously, and wants to go deep into the teachings, has to undergo initiations that must tend to set him apart from his believing but less committed fellows.

Indeed, many of the doctrines are difficult and subtle in the extreme. Central to Buddhism in all its forms is the idea that every soul has the capacity to reach the state of enlightenment, and thence *nirvana*—the extinction of its separate identity in union with the cosmic soul—in other words to become a Buddha. The Mahayana goes further, and adds a principle of compassion, so that no enlightened soul can be content to accept *nirvana* for itself while a single other soul remains bound to the wheel of mundane existence with its perpetual suffering—suffering being the very nature and concomitant of separation from the Soul of all things. Hence the ideal of the Bodhisattva, who might be defined as a potential Buddha—an enlightened soul which for aeons forgoes *nirvana*, returning to the world in bodily form over and over again, to work for the liberation of all souls.

This central principle, it is true, is not difficult to grasp. But from it emanated a most complicated system of Buddhas and Bodhisattvas—Gautam Buddha, or Sakyamuni, being considered as but one of a series of historical Buddhas of different eras. In Buddhism's early years, Sakyamuni was conceived of as the central one of a series of seven; later came the idea of a thousand Buddhas, of whom Sakyamuni was the fourth—thus there remain 996 ages to be fulfilled, each of which will have its own Buddha. (The thousand Buddhas are a recurrent theme in the wall paintings of the *gompas*). To add to the complexity, the very idea of Buddha-hood ceased to remain a unified one, and there appeared the concept of five Buddhas—or it is perhaps clearer for the uninitiated to regard them as five aspects of Buddha-hood—known as the *Dhayani* Buddhas, or Buddhas of Meditation, whose cosmic nature is demonstrated by the fact that while one was associated with the centre of things, the others radiated out to the four points of the compass. Later, with the development of the Vajrayana school, tantric elements were adopted from Hinduism. These implied the introduction of a feminine principle, in a state of simultaneous polarity and fusion with the masculine one; accordingly a system of female deities came to be associated with the Five Buddhas. The circular design of the mandala was an attempt to express in graphic terms the essentially abstract relationships between all these symbolic concepts.

This brief description of a few salient points does no more than hint at the enormous complexities of the Vajrayana school, which established itself in Tibet from about the eleventh century as a mystical and esoteric religion relying largely on practices and initiations derived from the secret texts of the Tantra. Historically too, Buddhism in Tibet had to contend with the pantheistic and shamanistic Bon religion, which was characterized by a highly developed cosmic system, and a multiplicity of gods and demons. Buddhism as it spread made no attempt to suppress this ancient cult altogether, but rather absorbed as many of its beliefs and practices as were not actually in conflict with its own. Thus many of the Bon deities appear in the Buddhist pantheon, where they have the position of *Dharmapalas*—Guardians of the Law; it is they, with their fearful aspect, who play such a large part in the annual dance-dramas held by each monastery on the days of its own particular festival.

All this resulted in an immensely difficult and ramified system of Buddhas and Bodhisattvas, gods and goddesses, beliefs and rituals, magic and mysticism, in which ultimately the whole cosmic order, and the human person in his totality—body, spirit, senses, mind, emotions—are involved. There can be no short cut to the study and absorption of Tibetan Buddhism, and it is hardly surprising that the Buddhist laity seem for the most part to be content with an uncomprehending observance of outward forms, based on a few simplistic beliefs, and show little understanding (at an intellectual level at least) of the complexities of their faith. On the other hand, it has been suggested that the tranquillity and balance of the Ladakhi character may be derived from Buddhist attitudes—if not thought-out and articulated beliefs—and particularly from the central idea of compassion for all living things, and the lack of value set on the self as an entity to be cherished. These ideas, indeed, may have failed to have a similar effect on the mentality of all the communities professing themselves to be Buddhist: the Khampa of eastern Tibet, for instance, have a long-standing reputation as freebooters, and latterly as the core of effective resistance against the Chinese occupation, and cannot be thought of as devoting much time to the contemplation and cultivation of the Bodhisattva ideal. But it is still arguable that the Ladakhis have been open to the peaceful influence of Buddhism, and that their ways of life and thought have been deeply coloured by it.

While it is true that for the mass of the laity, and perhaps not a few of the monks too, their Buddhism implies rather a set of attitudes than a set of beliefs, it is equally true that among the lamas there is a minority who are wise and learned men of religion. The traveller who wants to go deep into Buddhism, or even to undergo particular initiations, would be well advised to consider coming to Ladakh to find a guru, as much as to the better-known centres of Buddhist learning in Dharamsala and Nepal. In the *gompa* temples with their images and *thangkas*, in the elaborate mandalas of the Alchi murals, in the rock engravings, even in the simple piety of the unlettered faithful, the serious seeker after the Buddhist way will find much to meditate on.

The spiritual leaders of Ladakhi and Tibetan Buddhism are the lamas, who are seen everywhere in their heavy terra-cotta robes. They have a great influence among the Buddhist laity, as preachers and teachers, and in their role as priests and ministers on all the solemn occasions of· family life—births, marriages, deaths, a child's dedication to the monkhood—and the great new year festival of Losar, which falls about the time of the winter solstice. They are also advisers on the efficacy of various actions the individual may take to hasten his liberation from the endless cycle of birth and rebirth, and exorcists with power to banish evil spirits.

The lamas live congregated in the monasteries or *gompas*, which are the focus of religious life and activity. The head lama of each *gompa* is a *kushok*, the incarnation of some holy man of long ago, who himself may be held to have incarnated the spirit of some blessed Bodhisattva. (The first Dalai Lama, for instance, came to be revered as an incarnation of the Bodhisattva of Compassion, Avalokiteswara; by the same token Avalokiteswara now walks the earth as the present Dalai Lama, the fourteenth of his line.) More often, the incarnation may be of the founder of that particular *gompa*, or of the order to which it belongs. The *kushok* enjoys the courtesy title of *Rinpoche*, Precious Jewel. During his boyhood he will be instructed in the mysteries of the faith by a wise senior lama who has the title of *lobon*. Like the monasteries of mediaeval Europe, many of the *gompas* are supported by endowments of agricultural land, and have a considerable organization devoted to administering their temporal affairs. For the rest, they traditionally receive a tribute in the nature of tithes from the villagers, always paid in kind.

South-west Ladakh, from Dras to the Fatu-La, has always been open to infiltration and invasion, and the conversion of the people to Islam must frequently have been by the sword or, as in the case of Shagkar-Chigtan, at any rate for political reasons. The Chigtan rulers—Sultans as they called themselves after their conversion—seem to have embraced Islam as a means of freeing themselves from dependence on the kings of Ladakh; this action was a contributory cause of the Balti invasion at the beginning of the seventeenth century. But the people of Chigtan, as we have seen, found it hard to abandon their ancient ways, and till very recently neither their social life nor their religious practice conformed completely to the norms of Islam. However, many of their deviant customs may not survive much longer as, with improved communications by road, the Aghas, the spiritual leaders of the Kargil Muslims, extend their authority to establish a more orthodox religion in Chigtan as well as in the rest of their jurisdiction.

The Kargil Muslims are Shias; and to judge by their influence on the people, the Aghas preach a puritanical, not to say fanatical form of their religon. It is clear to even the casual observer as he travels in this region that life sits heavy on the people—in striking contrast to the impression he will get from Buddhists and Muslims alike in central Ladakh. Leaving aside the fact that no *chang* is prepared or drunk among the Muslims—which is to be expected—the Aghas have abolished polo by edict in Kargil town, the centre of their authority (though it is still played in Dras and Shagkar-Chigtan); music is frowned upon, and dancing outside Chigtan non-existent. The Aghas themselves look abroad for spiritual guidance, not to Arabia, but to Iraq, stronghold of the Shia faith. Even now some Kargilis, especially those belonging to the Agha families, go to Iraq to complete their education. In contrast to Buddhist Ladakh, the women of Kargil are secluded, and have little say in the conduct of life.

The Muslim community of the Leh area is descended either from immigrants, or from marriages contracted by local women with Muslim merchants settled in Leh from Kashmir and Yarkand. This mixed community, Sunnis by persuasion, have an influence in the town out of all proportion to their fairly small numbers, partly because their mercantile background makes them one of the most prosperous groups. The most important of the immigrant-descended groups is the Balti community of the large village of Chushot, across the Indus, about fifteen kilometres upriver from Leh. Although they are believed to have come from Baltistan as much as 350 years ago, in the reign of Sengge Namgyal, they retain to this day the consciousness that they are Baltis, in some way separate and distinct from the Ladakhis among whom they live. Like the Kargil Muslims, the Chushot Baltis too are Shias, and many of them follow the injunctions of their faith with uncompromising strictness. But they are unlike the Kargil Shias in that they have not lost—or have imbibed from their Buddhist neighbours—the capacity to enjoy life. The Leh Muslims live in a way that is not so different from that of their Buddhist neighbours.

The Christian community in Leh and a few of the surrounding villages numbers no more than a few score. The first Christian missionaries to reach Ladakh were the Jesuits Azevedo, Oliveira and Desideri, in the seventeenth and eighteenth centuries[1]; but none of them made Ladakh the field of their labours, and their

---

[1]See Appendix I: The Jesuits in Western Tibet.

short visits left no mark. Christianity as we see it today was brought by the missionaries of the Moravian church, who arrived in Leh in 1885. It appealed here not, as in many other parts of India, to the poor and down-trodden but to members of Leh's social elite, so that the Christian community is one of high standing in the town. There is a church at Leh, and one at Shey, fourteen kilometres upriver. Services are trilingual, in Ladakhi, Hindustani and English. In dress, appearance and way of life, the Christians are virtually indistinguishable from the Buddhists among whom they live.

Indeed, with a very few exceptions, communal feeling as experienced often so bitterly in other parts of India, has so far been conspicuous by its absence. This may in part be due to the fact that Buddhism seems to be a genuinely non-violent religion with no tradition of holy wars or religious persecution, so that where Buddhists are in the majority they are content to live at peace with their non-Buddhist neighbours. But there are a few things that Buddhists, or at least their spiritual leaders the lamas, will not tolerate, like slaughtering animals, or even fishing, near a *gompa*; it is a tribute to the good sense and goodwill of all concerned that matters like this have only rarely led to friction.

In Leh—admittedly the most cosmopolitan place in Ladakh—there is a long tradition of intermarriage, dating right back to the days of the caravan trade when its bazaar was home to a colony of foreign merchants; and this has surely strengthened the good relations between the different religions. It is quite common for a particular Muslim or Buddhist of good family to have relatives belonging to the other community; while among the Christians, converts of only a hundred years' standing and in a decided minority, it is universal. On the whole fewer Muslim than Buddhist girls marry outside their religion; this is probably one of the effects of polyandry, which in the past would have encouraged some of the presumed surplus of Buddhist women to seek husbands of other faiths, at the same time discouraging Muslim girls from marrying Buddhists. The Leh Muslim community on the whole enjoyed a position of wealth and status which again would tend to keep the girls from marrying outside. In spite of all this, occasionally a Muslim girl did marry a Buddhist, touched perhaps by the influence of Buddhist society's liberal attitude towards love and marriage, and its willingness to allow a reasonable freedom of choice to women as well as men. Nevertheless here as in most other societies it is the woman who has been required to adopt her husband's religion rather then vice versa.

But even when it involves conversion, intermarriage never means breaking off relations with one's own community. It would be strange if it did, as even in the ordinary run of events relations between members of different communities are close, and everyone takes a keen interest in each other's social and religious ceremonies. Both, or all three, communities will be represented at any birth, marriage or funeral ceremony; and religious festivals provide an opportunity to greet the members of that particular community. Thus Losar, the Buddhist new year, sees a stream of callers of all three faiths at Buddhist homes, Id at Muslim homes, and Christmas at the houses of Christians. The callers carry with them *kataks*, the white scarves presentation of which is a custom throughout the region of Tibetan culture, denoting respectful greeting. Originally a Buddhist custom, in Ladakh it has become a secular one, and *kataks* are presented on religious and non-religious occasions alike. It seems appropriate that this, a Buddhist gesture symbolizing goodwill and respect, should have become in Ladakh a custom common to three different religions which are often antagonistic, but which here co-exist in harmony.

XII
The Gompas,
A Living Heritage

Not only spiritually, but also materially, the glory of Ladakhi Buddhism is undoubtedly the *gompas* or monasteries. '*Gompa*' means 'solitary place'; and a few of them, like Hemis and Ridzong, are certainly that. Many others are situated near, and usually above, a village, the pattern of whose houses they complement with their square piled-up outlines. Often built on a slope, or near the summit of a craggy hill, they rise tier upon tier, as much as seven or eight storeys, dominating the landscape all around. With their massive walls and small windows, they might be mistaken for fortresses, if it were not for the *chorten* and *mani* walls scattered about the approach, and the prayer-flags that flutter everywhere. Inside, they are a rabbit-warren of rooms connected by dark stairs and passage-ways, their gloom relieved by courtyards, sometimes small, sometimes spacious, from which rise wide and steep flights of steps to the principal places of worship, the *Lha-khang* and *Du-khang*. The apartments of the *Rinpoche*, the head lama, are always right at the top, a kind of penthouse; often from the adjoining roof-terrace a magnificent panorama of village, field, stream and mountain is spread out before the visitor. The *gompas* are living centres of worship, and the lamas go about their duties not presumably oblivious of the crowd of sightseers, but determined not to let it make a difference to their ancient-established routine.

Although they look and dress alike, the lamas of Tibetan Buddhism are divided into a number of different orders, and of these five are represented in Ladakh. Most people have heard of the red and yellow sects, but there is more to it than that. For a start, it is only the headgear which may be either red or yellow; without distinction of sect all the monks wear red, or rather brick-coloured robes. The monks of only one order wear yellow hats—and hats indeed are not an everyday article of dress; they are worn only on ceremonial occasions. The 'yellow-hat' order is more properly referred to as the Ge-lugs-pa, meaning Model of Virtue; it is the last-founded of all the monastic orders.

The earliest of the orders is the Nying-ma-pa. It is based directly on the teachings of Padmasambhava, one of the first and reckoned the greatest of the Indian sages who over a period of centuries brought Buddhism at different stages of its development from India to Tibet. The most famous of the Tibetan Buddhist texts, the Book of the Dead, is a Nying-ma-pa work. The Nying-ma-pa lays emphasis on solitary meditation, and its holy places are as often hermitages as monasteries. Thus its monastic organization has been less powerful than that of other orders. In Ladakh it is represented only by the monastery of Thak-thak.

The next order is the Ka-gyu-pa, or School of Oral Tradition, founded on the basis of the teachings of a line of initially Indian masters. The first of these was Tilopa, who incorporated into Buddhism the tenets and practices of the Hindu Yoga philosophy. Tilopa's most famous disciple was the Kashmiri yogi Naropa, head of the famous Nalanda monastery in Bihar; and he in turn was teacher of the Tibetan Marpa, who carried the doctrines into Tibet, towards the end of the eleventh century. Marpa was the first of a line of famous teachers in Tibet, of whom the best-known was his immediate successor Mila-Respa, considered to be the greatest of the Tibetan masters, not least because of his genius as a poet. Towards the end of the twelfth century, the single line of transmission split into a number of sects, which continued separate and distinct in Tibet until the eclipse of Buddhism there in the wake of the Chinese occupation of 1950s. Two of these sects are represented in Ladakh: the Dri-gung-pa which claims the monasteries of Lamayuru and Phiyang; and the Drug-pa, which was specially favoured by the kings of the Namgyal dynasty, and to which the monasteries of Hanle, Hemis, Chemrey and Stakna belong—all of them founded about the time of Sengge Namgyal. Both sects are named after the original monasteries of their orders in central Tibet.

The last of the important 'red-hat' orders is the Saskya-pa, which is based on the teachings of the Indian yogic master, Virupa, brought to Tibet in the eleventh century. It takes its name from one of its great teachers, Sas-kya. In its early years it acquired great political influence in central Tibet, but by the fifteenth century had declined in importance, leaving the way open for the later political predominance of the Ge-lugs-pa. It is represented in Ladakh by the small monastery of Matho.

The Ge-lugs-pa, the order of yellow-hatted lamas, is the fruit of the reform movement started about 1400 by Tson-ka-pa. As the starting-point for his reforms, Tson-ka-pa took the teachings and the monastic organization of the Ka-dam-pa sect, which had been founded in the eleventh century on the basis of Atisa's teachings. A Ge-lugs-pa delegation arrived in Ladakh in the reign of king Trags-bum-de, perhaps in the early years of the fifteenth century, as a result of which the first Ge-lugs-pa monastery was founded, at Spituk, eight kilometres down the Indus from Leh. Tikse and Likir, older foundations of the Kadam-pa school, were taken over by the Ge-lugs-pa not long after. Thus monasteries of the later-established Ge-lugs-pa order pre-date in Ladakh the foundations of any sect of the Ka-gyu-pa.

The oldest *gompas*, those dating from Rinchen-zang-po's time—Alchi and Lamayuru, and the less accessible Wanla, Mangyur and Sumdah—belonged at the time of their foundation to none of these Tibetan schools, whose establishment they antedate. They were at some stage taken over by the Ka-dam-pa, and when it fell into decline they were taken over again, this time mostly by the Ge-lugs-pa. The exception was Lamayuru, which was for some reason claimed by the Dri-gung-pa. Alchi, perhaps already by the fifteenth century abandoned as a centre of living worship, was in the care of the Ge-lugs-pa establishment of Likir.

The iconography of Vajrayana Buddhism is extemely complicated, and no more than the merest hints can be given here. However, in style and content, the wall paintings of the later *gompas* display a remarkable uniformity, so that what is said of one applies equally to all. Alchi is different. Its murals are not only of a very early date, but in iconography as well as in style quite unlike those of the later *gompas*. In Alchi we find, for instance, a much greater stress on the Five *Dhayam* Buddhàs; the relationships between them and their associated Bodhisattvas are carefully worked out in elaborate mandalas. There are some representations of goddesses, mostly Prajnaparamita ('Perfection of Wisdom'), who appears in some exquisitely beautiful forms; but there is no system of female deities associated with the Five Buddhas; and only in the Lha-khang Soma or New Temple is there a hint of the later tantric concept of the fusion of the masculine and feminine principles. As might be expected, there are one or two representations of the great translator, Rin-chen-zang-po, who is elsewhere conspicuous by his absence. The Alchi murals contain some fascinating vignettes of secular life, several in the form of scenes from the life of Sakyamuni, a few along with representations of the divinities, and one or two on their own. There is not much stress on the terrible 'Guardian Deities', except Mahakala.

The temples of the sixteenth century at Namgyal Tsemo and Basgo have murals that, in style and content, occupy an intermediate position between Alchi and the later *gompas*. The mandalas which, at Alchi, express a whole philosophy in graphic form, have disappeared, to be replaced by figures of deities and Bodhisattvas arranged more or less haphazardly. But much of the charming decorative detail remains, as also some illuminating scenes of secular life; the artists have clearly been given a much freer hand than they were later. This is true too of such original seventeenth-century murals as remain at Hemis, Stakna and Chemrey. In the main temples these have been replaced by more recent work; but there are still a few of them to be found in dark corners, in a style which is much more free and vigorous than the more frequently-seen orthodox one, and which does not yet seem to have been described or analysed.

It is the orthodox style of painting, practised to this day, that the visitor will become most familiar with. It expresses an elaborate iconography with a profusion of divinities, prominent among them the fierce *Dharmapalas*, Guardians of the Law; particularly noticeable is Mahakala, 'Great and Black', the divinity specifically associated with Time. Usually he has the normal number of limbs and heads, and he is girt with a leopard skin, while he tramples on the bodies of his enemies. In Tibetan he is called simply *Gon-bo*, the Guardian. Other guardian divinities are Yamantaka, god of death, also black, and represented with many arms; Shugdan, who rides a fierce beast; and Vajra-Bhairava, who is particularly associated with the Ge-lugs-pa. Every *gompa* has its *Gon-khang*, a temple dedicated to these fierce deities, usually a small structure painted red, which is forbidden to women. But they feature largely in the main temples too, often near the entrance. They are often represented in *yab-yum*—in a position of union with their female counterparts. This is a specifically tantric manifestation.

The verandahs of the *Du-khang*, or main temple of the *gompas*, are invariably decorated with representations of the Lords of the Four Quarters, and the *Samsara Chakra*—the Wheel of Life. The Lords are mythological figures of great antiquity, and are depicted as warriors, in the Mongol tradition. Lord of the North is Kuvera, a yellow figure who holds a banner in his right hand and a mongoose in his left. Vimdhaka, Lord of the South, is either green or blue, and instead of a helmet wears an elephant's head; he carries a sword. Dhritarashtra, who rules the East, is white and plays a lute; and Lord of the West is Virupaksha, who is red and carries a *chorten* in his hand. Despite the symbolic purpose of having the entrance to important temples watched over by these powerful Lords who between them hold sway over all the world, in practice their function seems often to be purely decorative. In them, it seems, their painters have escaped from the macabre horrors of the terrible Guardians, and equally from the benign transcendence of the Buddhas and Bodhisattvas, into as nearly a secular form as Tibetan art is capable of.

The Four Kings, clad in shining armour, sit in their flowery gardens, among flags, musical instruments, arms, gifts, jewels, corals, silks, precious stuffs, heraldic animals and symbolic ribbons, making music with lutes, flying banners, playing with exotic animals, secure lords of a distant, golden age.[1]

Of a more purely didactic purpose is the Wheel of Life, which is supported by a grotesque Yamantaka. Also known as the *Kala Chakra*, Wheel of Time, or *Dharma Chakra*, Wheel of the Law, this represents the cycle of existence which has to be endured time after time by all souls, until they somehow escape from it and attain *nirvana*. In the innermost of its three concentric circles are shown the three primordial evils: anger as a cock, desire as a serpent, and ignorance as a pig. In the middle circle, taking up most of the space, we see the six states of existence: from the upper left in a clockwise direction—the abode of the gods; the abode of the demi-gods; the abode of the dead; hell, where the wicked are shown undergoing horrible tortures; the abode of animals; and the abode of men. The outer circle, no more than a

[1]Fosco Maraini, *Secret Tibet* (London, 1952).

narrow rim, contains twelve symbols which, following each other
in a clockwise direction, demonstrate the eternal chain of cause
and effect. Starting from the blind man at the top, who stands for
primordial ignorance, we next find a symbol representing the
basic appetites which arise from that ignorance, and which lead in
their turn to the third state which is awareness. Out of this arises
the attribution of names and forms to things; this attribution
sharpens the six senses; the six senses yearn for contact with any
Other; desire for contact gives rise to sensation; from sensation
arise thirst and other physical desires; these desires lead to attachment; from one attachment arise others in an endless chain;
hence birth; and finally death—and so back to primordial ignorance. Some of the objects symbolizing these various concepts
seem less obvious than others: for instance it is not clear to the
non-Buddhist mind why two men in a boat should symbolize
awareness attributing names and forms to things. But the total
effect is arresting; and the detail repays study.

The most popular of the female deities represented in the
gompas are the Green and White Taras—in Tibetan Dolma Dol-
kar, and Dolma Doljan. Spituk seems to be the *gompa* with the
greatest devotion to the Taras; it has a whole room devoted to the
twenty-three manifestations of Tara. Otherwise they are not seen
very often.

Various of the great masters of the Mahayana are often represented as Bodhisattvas: Padmasambhava, Atisa and—only in Ge-
lugs-pa establishments—Tson-ka-pa, recognizable by his yellow
hat. Otherwise the Bodhisattva most commonly seen is Avalokiteswara (in Tibetan Chen-re-zig), the personification of Compassion. He is often shown with eleven heads, arranged as a
pyramid, and surrounded, as with an enormous halo, by his
thousand arms and hands, an eye in the centre of each palm.
These were given him, it is said, in consideration of the
tremendous size and difficulty of his task as a Bodhisattva, the
very principle of compassion, of helping an infinity of benighted
souls to reach enlightenment. He is also sometimes seen sitting in
the lotus position with four arms making symbolic gestures or
mudras, and one, or occasionally three heads. The Buddhist scriptures recognize 108 forms of Chen-re-zig; but these are the most
common. Another often-represented Bodhisattva is Manjusri
(Jam-Yang in Tibetan), who personifies wisdom. He sits in the

lotus position, with a mere two arms and a single head; in his right hand he wields the blue sword which vanquishes ignorance, and in his left he holds the book of wisdom. The Buddha-to-come Maitreya (Chamba), also possesses the usual number of limbs and heads: he is either standing, or sitting on a throne—poised to step on to the historical stage. All these three Bodhisattvas wear five-pointed crowns, and their look is benign and majestic. But they also have a terrible aspect, in which the crown is replaced by a headdress made of five human skulls, and the hair by wildly streaming flames. Either way they must be represented with the Six Precious Adornments: earrings, chains around the neck, chest and waist, and bracelets on the wrist and upper arm. These symbolize the six transcendental virtues: generosity, patience, energy, meditation, wisdom and self-discipline. Sakyamuni, the historical Buddha, on the other hand, is recognizable by the plainness of his appearance. He has elongated pierced ears, it is true, but not the earrings which stretched their lobes; his head is bare, with the hair in tight stylized curls; the body too is usually bare.

All these descriptions—which do no more than scratch the surface of the enormously complex symbolism of Vajrayana ico-nography—hold good equally of the images and of the wall-paintings which the visitor will see in the *gompas*. During his round of *gompa*-visiting, he may, if he is lucky, find *puja*, or worship going on once or twice. There are services morning and evening, and on particular occasions special *pujas* that last the whole day. Visitors are welcomed, and are often invited to sit quietly at the back while the service is going on. What the uninitiated can observe is a heavy rhythmical chanting, accompanied by symbolic hand-gestures or *mudras*. The *puja* is punctuated by bursts of music from shawms, cymbals, bells, drums, and the long horns that rest on the ground. At intervals, sticks of incense are distri-buted among the lamas, who are seated in lines facing the centre along the length of the *Du-khang*. Every now and then the mate-rials of worship are ceremonially brought in: water for the bowls in front of the images; butter for the lamps; tiny *chorten* kneaded from a dough of *tsampa* and butter. And the lamas themselves are refreshed with periodical servings of butter-tea. Even this homely touch is not really incongruous. It is a reminder that in the Vajrayana man in his totality is involved in his worship—not only his mind and spirit, but his body with its appetites too. The whole *puja*, even if its 'meaning' escapes the uninitiated observer, may still strike chords beyond the level of intellectual understanding. In its setting it can hardly fail to be apprehended as a link in a chain of belief and practice going back hundreds of years, and spreading over an area the size of Europe. It is part of the human heritage, and Ladakh is one of the few places where it survives.

There now follow some notes on particular *gompas*.

Namgyal Tsemo

Namgyal Tsemo, the peak above Leh, and site of buildings of historical and religious interest, can be approached by any of three routes. There is a zig-zag path visible from the bazaar leading up the front of the hill behind the Palace; this route, the most direct from the town, has the disadvantage of being in the sun for most of the day, and would therefore be very hot except early in the morning or during unusually cloudy weather. A steep path leads almost straight up the back (north side) of the hill from the hamlet of Chubi, whose establishment is associated with that of Tashi Namgyal's fort and temple on the peak. If transport is available, the most painless route is from that point on the Khardung-La road (leading from behind the Transport Depot and the Development Commissioner's office) where it crosses the ridge connecting Namgyal Tsemo hill with other higher ones to the east. From there a path, rather rough and narrow, leads at not too punishing a gradient up the ridge and round to the summit. The Namgyal Tsemo complex is uninhabited, but the temples are maintained by a lama from Sankar *Gompa*, down in the valley behind Leh, who comes up every day to light the butter lamps. He is to be found usually between six and seven o'clock in the morning, and five and six in the evening.

The buildings of interest are the Maitreya temple, and the *Gon-khang* and fort of Tashi Namgyal. The Maitreya temple is of uncertain date, but might go back to the time of king Trags-bum-de, who founded hereabouts a 'red monastery' or 'red college', with an image of Maitreya—though that, being 'in size such as he would be in his eighth year', cannot be the large and undistinguished image that stands there today. Francke, in 1909, found the wall covered with paintings, including one of the great Tashi-lunpo monastery in Tibet, and several inscriptions. These have since been destroyed, and in July 1978 the walls were in the process of being repainted; the right-hand one had been completed, with figures including Sakyamuni, Avalokiteswara, Padmasambhava, Tson-ka-pa and Green Tara. In subsidiary positions are Sron-tsan-gam-po, the strong man of ancient Tibet, with various manifestations of the White Tara—a juxtaposition less incongruous than it may seem, as his two wives, who were instrumental in converting him to Buddhism and establishing it as the official religion, were recognized as incarnations of the Taras.

The *Gon-khang* built by Tashi Namgyal in the mid- 16th century, is much more interesting but, as it is almost completely dark, the visitor should take a powerful torch with him. Women are allowed entry—perhaps only because the main images are completely veiled. This is the temple of which the Chronicle tells us that Tashi, having defeated the Mongol invaders, laid the corpses of the slain enemy beneath the feet of the images. The six-armed Mahakala (or perhaps Yamantaka) has a phallus which is superstitiously worshipped by barren women for the favour of a child, an offering being hung in the temple's antechamber.

Though the images are hidden, the wall-paintings have a lot of interest. Surprisingly, for a temple dedicated to the wrathful deities, these murals contain representations of gods and Bodhisattvas, mostly in their benevolent aspect. There is a sweetly smiling Tara, a Tson-ka-pa and a Sakyamuni, among others whose identification, even with the aid of a torch, is difficult. The fierce divinities are only on the entrance wall, to the right of the door as you enter. To the left, at about waist level, is the famous presumed portrait of Tashi Namgyal, part of a court scene in which drinking cups are prominent in the participants' hands, while at the bottom of the picture is a row of earthenware *chang* pots, identical to those in use today. Oddly, there seem to be two Tashi Namgyals: right next to the portrait which has been accepted as Tashi's, is another which is almost its mirror-image—the features seem to be identical, only some details are different, and the presumed Tashi's turban is a fraction larger. This is puzzling: such a 'twin' representation must have had some symbolic meaning; but whatever that might have been, it has been obscured by the passage of time. The style of painting and the sitter's face call to mind Persian, rather than Tibetan art. The narrow slanting eyes are perfectly appropriate to the Persian style; and the fine thin features are unlike anyone's idea of the flat-faced Tibetan. The crafty and ruthless politician is implicit in every line. The dress and turban are in the Mughal style which, brought from Kashmir, was current among the Ladakhi nobility at the time. Just to the right of this miniature court scene is a mounted figure, dressed and turbanned in the same way, smiling, and with blunt and coarse features, very different from the fine face of the king.

The complex of buildings is completed by Tashi Namgyal's fort—the first known royal residence at Leh. It is now in ruins; in the uppermost room, reached by a scramble up crumbling steps and through broken walls, there are the remains of murals in circular forms, and traces of painted decoration on the woodwork of the windows. From here, as from practically every point on the peak, there is a magnificent panoramic view over Leh, the flat roofs of the town, the green expanse of the oasis, and across the Indus to the seamed and folded flanks of the Zanskar range and the commanding peak of Stok Kangri. Did Tashi Namgyal appreciate the view? Or was it rather a matter of designing a building to get the sun and avoid the wind sweeping down from the snows of the Karakoram to the north? For whatever reason, the fort's only windows are in its south-facing wall.

At the back of Tashi's fort are walls, the remains of even more ancient fortifications, which according to Francke used to be locally known as the Dard Castle. If this name is an authentic reflection of historical fact, it means that they are the remains of a fort dating from before the establishment of a Tibetan ruling class in Ladakh—that is, from more than 1,000 years ago.

Sankar

Sankar is one of the few *gompas* to have definite visiting hours, morning and evening, and though it is possible to poke about the courtyard and the verandahs during the day, visitors wanting to enter the *Du-khang* out of hours will be warned off in no uncertain terms.

The village and *gompa* of Sankar are an easy half-hour's walk from Leh, up the valley behind the town, in the lee of the Khardung-La. The *gompa*, a pleasing cluster of buildings and *chorten* nestling among trees on the edge of the village, is a relatively modern foundation, a daughter house of Spituk, and is the residence of Spituk's head lama, the Venerable Kushok Bakula, seniormost of the incarnate lamas of Ladakh by virtue equally of personal authority and of the antiquity of his spiritual ancestry. From 1970 to 1977 he represented Ladakh in Parliament.

The verandah of the *Du-khang* is decorated with the usual Lords of the Four Quarters and Wheel of Life, in pleasantly mellow renderings, also the Old Man of Long Life. Unfortunately, visiting out of hours (in the course of an afternoon walk, rather than with the serious intention of a *gompa* visit), I was not admitted to the ground floor of the *Du-khang*, or to its upper verandah, which happened to be full of activity that day in preparation for the forthcoming visit of His Holiness the Dalai Lama. Throughout the *gompa* windows were being polished and woodwork painted; in the upper verandah there was polishing of the brass vessels used in worship, and the busy humming of a sewing machine as one of the lamas ran up new window-frills. The upper storey of the temple, a kind of mezzanine running round all four sides, from which it was possible to peer into the main chamber beneath but not to distinguish anything in the gloom, had its walls bare, stripped for repainting. A few large canvases were on display, with figures and writing not integrated into any definite design; they seemed to be in the nature of guides or instruction manuals on iconography.

Spituk

Spituk *gompa*, founded early in the fifteenth century apparently on the site of an eleventh-century monastery, was the first Gelugs-pa establishment in Ladakh, and this is reflected in its name which in Tibetan means 'Effective as an Example'. The *gompa* is situated almost at the summit of a small but precipitous and craggy hill, about eight kilometres down the Indus from Leh, above the fields and houses of Spituk village. Even more than most *gompas*, it seems to be a maze of dark passages, stairs up and down, and unexpected shrines in odd corners.

The *Du-khang* or main assembly hall follows the pattern of all such buildings without any features of particular interest. At a higher level, near the private appartments of the *Kushok*, there are three more devotional rooms, one dedicated to Tson-ka-pa which is also a library of his works. The most interesting and unusual of these is sacred to the goddess Tara, and holds images of her twenty-three manifestations. These are exquisite pieces, old and of superb workmanship.

The *gon-khang* is a little apart from the main *gompa* buildings, at the very summit of the hill. It is said to contain impressive images of the usual fierce guardian divinities. Near it is a small *chorten*-like structure also painted red; and there are the remains of ancient walls belonging either to the earlier monastery or to a hill-top fort. Near the foot of the hill, to the north-west, there are some rock-engravings in very flat relief of Tson-ka-pa and some of his disciples, with beside them a large but now very indistinct figure which must be that of some Buddha or Bodhisattva.

Phiyang

Phiyang village must be one of the prettiest in all Ladakh. Its cultivated area covers with a pattern of terraced fields the floor of a valley carved out by a rushing stream in the alluvial deposit— barren elsewhere for lack of water—on the right bank of the Indus about fifteen kilometres downstream from Leh. The *gompa* is on the summit of a small hill dominating the village.

Phiyang *gompa*, one of the two Dri-gung-pa monasteries in Ladakh, was founded by king Tashi Namgyal in the third quarter of the sixteenth century. It may have been part of an attempt to atone for the crime by which he ascended the throne—having his elder brother's eyes put out. At the spot on the road from Leh from which Phiyang *gompa* could first be seen, he erected a large prayer-flag-pole—of the same kind no doubt as those that still stand in the main courtyard of most *gompas*. This was to be a place of sanctuary for anyone guilty of a crime against the king's person or property: the criminal on the run, if he reached this spot, would be free of his crime. It is not difficult to imagine Tashi considering a possible personal application.

One thing that may strike the experienced *gompà* visitor is an impression of neatness and cleanness about Phiyang and, inside the shrines, an unusual amount of light. Most of them are so constructed as to let in enough daylight to examine the paintings and images without the help of torches; and the paintings themselves are for the most part new and fresh, in bright glowing colours. Evidently much care is lavished on the upkeep of this *gompa*; the paintings, as soon as they show signs of becoming shabby, are replaced—always of course squarely within the bounds of the traditional iconography. The execution, which visitors may be lucky enough to observe in progress, is impeccable; and some of the purely decorative elements—on lintels and door-posts, for instance—are quite exquisite. Here is the proof that religious art in Ladakh, even if not a developing tradition, is still very much a living one.

Among the treasures of Phiyang are a collection of Kashmiri Buddhist bronzes which, as Snellgrove points out, 'by the very nature of the case cannot be later than the 14th century or so'; and a few pieces of old arms and armour. The full collections of these may not be on display at any particular time. It is worth making the ascent to the roof of the *gompa*, both in order to see better—by peeping through an open casement—the paintings on the upper part of the main shrine's walls; and for the sake of the vista spread out before one—to one side the fields and houses of the village, lying like a jewel in a fold of the bare mountain slopes; and to the other the ground falling gently to the Indus, and beyond it the ridges and folds of the Zanskar range.

Shey

Shey, on the main road up the Indus, about fourteen kilometres from Leh, was the ancient capital of Ladakh; and even after Sengge Namgyal built the more imposing palace at Leh, the kings continued to regard Shey as their real home—as is shown by the insistence that the heir apparent should always be born there. However, during the last two centuries of the Namgyal dynasty, it was eclipsed in importance by Leh with its more convenient position at the foot of the Khardung-La, right on the summer route to Yarkand, and consequent development as a great entrepôt. After the Dogra conquest, when the Namgyal family was stripped of its position and power, Shey as a royal seat was abandoned.

Tradition has it that Shey was the capital of the pre-Tibetan kings of Upper Ladakh, supposedly the descendants of Kesar;

the remains of ancient fortifications bear witness that it must have been a place of importance well before its first mention in the Ladakh Chronicle, about the fifteenth century. Its advantages as a strategic centre are obvious, for the fortifications are on the ridge of a spur running out from the Ladakh range to within a kilometre of the Indus, offering long views both up- and down-stream, and leaving only a narrow, easily defensible space between the tip of the spur and the river. At one time much of this space was occupied by an artificial lake which must have formed part of the system of defences. The remains which are fairly extensive have been reduced by weather and time to bare walls, open to the sky; many of them are pierced with loopholes. There is also a later palace, similar in outline to the one at Leh but smaller, of whose construction there seems to be no record. The importance which was attached to Shey—the heart of Ladakh's heartland—is attested by the enormous number of *chorten* about the village, particularly around the palace complex, and on the barren plain to the north of the road.

Incorporated in the palace buildings is a temple housing an enormous copper-gilt image of Sakyamuni, attributed to Deldan Namgyal. These huge images lack aesthetic appeal, but their very size gives them a kind of majesty. Both those at Shey sit in two-storey temples, of which the upper storey is the focal point for worshippers and visitors. The palace temple is dingy in the extreme, but its dinginess bears witness to the fact that the image is an object of living worship, for the blackness on the walls comes from the smoke of the innumerable butter lamps that have been lit in front of it over the centuries. Some are kept burning day and night, and an enormous one is filled with enough butter to keep it alight for a year: it is a beautiful thing, made of some dull metal like pewter, and studded with huge turquoises. Through the patina of soot it is possible to make out a little of the wall-paintings. Though their subject-matter can be guessed rather than discerned, it is clear that their quality is very fine and that, if the walls could be cleaned without erasing the pictures, real works of art would be revealed. There are a few other images, two of them of tantric divinities. The lower storey has a library of sacred books, and the walls are painted with representations of the Thousand Buddhas.

The rest of the palace has little to offer beyond some attractively carved wooden lintels and a number of derelict rooms. In one of these however, immediately above the stairs leading to the lower entrance of the temple, there is an unexpected and surprisingly decorative object—a stove built of stone which, as befits a royal kitchen, is adorned with carved scroll work. It is dilapidated, but must once have been beautiful.

Shey's other main site is not more than three or four hundred metres from the palace hill, but it is easy to miss, as outwardly it looks more like a superior dwelling-house than a temple. It is approached through a group of *chorten*, one of which has a number of carved stones placed around it—presumably gathered from various places and brought together here as an act of piety. (There is a similar engraved stone at the roadside, just where the track up to the palace leaves the road.) The main attraction, here as at the palace, is a **gigantic** Sakyamuni image, probably erected at the instance of Sengge **Namg**yal. There is a tradition that it was built by craftsmen specially brought from Nepal by Gyal Katun, Sengge's Balti mother. While very similar to its fellow in the palace, this one is rather more pleasing; the temple, which was rebuilt around it a few years ago, has a clean fresh appearance, and is designed so as to let in a good deal of light. The paintings on the walls, probably done faithfully to the same designs as in the original temple, are bright without being garish. They represent the sixteen *arhats*, Buddha's original disciples, along the two side walls; and at the back two more disciples flanking the three great preachers, Padmasambhava, Atisa and Tson-ka-pa. On the front wall various deities are represented. In the same complex are a couple of small tantric shrines, and a temple of the Buddha Amitabh (Boundless Light)—one of the Five Buddhas. Here too the walls are painted with representations of the Thousand Buddhas. This temple has not been restored.

The only other important monument at Shey is the one which most visitors will have seen first of all. It is an engraving on the rock-face right beside the road where it makes a sharp turn round the lowest spur of the palace hill. It represents the Five Buddhas of Meditation—five manifestations of Buddha-hood rather than separately conceived historical figures—distinguished by their several *mudras* or hand-gestures, and by their animal vehicles, shown beneath them. Each stands on a lotus, and a congregation of the faithful completes the carving. This probably dates from early in the period of Tibetal cultural influence.

Tikse

Tikse is one of the largest and most impressive of the central Ladakh *gompas*, a complex of buildings on a crag rising in tier upon tier above the village which it at the same time dominates and completes. A motorable track connects the monastery to the road, and takes the visitor up to the very base of the main courtyard and temple buildings.

Directly to the visitor's right as he enters is a two-storey temple painted red. This temple, which was dedicated by His Holiness the Dalai Lama in September 1980, houses an immense image of Maitreya in an unusual manifestation known as Chon-kor. This Maitreya, instead of standing, or sitting European-style on a raised throne, sits in the lotus position. The murals behind the image represent scenes from Maitreya's life, and were executed by monks from the monastery of Ling-shed deep in the mountains on a tributary of the Zanskar River; while the decorative work on the capitals of the wooden pillars and round the doors and windows (which let in a good deal of light) is from the hand of local artists. To a sophisticated eye, these new paintings, and similar ones eleswhere, may seem on the garish side. But to the monks and lay worshippers in these temples, aesthetics are an irrelevant consideration: the execution of these paintings is a work of piety and merit; completed they are a support and aid to worship (like the stained glass of European churches); and even the outsider will appreciate that the effort and devotion that have gone into them are encouraging signs of a living and flourishing religion.

The *Du-khang*, at the other end of the courtyard, up a steep flight of steps, presents a striking contrast to the Maitreya temple. It is dark and rather shabby, and though a few of the murals on the right wall seem to have been touched up, on the whole the paintings and images have been left as (presumably) they were originally. Most of the paintings are of the terrible deities, some of them in *yab-yum*. The left wall is covered with wooden book-racks containing volumes of the scriptures. Instead of an image in the place of honour in the centre of the main altar, there is (or was in September 1980) a blown-up photograph of His Holiness the Dalai Lama. Flanking this are several small images in gold, of Tibetan workmanship. A small dark chapel behind the main altar houses a big Sakyamuni image, together with a four-armed Avalokiteswara and a Tson-ka-pa. This chapel has the remains of murals in a more free and less formal style than those in the main temple, showing grotesque animal figures. Like all such *Dukhang*, this one is in regular use for worship, and on a shelf to the right of the door there is a set of enormous copper pots, for serving tea during the *puja*. They are entirely undecorated, but of a beautiful strong rugged shape, and come originally from Tibet. The verandah has the conventional Lords of the Quarters and Wheel of Life.

The *Gon-khang* is the usual small, dark, gloomy chamber. Women are admitted but only because the faces of the deities are kept veiled. The roof terrace affords a stunning view, upriver to Stakna and down to Shey, across to Chushot and Matho—the fields and villages of Ladakh's most extensive fertile tract. In September men and women are reaping the barley, and their voices drift up to the watcher on the roof, singing the immemorial songs of harvest.

Tikse was established during the original period of Ge-lugs-pa expansion in Ladakh, probably about the middle of the fifteenth century, and very likely on the site of an earlier Ka-dam-pa foundation. It may have had its origin as a daughter house of the small chapel of Stagmo seven kilometres north.

Hemis

Its two-day festival has given Hemis a particular reputation with outside visitors, though indeed it is by no means the most attractive of the *gompas*, nor the one with the most peaceful or 'religious' atmosphere. Though all the *gompas* have their festivals, which take the form of dance-dramas, the so-called 'devil-dances', Hemis's is the only one to take place in summer, which is why it has become so well-known. The symbolism behind these dance-dramas appears to be little understood by many of the lamas themselves, and contradictory interpretations have been offered both by them, and by various western spectators. In the Hemis

festival, which is dedicated to Padmasambhava, what the visitor
can observe is a series of scenes in which the lamas, robed in gowns
of rich, brightly-coloured brocade and sporting masks sometimes
benign and sometimes bizarrely hideous, parade in solemn dance
and mime round the huge flagpole in the centre of the courtyard,
to the plaintive melody of the shawm, the moan of the eleven-foot
horns, the boom of drums and the clash of cymbals. The solem-
nity is varied by comic interludes in which dancers in the guise of
skeletons bound into the arena, performing grotesquely agile
gymnastics. In the climactic scene, towards the close of the first
day, a doll, moulded out of *tsampa*, is ritually dismembered by the
demons, and its fragments scattered to the four quarters of the
compass. This has been variously interpreted as referring to the
assassination of the apostate Tibetan king, Lang-dar-ma, by a
Buddhist monk, in AD 842; as the annihilation of the evil in the
individual soul, and its purification; as the dissolution of the soul
and its merging with the totality of things; and as the dissolution
of the body after death. Thus the supposed 'demons' may
perhaps represent not the forces of evil at all, but rather the
righteous Guardians, in their terrible aspect. The 'meaning', indeed, may be any or all of these things. While the lay Ladakhi
spectators who flock devoutly to the festival will be vague about
what they 'understand' of the drama enacted before them, it
clearly has a hold on their imaginations that goes deeper than
words or concepts. Every twelve years, the festival takes on a
special dimension when the monastery's greatest treasure, an
immense *thangka* of Padmasambhava, embroidered not painted,
and adorned, it is said, with pearls, is ritually exhibited. Its next
unveiling is due to take place in 1992.

Founded in the 1630s by Stag-tsang-ras-pa under the royal
patronage of Sengge Namgyal, Hemis is the largest and richest of
the Ladakh *gompas*. It is situated a little way up a side-valley in the
mountains of the Zanskar Range, about forty kilometres up the
Indus from Leh. Although easily accessible (it is the only *gompa* to
which there is a regular bus-service for tourists in the season), it
has a secluded situation, being tucked into a corner of the winding
glen, and nestling almost into the mountainside. Thus the
approaching visitor only catches his first glimpse of the monastery when he has come within a kilometre of it. A pavilion with a

walled garden, built no doubt to accommodate the Namgyal kings and princes on pilgrimage to their favourite *gompa*, has been converted into a restaurant and picnic-spot; and a few level patches beside the stream offer possibilities for campers. Of all the *gompas* Hemis is the one which most gives the impression that it is conscious of being on show: the lamas are cleaner and better-dressed than elsewhere, and a few of them speak English.

The main courtyard, where the dance-drama takes place, has a colonnade along two sides, under which the musicians sit; above are galleries for privileged spectators. The balconied windows of the main building's four storeys become boxes for specially invited guests, while the *Du-khang* serves as the green room; it is from its door and down its steep steps that the dancers emerge on to the stage of the courtyard.

The visitor who comes at any other season to see the *gompa* rather than the drama will find little of interest in the *Du-khang*. The altar has a fierce divinity partly veiled; and the remains of original seventeenth-century murals are badly damaged. In September 1980, one wall was stripped preparatory to repainting. The verandah has been remodelled recently, and the ususal paintings of the Wheel of Life and the Lords of the Four Quarters are executed in an unusual rather naïve style. They are accompanied by the Old Man of Long Life, pouring himself a cup of tea, and a symbolic composition in which an elephant supports a monkey, who carries on his back a rabbit, who in his turn supports a bird who pecks fruit from a tree.

More rewarding is the *Tshogs-khang*, the temple on the left as you stand in the courtyard facing the main building. Here the principal feature is an enormous silver *chorten* said to have been dedicated by Lama Shambhunath, probably the third *Kushok* in line from the monastery's founder, Stag-tsang-ras-pa. This would place it about the first half of the eighteenth century. It is encrusted with huge flawless turquoises and other stones, and stands behind a fine image of Sakyamuni. There are several other *chorten*, one of which claims attention for its elaborate design, quite out of the ordinary. The front wall near the door is painted with fierce divinities, and the sides with Sakyamunis and the Thousand Buddhas. On the back wall and practically hidden by the row of silver *chorten*, the torch's beam reveals damaged paint-

ings in the freer style of the time of the monastery's founding; as
far as can be made out, figures are grouped in composition round
large Sakyamunis. The verandah is conventionally decorated
with the Lords of the Quarters, and an elaborate Wheel of Life.

Chemrey

Chemrey is situated to one side of a tributary valley of the Indus,
just off the road leading to the Chang-La, about forty-five
kilometres from Leh. Though most of the books, including the
Ladakh Chronicle, tell us it was founded by the great lama Stag-
tsang-ras-pa under the patronage of Sengge Namgyal, Professor
Luciano Petech has shown that it was actually founded after
Sengge's death as a funeral act of merit for him. The building was
started in March 1644, and completed in 1645 or 1646.

Overlooking fields and houses, the monastery is perched pic-
turesquely atop a small hill, down one side of which spill the
monks' dwellings. A motorable road winds round up the back of
the hill almost to the main entrance. The main *Du-khang*, a large
rather bare temple, has images of Stag-tsang-ras-pa and other
Drug-pa lamas, together with a fine silver *chorten* about fifty years
old made at Chiling. The murals are mainly of manifestations of
Sakyamuni, as is common in Drug-pa temples; there are also fine
mandalas of Kalachakra and Akshobya. Twenty-nine volumes of
the scriptures have title pages whose lettering is in solid silver of
exquisite craftsmanship, the text in pure gold. A smaller temple
upstairs houses a nondescript collection of images of Drug-pa
lamas. Under a thick layer of grime from the smoke of innumerable butter lamps can be discerned the decaying remains of murals in the relatively free style characteristic of the earlier monastic
paintings—interesting and individual faces flickering into
momentary life among the grime and the shadows in the fitful
beam of a torch as it sweeps over them.

At almost the very top of the *gompa*, a new *Du-khang* has been
built recently, to house an ancient image of Guru Rinpoche.
Large, and of seemingly undistinguished workmanship, its forehead is studded with a huge and flawless turquoise. In September
1980 the walls were still largely bare, not a quarter of their area yet
having been covered with paintings. The young master painter, a
man of not more than 40, who showed no irritation at being
interrupted in the minute and finicky task of painting the details

of a Tara's necklace, told us that, because of the cold at Chemrey, he could work there for only about three months in the year. What he had done so far had taken two months already, even with the help of his four apprentices, and he expected that it would be 1982 at least before the whole was completed.

Thak-Thak

This small *gompa*, above the village of Sakti a few kilometres beyond Chemrey, was founded in the reign of Tshe-wang Namgyal—that is, in the second half of the sixteenth century—around one of the many caves where the Indian sage Padmasambhava is said to have stayed and meditated during his journey to Tibet, where he was the first to bring the gospel of Buddhism. It is the sole representative in Ladakh of the Nying-ma-pa, the oldest of the Tibetan monastic sects.

The *gompa* is constructed against the mountainside around Padmasambhava's cave. This, made into a temple, is an excessively dark and gloomy chamber, the low rocky ceiling and the walls being absolutely black from the smoke of the numberless butter-lamps that have burned there over the centuries, while even the uneven stone floor is grimy, and feels sticky to the touch of bare feet. The grime has completely obscured the paintings that once adorned the walls. Another cave a little further down has been made into a kitchen, where, on immense stoves, food is cooked for the pilgrims who flock to the gompa's annual festival.

The verandah of the *Du-khang* has the usual paintings of the Four Lords, while the walls of the temple itself are covered with recent paintings of fierce divinities. A new temple a little way below the main *gompa* complex was consecrated in September 1980 by His Holiness the Dalai Lama. At that time it was incomplete, insofar as the walls had yet to be painted; this work is likely to take a year or two.

Stakna

Stakna appears to be the earliest of the Drug-pa foundations in Ladakh, having been established before the arrival on the Ladakh scene of the great lama Stag-tsang-ras-pa, the founder, under Sengge Namgyal's patronage, of Hanle and Hemis, and later of

Chemrey. Associated with the *gompa*'s early history is the name of
Nawang Namgyal, one of Sengge's half-brothers, the sons of
Jamyang Namgyal's first marriage, who entered holy orders in
1630. He is said to have 'restored' the building—perhaps replac-
ing an originally more modest structure with the present impressive pile. It was later endowed by Delegs Namgyal; but in the
eighteenth century seems to have lost ground to Hemis in the
matter of royal patronage and political importance.

Stakna's situation is dramatic, on an isolated rock sixty metres
high, which rises from the almost dead flat of the Indus valley a
few kilometres above Tikse. Even from a distance it makes its
presence felt. It is on the left bank of the river and therefore,
although it is quite close to Tikse, it has to be approached from
Chushot, after crossing the river at the Choglamsar bridge.

The *gompa* buildings, crowning their rock, are not extensive but
are beautifully maintained. A small courtyard has steps leading
up to the *Du-khang*, whose principal feature is a silver chorten
manufactured in Chiling a mere twenty years ago—an object of
exquisite craftsmanship studded with great flawless turquoises.
The murals are nothing out of the ordinary, being in the familiar
style and therefore presumably of fairly recent date. But a small
chapel behind the chorten and its attendant images has paintings
which probably date from the *gompa*'s foundation, their style
much more free and alive and individual. Unfortunately it is
almost completely dark, so even a powerful torch can do no more
than pick out odd faces and figures. But even from these partial
and incomplete glimpses it is clear that the paintings are of ex-
ceedingly high quality, and would certainly repay detailed study.

The *Gon-khang* is closed to women; no doubt it is the usual small
gloomy chamber, filled with the hideous-seeming forms of the
terrible Guardians. As might be expected from the *gompa*'s situation, there are stupendous views from the roof, both down and up
the Indus valley, taking in Shey, Tikse, Chushot and Matho,
with the bare slopes of the Ladakh range to the north, and the
tremendous snow-capped peaks and ridges of the Zanskar range
to the south.

Matho

The village of Matho is situated at the mouth of a gorge running
out of the depths of the Zanskar Range, across the Indus and

directly opposite Tikse. The gorge must have been formed remote ages ago by a huge torrent, traces of which still remain in the form of a wide pebbly river-bed, down the middle of which a small stream trickles sadly. The houses are scattered widely among the fields; and more than any other village Matho seems to be home to a goodly number of that handsome bird so character-istic of Ladakh, the Bactrian magpie.

The *gompa*, the only representative in Ladakh of the Saskya-pa sect, is said to be one of the few in which the number of lamas is not on the decline, rather the contrary, the number of novices auguring well for the future. Nevertheless, the buildings have a somewhat run-down appearance—possibly indicating a greater emphasis on spiritual discipline than on the upkeep of material objects. There is however a new *Du-khang*, built about twelve years ago. This unfortunately was locked up on the day of my visit, as a death in the neighbouring village of Chushot had taken most of the lamas away to conduct the funeral ceremonies. The solitary lama in evidence had the keys only of a small chapel on the topmost storey, and of the *gompa* 'museum' in an adjacent room. Both contain numerous old and very beautiful *thangkas*, most of which, sadly, are in an advanced state of deterioration. Many of them are in the form of mandalas, and the oldest ones are said to have been brought from Tibet at the time of the monastery's foundation, perhaps in the first half of the sixteenth century. In the museum are displayed the robes and masks worn by the lamas in the dance-drama at their annual festival, while the small chapel has images of Saskya-Pandita and other Saskya-pa lamas. The verandah of the new *Du-khang* has paintings of the Lords of the Quarters in a unusually plain and sober rendering.

Matho *gompa* is famous for its annual festival of the oracles which takes place around the Buddhist New Year, usually in the first half of March. The oracles are two lamas, chosen by lot every three years who, when purified by months of fasting and medi-tion, become the receptacles for the spirit of a particular deity. Once possessed by the god the oracles are said to perform all sorts of dramatic feats, cutting themselves with knives, and cavorting blindfold along the parapets of the gompa's topmost storey, im-mune from any danger of falling from the great height to the rocks of the valley below. In this state they answer questions about the welfare of Ladakh and of Matho in the year following, and also questions put by individuals about their own particular spiritual and material welfare. The spirit is said however to be able to detect questions put by sceptical observers with the object of testing him, and to react to such with a frenzied display of anger.

Stok Palace Museum

Stok Palace, seat of the Namgyal family after they had been deprived of their royal authority by the Dogra conquest, now houses a museum in which the family's heirlooms and relics are displayed, a poignant evocation of Ladakh's vanished past as an independent kingdom.

Religion was never far from the surface of Ladakhi life, and there are many religious objects in the museum. These include fine old *thangkas*, one set of thirty-five representing the life of Sakyamuni which is said, according to inscriptions on the back, to date from the reign of Tashi Namgyal in the middle of the sixteenth century, and to be authenticated by Tashi's own hand-print on the back of each. They look as bright and fresh as if painted yesterday, which is accounted for by the claim that they have not been displayed until the present, but lay carefully packed up for 400 years. In the two royal chapels, one of them attached to the king's bedroom, are images in bronze and gold. One of these, an Avalokiteswara, is said to come from Bhutan, though if it does it can hardly, as claimed, belong to the seventh century, since Buddhism reached Bhutan much later than that. Bronzes in distinctly Indian, or rather Kashmiri, style can hardly be later than the fourteenth century, the period when Buddhism was eradicated in Kashmir.

Although in no sense priest-kings, the Namgyal rulers did exercise some priestly functions, presiding at religious ceremonies of state; and their *puja* instruments—bell, *dorje* and cymbals—are preserved, as is a round papier-mâché hat with a knob on top, as worn by the lamas in some episodes of the dance-dramas. Some of the masks from these dramas are also here. A volume of the scriptures has its cover and pages filled with lettering in pure gold; while wooden blocks for printing prayer-flags, and the rolls that are inserted into the prayer-wheels, are covered with endless repetitions of *Om Mani Padme Hum*.

Of equal interest are the objects evoking the secular aspect of Ladakh's past. There is a collection of the instruments of war—quivers, arrows, guns, swords and shields; and of government—

coins and seals. Some objects are associated with particular members of the Namgyal family. A sword with its blade twisted into a knot is said to have been thus contorted by the enormous strength of Tashi Namgyal, while a fez-like hat is said to have been worn by the fourteenth century prince Rinchen, perhaps the first Muslim ruler of Kashmir. Items that would have been in use in the kings' daily life are silver and copper pots for serving tea and *chang*, and some exquisite cups in jade and porcelain, clearly of Chinese manufacture. For their more personal use, there is a chatelaine, made of gold, with a toothpick and special instruments for cleaning the nose and ears. Among the queens' ornaments are Gyal Khatun's necklace, or rather stomacher, since its thirteen rows of silver beads descend low on the body; the royal *perak*; and a stunning turquoise-studded shoulder ornament continuing into a veil of pearls for the head, which is said to have belonged to Jovo Kunjo, wife of the redoubtable seventh-century king of Tibet, Sron-tsan-gam-po, and to have been brought to Ladakh in the eighteenth century by Nyilza Angmo, wife of king Deskyong Namgyal. The regalia of Ladakh consist of an unusual turban-shaped crown, and ceremonial gown and boots.

Basgo

Basgo was an important centre in the old days, having been the capital of Lower Ladakh when the kingdom was divided in the fifteenth and sixteenth centuries, and the seat of that branch of the dynasty which eventually unified Ladakh and took the surname Namgyal (Victorious). It is mentioned as Ladakh's capital in the first European account of Ladakh, by the Portuguese merchant Diogo d'Almeida just before the great Balti invasion around the turn of the sixteenth and seventeenth centuries; and it was at Basgo, strategically situated where the near approach of the mountains to the river turns the Indus valley into a gorge, that the advance of the invading Tibetan and Mongol armies was checked in 1680. Ruined fortifications bear witness to the palace's strength against siege, which it withstood for three years at that time, being said to have enjoyed a perennial water-supply. Now the broken walls and towers rear up roofless and derelict, hardly distinguishable from the wind-eroded pinnacles on which they stand.

As with the other royal residences at Leh and Shey, the palace at

Basgo also incorporates places of worship. The largest of the three shrines, all of which are dedicated to Maitreya, has been described by Snellgrove as 'after Alchi perhaps the most beautifully painted temple in Ladakh'. Built by Tshe-wang Namgyal, it is the only temple in Ladakh with original surviving sixteenth century murals. The image, a large one of whose face no more than an oblique foreshortened glimpse can be had from the main chamber downstairs, is also reckoned unusually fine. It is flanked by two Bodhisattvas. The paintings relegate the fierce divinities, the Guardians, to a subservient position, even Mahakala's usual place above the main entrance being usurped by the Bodhisattva Vajrapani. The Lords of the Quarters have been translated from their usual place outside the main door, to a position beneath the Bodhisattva, where they are accompanied by fierce divinities; below these again there is a narrow frieze showing court scenes of the temple's builder Tshe-wang Namgyal and his family, dressed (like Tshe-wang's uncle, Tashi Namgyal in a similar scene in the *Gon-khang* at Namgyal Tsemo) in the Kashmiri–Mughal style.

Large figures on the side walls are arranged more or less haphazard, in the style of later temples at Tikse, Hemis, Chemrey and elsewhere, rather than in any manner reminiscent of the coherent patterns of the Alchi mandalas. Clockwise from the entrance they are Sakyamuni; another similar Buddha-figure; Atisa (a rare representation); Buddha-figure; and on the right-hand wall Vajradhara; Buddha-figure; Padma-karpo; Avalokiteswara. This last figure seems to have been repainted in the later more conventional style. On the back wall, behind and to the right of the images, Snellgrove found paintings of Padmasambhava and Mila-Respa; but at the time of my visit six years later these were covered with *thangkas*—some good old ones in a fair state of preservation. The detail filling in the wall space between the main figures is engaging and repays study. Here we find mermaids and elephants; ducks and dogs and lions. There is a decorative frieze of *chorten*, and the ceiling is made of painted panels, reminiscent of those in the Alchi *Du-khang*.

The Ser-zangs ('gold and copper') temple is called after a set of the Buddhist scriptures, the Kangyur and the Tenjur, in these materials, dedicated as an act of merit by Sengge Namgyal. Entrance to the main chamber downstairs is by a beautifully carved doorway, and here too the main image is of Maitreya. A glass case houses some ancient images, one clearly of Indian (Kashmiri) origin, and one an exquisite little brass studded with turquoises, in the Tibetan manner. The walls are mostly covered with the racks containing the volumes of the Kangyur and the Tenjur; what little can be discerned of the paintings suggests work in a style reminiscent of the big Maitreya temple.

From an upper verandah there is a view of the image's head, protected by a modern structure of wood and glass, newly painted in rather garish colours. The alcove behind the head is painted with representations of the Ka-gyu-pa masters—Tilopa, Naropa, Marpa and Mila-Respa. The verandah's walls have murals in poor condition, with Buddha-figures in a landscape of palaces and cities, many of the buildings having roofs with tip-tilted corners like pagodas; there are glimpses of the sea, and a river in which people bathe; there are musicians, and elephants.

The third temple in the Basgo palace enclave is a small shrine, sacred like the other two to Maitreya. It was dedicated by Skalzang Dolma, Sengge Namgyal's wife. The murals, again in poor condition, show a Sakyamuni behind the main image; and on the side walls fierce divinities in *yab-yum*, together with one Ge-lugs-pa lama, looking uneasily out of place in this complex otherwise dedicated to the Drugpa.

Likir

Likir is situated at the head of the village of the same name, which straggles down the valley of a side-stream flowing into the Indus between Basgo and Saspol. It is reached by a motorable track, about five kilometres from the main road to the *gompa*, which is the usual impressive pile on the top of a low hill. It seems to have been founded in the twelfth century, when it was presumably associated with the Ka-dam-pa order. It was refounded in the fifteenth century as a Ge-lugs-pa establishment, and at some stage it took over responsibility for the monastic buildings at Alchi, when they ceased to be a living centre of religion and worship. The present buildings date from the eighteenth century, the earlier structure having been destroyed by fire.

Likir seems to be a well-maintained *gompa*. Its head lama is a brother of the Dalai Lama and, though not permanently in residence, comes from time to time to conduct the more important *pujas.* The main *Du-khang* has every appearance of being in regular use for worship; it contains on either side the wooden racks with pigeonholes in which the volumes of the scripture are kept. There is another smaller *Du-khang*, with an image of eleven-headed Avalokiteswara, and new paintings on the side walls, representing benevolent Bodhisattvas, and the sixteen *arhats.* Upstairs, adjoining the private apartments of the head lama is a small *puja*-room or chapel, to which visitors may be admitted; it has a number of very beautiful images, framed in wood-carving of superb workmanship. Both this room and the *Gon-khang* (to the outer chamber of which women are admitted) have a large number of *thangkas,* some new, others obviously very old. Of the old ones, a few are in a bad state of repair; but some have been no more than mellowed by the effects of time, and are things of great beauty.

Alchi

It seems presumptuous to essay a description of Alchi after the detailed account given by Snellgrove and Skorupski in their definitive *The Cultural Heritage of Ladakh.* For the aspiring Buddhist, the historian or the art critic, reference to their work will be indispensable; and much of what I have to say is based upon it. But the more casual visitor, without such specialized interests, may be glad to have a more general account, for he will not have time to make a minute examination of every detail and yet may like to have a broad idea of what he is seeing.

The village and *chos-kor* ('religious enclave') of Alchi form an oasis cradled in a bend of the river just opposite Saspol. From the main road, about four kilometres from Saspol towards Khaltse, a motorable track leads down to a bridge and over the dunes of the desert till the oasis with its fields, green or golden according to the season, its poplar spires, its houses and monastic buildings, gradually unfolds itself. Alchi is one of the few places where there is provision for visitors to spend a night or two, in an inn somewhat inappropriately named the New Gay Time, whose amenities may be presumed to be of the most basic. For Alchi, even more than for other *gompas,* it is important to go equipped with a good torch because most of the temples have no light, except what can filter through the open door. An electricity line crosses the river from

Saspol, and the temples are wired, with naked bulbs hanging incongruously from the ceiling. In common with other places where there is electricity, Saspol is illuminated only at dusk, when the generator is set going. But serious visitors, willing to pay for some kind of light, may consult the Tourist Officer at Leh a day or two ahead of their visit, as to the possibility of having the generator specially set going for them. Even then they should not leave their torches behind.

The extent and richness of the *chos-kor* testify that in its day Alchi must have been a religious centre of great importance. Local tradition credits its foundation to Rin-chen-zang-po; but inscriptions show that it was founded in the eleventh century by Kal-dan Shes-rab whose name shows him to have been a member of one of the Tibetan noble families who migrated west with Nyima-Gon to establish the Ladakhi kingdom. He was a graduate of Nyar-ma (near Tikse; now a heap of rubble, barely distinguishable from the stones of the encroaching desert), one of the few monasteries known for certain to have been founded by Rin-chen-zang-po. Thus, though the Great Translator was not himself directly involved in the establishment of Alchi, it was nevertheless clearly an important landmark in the movement known as the Second Spreading, of which he was the foremost figure. Along with Tabo, in the Spiti district of Himachal Pradesh, it is the most notable monument to that movement. The extraordinary state of preservation in which many of its murals remain can be attributed to the fact that perhaps as early as the sixteenth century, it was abandoned as a living centre of worship for reasons altogether unknown. Responsibility for its maintenance was assumed at some point by the Ge-lugs-pa monastery of Likir, and it is Likir monks whom the visitor will find in attendance today.

Thus we have at Alchi a remarkable record of Buddhist iconography at the time of the Second Spreading—that is, in the eleventh and twelfth centuries—unrivalled except for Tabo. It is true that at this time Buddhism was still flourishing in India, but before long it went down before the onslaught of resurgent Hinduism south of the Himalaya, and Muslim domination in Kashmir. It is only as a result of the efforts of the Second Spreading's Tibetan agents that we can today, at Alchi and Tabo, remote corners of what was then the Western Tibetan Empire, gain some idea of Buddhist iconography of that period. The style is quite different from that of the later *gompa*-paintings, whose inspiration was all from Tibet; and the content, while obviously overlapping with these, has a quite distinct emphasis.[1]

The Alchi *chos-kor* is an irregularly shaped enclosure consisting of small courtyards, connected by narrow alleys, in which are disposed five main places of worship containing paintings and images whose richness has only recently come to be appreciated. Furthest down the gentle slope from the approach, there are two small and relatively bare temples, the Manjusri *Lha-khang* and the Lotsawa *Lha-khang*. The fourfold Manjusri image in the temple of the same name is, according to Snellgrove, surely the original; but it has recently been painted in garish primary colours. The murals of the Thousand Buddhas have a certain monotony about them, but the ceiling, made of decorated panels, is attractive. The Lotsawa *Lha-khang*, as its name implies, has an image, and also a painting of the Great Translator, Rin-chen-zang-po; these are rarities, as this scholar who did so much to revive Buddhism in Tibet when it had fallen on evil days, is noticeably absent in the later *gompas*. The central image is of Sakyamuni, with Avalokiteswara on one side and Rin-chen on the other. Here for the first time we see those curiously rococo decorative motifs that recur in the bigger temples, the *Du-khang* and the *Sum-tsek*; just under the ceiling there is a frieze of geese, waddling along in profile, together with an effect as of looped curtains, while disporting themselves on the walls are mythical birds and sea monsters.

The real riches of Alchi are in the *Du-khang*, the main assembly hall, and the *Sum-tsek*, the unique three-storey temple. Neither of these is impressive in terms of size; but with every square inch of wall-space covered with paintings in a style that survives hardly anywhere else, and in colours yet vibrant, they are treasure-houses of an otherwise vanished art.

The *Du-khang* is approached through a court which has colonnaded verandahs with wooden pillars, and three small shrines near the temple entrance. The cloisters are decorated with paintings of the Thousand Buddhas, while near the outer gate are a Wheel of Life and a Mahakala. Small secular scenes, including

[2]See above, pp. 40, 161–2.

ships, appear in the interstices of the main paintings; while the goose frieze, along with the looped hangings, appears along the top of the wall. All this is in a poor state of preservation, being executed in some smudgeable chalky material. Of the small shrines, that on the left has an image of eleven-headed Avalo-kiteswara flanked by other Bodhisattvas, behind a carved wooden screen of modern workmanship; while the one to the right holds a gigantic four-armed Maitreya. In this shrine appear the only examples at Alchi of paintings in the later 'Tibetan' style.

The *Du-khang* proper, a smallish chamber, completely dark except for whatever daylight can filter in through the open door, is dedicated to the Five *Dhayani* Buddhas, and among them parti-cularly to Vairocana who is associated with the Centre of things. His image is surrounded by a frame of exuberantly carved wood in the midst of whose scrollwork are the half concealed figures of *apsaras*—heavenly nymphs—musicians, elephants and mythical animals, as phantasmagoric as creatures in a dream. Most of the wall space is covered with the elaborate mandalas that mark so striking a contrast between Alchi and the later *gompas* with their more (seemingly) haphazardly arranged murals. The spaces be-tween these are closely filled with decorative motifs of that curiously rococo nature seen earlier in the Lotsawa *Lha-khang*—scrollwork, and stylized flowers, and small roundels, one of them rather incongruously framing a Sakyamuni—which seem to de-note a style of art in full bloom, if not teetering on the edge of decadence.

To many visitors, the six superb mandalas, the walls' principal adornment and, in their mystical significance, the *raison d'être* of the whole *oeuvre*, may have less interest than the little scenes of secular life that appear on either side of the main entrance. As at Basgo, and in the *Gon-khang* at Namgyal Tsemo, these are minia-tures at or a little below eye-level. To the left of the door a king and queen are carousing, accompanied by lesser figures that may represent princes or courtiers. Their dress is in an archaic Central Asian style. Below and to the right of this, a damaged painting seems to represent a battle. In the corresponding position on the other side of the door, further scenes, presumably of secular life, are almost obliterated, though something remarkably like a palm tree can just be distinguished. (This, if truly a palm tree, corrobo-rates the inference from the style of the Alchi paintings that they

were executed either by Indian craftsmen, or by local men—or
possibly Tibetans—trained in India. Either way, the artist's experience seems to have extended beyond Kashmir—the main
source of Rin-chen-zang-po's inspiration—down into the plains
of India.) Near the Mahakala above the door can be made out
heraldic-seeming beasts, mythical figures on different kinds of
mounts, one of them astride a yak, and a mounted warrior with
his attendant shield-bearer. As in the Manjusri *Lha-khang*, the
ceiling is made up of decorative panels, and the wooden pillars
have carved capitals.

The riches of the *Du-khang* are extraordinary; but even they are
surpassed by the *Sum-tsek*, the three-storey temple, a shrine which
resembles no other in the Himalayan world or elsewhere. The
ground-floor chamber has the central part of its roof cut away in a
square which admits a little daylight; the heads of three gigantic
Bodhisattva images extend up through openings in the ceiling to
the second storey, the ladder to which is no more than a stout
tree-trunk, with barely adequate notches as rungs. (Visitors are
forbidden to ascend, on account of the structural unsoundness of
the building.) The third storey, to which there is no access, consists merely of the walls of the canopy-like roof which shelters the
whole.

Thus even from the outside the *Sum-tsek* has an unusual look,
made all the more striking by the elaborate wooden carving which
surmounts its facade. Inside, the centre of the lower chamber is
occupied by a stucco *chorten*, while the three Bodhisattvas are
ensconced in alcoves in the side and back walls. In a clockwise
direction, they are Avalokiteswara, Maitreya and Manjusri.
Although the heads of these images are invisible from below, they
immediately attract the visitor's attention by the curious garments
they wear, draped about their legs from waist to knees. Each of
these is covered with a series of beautifully executed miniature
paintings the like of which do not seem to be known elsewhere,
and which, even apart from their rarity value, are full of interest.
Avalokiteswara's robe has a series of small scenes depicting
palaces and shrines which may, in Snellgrove's interpretation,
represent important places of Buddhist pilgrimage. Maitreya's
robe is adorned with roundels representing events of Sakyamuni's life; while, unique among the Alchi paintings, Manjusri's robe
shows the direct inspiration of the Tantric tradition, the 84 Mas-

ters of the Tantra being accompanied by scenes figuring some interesting nudes. Secular scenes appear on the walls of Manjusri's alcove; while Avalokiteswara's is filled with deities and mythical figures, including an exquisitely beautiful Prajnaparamita, the goddess Perfection of Wisdom. Another Prajnaparamita appears on the second storey, above the head of the Manjusri image; above Avalokiteswara is an eleven-headed Avalokiteswara, and above Maitreya, Vairocana, one of the Five Buddhas. The rest of the wall-space on all three storeys is devoted to mandalas, delicate scrollwork filling up every unoccupied corner.

Inscriptions show that some repair and restoration work was done in the *Sum-tsek* in the sixteenth century, during the reign of Tashi Namgyal; thus the date of the paintings as we see them is uncertain. But on the whole, the sixteenth century restorers seem to have been scrupulous in their adherence to the original style, perhaps doing no more than to touch up faded colour, or sharpen blurred outlines. For the most part, the style remains perfectly distinct from work being done in the same period at Basgo and Leh (Namgyal Tsemo). Exceptions noticed by Snellgrove are the Mahakala over the main doorway, the Prajnaparamita on the second storey, especially her attendant figures, and the eleven-headed Avalokiteswara, also upstairs, whose attendant goddesses, Snellgrove notes, 'would scarcely be out of place in Mughal miniatures or for that matter in Nepalese painting of the sixteenth century and later.'[3]

After the splendours of the *Sum-tsek*, the *Lha-khang Soma*, or New Temple, comes as something of a disappointment. Not only its name but also the style of its paintings testifies to its being less ancient; here there is no attempt to emulate the formal perfection of the *Sum-tsek*'s or the *Du-khang*'s mandalas, or the rococo whimsy of their decorative panels; we are in a different world, and the walls are crowded with figures, many of them deities in *yab-yum*, the only examples of such at Alchi.

Alchi is special, something more than the sum of its five temples with their wonderfully varied paintings. The *chos-kor* lies in the midst of the oasis, hidden among the desert's dunes, like a jewel in its setting. There is an atmosphere of peace, which it seems a shame to desecrate with the sound of the petrol engine; while

[3]Snellgrove, *The Cultural Heritage of Ladakh*, p. 56.

more than anywhere else in Ladakh, the tourist's anorak and camera seem out of place, an intrusion. What manner of men were the monks who built it, expressing in paint on its walls their vision of cosmic reality, for unimagined generations after them to wonder at? And for what reason, after centuries of quiet meditation and worship, did their successors abandon the marvellous monument they had raised, in this setting seemingly so perfect for the contemplative life? We shall never know, nor shall we fully understand what miraculous chain of circumstances preserved it almost undamaged, in this remote spot, unknown and uncared for except by a community of monks thirty kilometres away on the other side of a rushing river, over centuries and through a history of raids and invasions by the avowed iconoclasts of Islam. What we do know is that its mud-plastered walls having survived against all odds, the paintings they bear are one of the world's masterpieces of art and religion, part of the heritage of us all.

Ri-Dzong

The 'reformed' *gompa* of Ri-dzong was founded only a hundred years ago, to give full expression to the monastic ideal of the Ge-lugs-pa. It has maintained its strict adherence to the rules of monastic life, and has the distinction of being the only one of the major central Ladakh monasteries to have remained so far off the beaten track that even now it cannot be approached except on foot. The track to Ri-dzong leaves the main road along the Indus at Ule-tokpo, between Saspol and Nyurla, to follow the valley of a tributary stream; a couple of kilometres up it, visitors must leave their vehicle and continue on foot for a further few kilometres, the valley narrowing to little more than a winding gorge. The *gompa* is situated at a point where two spurs approach each other from either side, and the gorge is further blocked by a ridge of debris, deposited by some cataclysm, landslide or earthquake, geological ages ago. Thus the *gompa* buildings, rising high above the footpath, fill the whole width of the gorge, blocking any further view. Far from any other human habitation it is truly, in the literal translation of the word *gompa*, a solitary place, and this is emphasized by its name, which means 'mountain fort'.

The monks here are laid under a much stricter discipline than in most *gompas*, even Ge-lugs-pa ones. This is the only monastery in which they do not have individual cooking arrangements, but eat from a communal kitchen—though not all together in a dining hall or refectory; the food is served to each monk separately in his own quarters. There are about thirty monks at present, and twelve *chomos* or nuns, who have their own establishment at the *chomoling* a kilometre down the gorge. The *chomos* come up to the *gompa* once or twice a month for special *pujas*, otherwise they remain in the precincts of the *chomoling*, conducting the everyday services themselves.

The most interesting feature of Ri-dzong from the visual point of view is its murals which, while not differing in any tangible particular from other 'recent' work of the same type, nevertheless do betray an individual style. The figures in a landscape, in a series of scenes from the life of Sakyamuni which adorn the walls of one large temple, have an indefinable quality of being different—in more subtle colours than usual, they have the delicacy and charm of figures on a willow-pattern plate. They were executed by Lama Tshul-tim Nyima, founder of the *gompa*.

Otherwise, this *gompa*, being modern, has relatively little aesthetic or antiquarian interest. The silver *chorten* in the same large temple is said, surprisingly, to have been made not at Chiling, but at Mangyur, a village deep in the mountains across the Indus from Ri-dzong. The *thangkas* here are good but some of those in other smaller shrines are garishly modern.

The art-historian or antiquarian, bent on seeing what he can of Ladakh's monastic treasures, may be forgiven for giving Ri-dzong a miss. But its lamas have an air of peace and dedication all too rare in many of the other *gompas*, which, to anyone seeking to grasp the inwardness of Buddhist monastic life, may prove an inspiration.

Lamayuru

As a monastic site, Lamayuru, properly called Yung-Drung ('Swastika') is believed to be the oldest in Ladakh, and to have been a holy place of the Bon-chos before the advent of Buddhism. As an integral part of the village, perched on a spur high above the valley bottom—just off the main road as it descends from the Fatu-La to Khaltse—it is one of the most spectacularly picturesque of the *gompas*; inside, however, in spite of its antiquity, it has less to offer than many others, nor does it have a particularly appealing atmosphere.

The oldest part of the structure is a small temple, whose iconography places it squarely in the time of the Second Spreading. The main image is Vairocana, whose cult is 'typical of Rin-chen-zang-po's time, especially of the monasteries associated with him'.[4] The other four *Dhayani* Buddhas occupy a subordinate position. The carved doorway, and the paintings, now much worn and defaced, are distinctly reminiscent of Alchi. As far as the murals can be made out, there is a mandala, and some fierce divinities in *yab-yum*. This small temple, which shows no sign of being in use for worship, is not on the regular 'tour' of the *gompa*, being in fact quite a distance away from the *Du-khang* and the other main shrines, down narrow alleys and dark steep uneven staircases. Those visitors who are determined not to miss anything may be shown it on demand.

The main *Du-khang* is built around the opening to the cave in which, it is said, the sage Marpa rested and meditated. The cave mouth is in the right-hand wall, and a torch flashed inside shows life-size images of the sage and his principal disciple Mila-Respa. Lamayuru, unlike the other foundations of Rin-chen-zang-po's time, was not taken over in the fifteenth century by the Ge-lugs-pa, but at some point passed into the hands of the Dri-gung-pa, a sub-sect of the Ka-gyu-pa 'red-hat' school. The main image in the *Du-khang*, as well as in the inner shrine behind the main altar, is of the Dri-gung-pa guru, Skyoba Jigsten Gonbo; also in the inner shrine is a modern set of the twenty-one manifestations of Tara, in copper-gilt, made only a few years ago in Aligarh. To one side an enormous *chorten* behind glass, apparently in carved and painted wood, proves itself to be moulded in coloured butter; it is said to have been made about 1975. This, along with its allegedly century-old companion piece in another temple nearby, is the only example I have come across in Ladakh of this rather ésoteric art-form, which is reported to have been common in the *gompas* of old Tibet. Apart from some old and worn *thangkas*, the *Du-khang* has little of interest to offer. The inside walls are not painted, though the verandah has the usual Lords of the Quarters and Wheel of Life, in obviously recent renderings.

[4]Ibid., p. 91.

A small temple on a higher level, besides its ancient butter sculpture, has images of Marpa and Mila-Respa, and three silver *chorten*, the largest of them said to have been made at Chiling about sixty years ago. The murals are in the usual conventional style, and represent mostly fierce divinities.

The Mulbekh Gompas

There are a few *gompas* in or near Mulbekh, though these have nothing like the richness and variety of the central Ladakh ones. As few travellers stop to see them, they have no regular opening hours, nor do the lamas seem to expect visitors.

Mulbekh *gompa* itself I can give no account of. It is spectacularly situated on the very pinnacle of a crag 200 metres above the main road, with a footpath winding up to it from behind. My proposed visit was abandoned at the foot of the ascent, when women working in the fields told us that the lamas had come down to the village to perform a *puja*, and would certainly have locked up behind them. There are indeed said to be two *gompas*, one belonging to the Drug-pa and one to the Ge-lugs-pa; they incorporate— or are incorporated in—the 'palace' of the erstwhile rulers of Mulbekh.

Shergol is situated a couple of kilometres off the main road, on the other side of the Wakha River, up a side valley. An unmade track leads across a wooden bridge and up to Shergol village whose fields and dwellings slope down to the stream, while on the other side of the track a footpath snakes across the desert to the bluff, half way up which the monastery is perched. A Ge-lugs-pa foundation, its only temple seems to be a small shrine with an eleven-headed Avalokiteswara image, accompanied by several Ge-lugs-pa masters. There are also three Tara images carved in wood, of Tibetan workmanship. The wall-paintings are old and mellow, and represent Ge-lugs-pa sages, Taras and fierce divinities. Two panels have recently been stripped to make room for paintings of the present Dalai and Panchen Lamas. From the verandah, hanging over the valley below, the view of ridges and peaks is breath-taking—more of an aid to meditation and worship perhaps than the dusty images and faded murals within.

The *gompa* of Ngari Rinpoche stands just off the main road a little before it leaves the Wakha valley and starts the ascent to the

Namika-La. It stands by itself among fields, square and uncompromising, related neither to a village nor a mountainside. It
consists of no more than a single temple with, presumably, the
lama's living quarters tucked away somewhere at the back. It was
built in 1975 by the lama who still officiates there; the Ngari
Rinpoche to whom it is dedicated is the Dalai Lama's younger
brother, the head lama of Likir Gompa. The sole image is of Cho
Rinpoche; the wall-paintings depict Sakyamuni in various poses,
in a pagoda-filled landscape.

There could be no greater contrast than that between this
modern structure and the *gompa* of Gyal, up the Wakha Valley a
few kilometres beyond the point where the road turns off it to
approach the Namika-La. The visitor will do well to leave his
vehicle where the track on up the valley leaves the main road, as
this is agonizing even by Ladakhi standards. Either way, the last
stretch has to be covered on foot, by a narrow path running
through fields. The mountains begin to close in; and the village
nestles beneath cliffs of sand-coloured conglomerate. The *gompa*
which but for its nearness to the village might more aptly be
described as a hermitage, so tiny is it, is incredibly situated, thirty
metres above the village, not on top of the cliff but perched
precariously on a man-made platform supported by two of the
cliff's natural buttresses. The steep passage up to it passes behind
and then through one of these. Once at the top, there is nothing
but a verandah, which serves as the lama's living quarters, and a
tiny chapel, partly carved out of the rock itself, with images of
Sakyamuni and eleven-headed Avalokiteswara. Pigeon-holed
racks to hold the scriptures line one wall, but there are no paintings. The verandah is painted with the Wheel of Life, and the
Eight Auspicious Signs.

But here, the external man-made signs of religion mean nothing. No-one need visit Gyal to see paintings or images. Rather
there is an atmosphere of deep peace in which it might be possible
to approach an intuitive understanding of what it is that the
lamas, and all men, are seeking. In this eyrie, solitary yet not cut
off from the world, for comforting sounds of the village's life drift
up faintly from below, and with the mountains over the river so
near that you could stretch out your hand and touch them—here,
if anywhere, a man might come close to the heart of things.

Appendix I

The Jesuits in Western Tibet

In 1625 Tsaparang, the capital of Guge, became the headquarters of a Jesuit mission under the Portuguese priest, Antonio de Andrade. In the days of Nyima-Gon, founder of the first Ladakhi dynasty, Guge had been part of the Ladakhi empire; later, allotted to one of Nyima-Gon's younger sons, it became a kind of vassal state of Ladakh. By the seventeenth century it appears to have been more or less independent. Tsaparang was situated on the upper waters of the Sutlej, now a few kilometres inside the Tibetan border.

The arrival of the Jesuits at this remote spot is a strange enough story; the sequence of events leading up to it can be traced back as far as the early middle ages. From that time, rumours had been trickling through to Europe of 'lost' communities of Christians in central Asia, vaguely associated with the name of the mythical emperor Prester John. These reports did have some factual basis in that communities of Nestorian Christians did exist in central Asia in the middle ages, though Prester John was probably a figment of the imagination. The Nestorians seem to have disappeared by the seventeenth century; but similar reports came to the ears of the Jesuits who, with their headquarters in the Portuguese colony of Goa, had embarked on missionary work in India about the end of the sixteenth century, establishing a series of missions at the courts of the Emperors Akbar and Jahangir. These later reports may have been based on seeming similarities between certain Catholic rituals, and some of those of Tibetan Buddhism, as seen perhaps by pilgrims to the Hindu holy places of Mount Kailash and Lake Manasarowar in south-west Tibet.

In 1624 Andrade, one of the priests in residence at the court of Jahangir, found an opportunity to test the truth of these rumours by travelling into the fastnesses of the Himalaya. In Delhi, he fell in with a party of Hindu pilgrims bound for the sacred shrine of Badrinath in Garhwal; disguising himself as one of them, and taking only one companion, Brother Manuel Marques, he joined their caravan. Reaching Badrinath, the Jesuits parted company with the pilgrims, and continued, skirting the slopes of the mighty mountain Kamet, over the 5,600 metre Mana Pass into Guge, reaching Tsaparang probably some time in July 1624. Here they met with an unexpectedly warm welcome. The king of Guge seems to have been impressed that the two travellers had undertaken a journey of such hardship from purely religious motives, and received them hospitably. Andrade, for his part, soon realized that here were no lost Christians; but it began to dawn on him that the kindly disposition of the king might be turned to account for the opening up of a new mission field. He left Tsaparang at the end of August with a written commission from the king appointing him his Chief Lama, and giving him 'full authority to teach the holy law to our people'. He was back in Agra early in November with two boys from Tsaparang; and having obtained the necessary sanction from the Provincial head of the Jesuits at Goa, set out again in June 1625, arriving at Tsaparang in the third week of August.

The Guge king fulfilled his promises of the previous year, and himself laid the foundation stone of the church of Our Lady of Hope. For about five years the missionaries, never more than five of them, pursued a strange and lonely existence in this petty Tibetan capital, which cannot have been much more than a rude village; however all difficulties were smoothed away by the enthusiastic patronage of the king. The number of converts made is not known, but it must have been small. The king's encouragement, on which the missionaries' hopes were chiefly founded, fell short of receiving baptism himself. A sub-station of the mission may have been opened at Rudok, more than 150 kilometres north of Tsaparang; and the king of Tsang, the province adjoining Guge to the east, as well as the king of Ladakh, the great Sengge Namgyal himself, expressed interest in the 'lamas from the west'.

However, in spite of their modest successes and their apparent security, the position of the missionaries, isolated amid an alien though not immediately unfriendly people, and in a situation in which they were liable to be caught up in the cross-currents of politics unconnected with their own purposes, was in reality precarious. The first misfortune to befall the mission was the recall of Andrade on his appointment as head of the whole Jesuit province of Goa. This deprived the little settlement of an enterprising and sagacious leader, who might have been able to pilot it through the troubles ahead. For the very patronage of the king, though it formed the sole support on which all their efforts depended, was to prove both his undoing and theirs. This ruler had for years been at odds with his brother who was head of Guge's religious establishment. The favour shown by him to the propagators of an alien faith strained their already fragile relationship to breaking-point. On top of this, there was an ancient feud with the king of Ladakh, whose sister, according to Andrade's account, the king of Guge had married as his second wife, and then repudiated. This had happened years before Andrade arrived but the facts would have been common knowledge during his time in Tsaparang, and there is no reason to doubt the accuracy of his report. His story implies that the Ladakh king had made this slight the pretext for making war on Guge, which had been suffering from the depredations of the Ladakhi army for eighteen years. The presence of the Jesuits seems to have had a catalytic effect, helping to precipitate the crisis that now ensued. Certainly they and the Christian converts along with their patron the king were the chief sufferers. Taking advantage of the king's protracted illness the lamas, raising the cry of 'Religion in danger', incited the army to revolt, called in the Ladakh king, and offered him the crown. The Guge king was tricked into surrender, and carried away by the Ladakhis into honourable exile in Leh. Two of the missionaries were also taken prisoner to Leh, but later released and allowed to return to Tsaparang; no record remains of their visit to Ladakh. All these events took place in 1630.

The Tsaparang mission never recovered from this catastrophe, and was finally closed down in 1635, though a watch was kept on the situation till about 1640 to see whether there was any possibility of resuming operations. Brother Manuel Marques, Andrade's original travelling companion, who had crossed the Mana Pass no fewer than nine times on his journeys in and out of Guge, is last heard of in 1642, held a prisoner in Tsaparang by the new Ladakhi administration. He probably died there, a solitary and unhappy death.

From our point of view, the great interest attaching to this episode is that it provided the occasion for the second documented visit of a European to Ladakh. (A Portuguese merchant, Diogo d'Almeida, seems to have spent some time in the country about 1600.) When Andrade, now head of the Jesuit mission province of Goa, received in 1631 the first reports of the revolution at Tsaparang, he appointed as Visitor to the mission Father Francisco de Azevedo, ordering him to proceed immediately to the spot and investigate the situation. This Azevedo did; but he did more. He realized that the only hope of reestablishing the mission would be to gain the favour of the king of Ladakh, Sengge Namgyal himself. This was the object of his journey to Leh.

With the possible exception of the mission members taken prisoner by the Ladakhis the previous year, Azevedo and his companion Father John de Oliveira were the first Europeans to cross the bleak upland plateaux of Rupshu and Chang-Thang. Like their successors, they were impressed by the absence of vegetation; but Azevedo noted an abundance of wild-life: 'hyacas' (yaks), wild asses, mountain goats, hares; pigeons, ravens and eagles. They left Tsaparang on 4 October, when the season was already well advanced; and reached Leh on 25 October, after a journey for whose hardships even the severity of the Mana Pass could have been little preparation. Azevedo penned the first recorded description of Leh:

It is built on the slope of a small mountain and numbers about 800 families. Half a mile lower down but still quite visible flows the river that goes to Lahore [*sic*]. By the town itself passes a mountain stream which works a large number of water-mills; a few trees are also found here.

In his account of his first interview, Azevedo describes the person of Sengge Namgyal:

He is a man of tall stature, of a brown colour, with something of the Javanese [meaning presumably Mongoloid] in his features, and of stern appearance. He wore a rather dirty upper garment of some red material, a mantle of the same, and a threadbare cap. His hair hung down to his shoulders, either ear was adorned with turquoise and a large coral, whilst he wore a string of skull-bones round his neck to remind himself of death. He was sitting cross-legged on an ornamental carpet of crimson velvet.

The two priests were received courteously, and regaled with butter-tea and *tsampa*.

Although the Tsaparang mission was not able to recover from the disastrous events of 1630, Sengge did send Azevedo and Oliveira away with kind words, and a promise that the missionaries might continue their work in Guge, Rudok and even in Leh. After a stay of only fifteen days, the two priests left Leh on 7 November—a terrible season to travel far over those bleak and bitterly cold upland wastes. They completed their amazing journey by pioneering—as far as Europeans are concerned—the route down to Kulu Valley and the Punjab, via the Thung-Lung, Lunga-Lacha, Bara-Lacha and Rohtang Passes. They finally crossed the Rohtang Pass, floundering through breast-high snow, and being forced to bivouac on the slopes of the pass as they could not get down to the valley before nightfall. At this point Azevedo nearly died; but it was the last of the perils they faced on this gruelling trek, and the next day they descended to the gentle landscape of the Kulu Valley. They reached Agra on 3 January 1632, having accomplished the journey from Leh in just short of two months.

The story of the Tsaparang mission and Azedevo's visit to Leh was unknown to nineteenth-century writers on Ladakh, for the records lay in the obscurity of the archives of the Society of Jesus in Rome until 1924 when C. Wessels SJ published his *Early Jesuit Travellers in Central Asia*. However, in the headquarters of the mission province of Goa, the memory remained alive throughout the seventeenth century, and with it the hope that some day the mission might be revived. The opportunity did not arise till 1714 when two priests, an Italian, Ippolito Desideri, and a Portuguese, Emanuel Freyre, set off from Delhi over the Pir Panjal into Kashmir en route for Tibet. Desideri was the moving spirit of the enterprise but he was only 29, and Freyre, his senior in age and Indian experience, was the nominal leader of the expedition.

They wintered in Srinagar and set off towards the end of May 1715 to cross the Zoji-La, which they did on 30 May in a blizzard. They were the first Europeans to travel what is now the 'orthodox' route into Ladakh but events were to show that their idea of the region's geography was of the haziest. They did not reach Leh till 20 June—which means that their journey took considerably longer than the sixteen days between Srinagar and Leh reckoned by travellers of the nineteenth century, and indeed up till the time of the construction of the motor-road in the 1960s. (Sven Hedin, admittedly a traveller extraordinary, made Srinagar from Leh in

eleven days in 1902, in the middle of winter.) Notwithstanding
the mercantile connection between Ladakh and Kashmir, the trail
was evidently quite rudimentary; to the extent that Desideri believed that no pack animal could traverse it, and that all baggage
had to be carried on men's backs.

However, on their arrival in Leh, the two priests were cheered
by a warm reception from the king, Nyima Namgyal; and, like
Andrade before him, Desideri began to dream of settling down in
this hospitable atmosphere and embarking on missionary work.
But Freyre, his superior, had different ideas. He took a narrower
view of the purpose of their journey, as simply to search for traces
of Andrade and his work; finding none, he was only anxious to
return to the plains of India, which were home to him. But
appalled by the hardships of the journey from Srinagar he was
not prepared to return by the same perilous route, and started
casting about for an alternative. His ignorance of trans-
Himalayan geography made him decide, astonishingly, that an
easier way to get back to Hindustan would be by way of Lhasa. He
overruled Desideri, and after a two-month stay in Leh they left
like Azevedo at the beginning of winter, reaching Lhasa seven
months later. From the Tibetan border onwards, their party was
attached to the entourage of a beautiful Tartar princess, widow of
the late military governor of Gartok, who had taken over the
command on her husband's death and had now been recalled to
Lhasa. In spite of this unlooked-for good fortune one wonders if
Freyre, a man at once weak-willed and cantankerous, ever had
any doubts about the wisdom of his decision to travel east, as the
caravan crawled across the interminable steppes in the biting cold
of winter. He left Lhasa almost immediately to return to the plains
of Hindustan, but Desideri remained for five years, witnessing
and recording the dramatic political events which laid the foundation of Chinese claims to suzerainty over Tibet, and immersing
himself in the study of Buddhism, the better to refute its 'false
doctrines'. His *Relazione* thus provides a unique insight into the
life of the Tibetans and the mysteries of Tibetan Buddhism which
has not been superseded by modern studies in any European
language. The tragedy is that it lay unnoticed for almost two
hundred years, until the early years of this century.

Obviously Desideri's account of Ladakh is by no means the most
interesting or important part of his *Relazione*; and in insight and

fullness of detail it falls far short of the one given by Moorcroft a hundred years later. Yet every scrap of information reaching us from this early date has its interest and Desideri gives us a valuable glimpse of Ladakh at that time.

In his account of Srinagar, Desideri had occasion to talk of shawls, and he knew that the raw material from which they were made came from Ladakh, though he was wrong in supposing pashmina to be produced from sheep. His is the first description of a crossing of the Zoji-La, and of the *jhoola* type of bridge, made of ropes of twisted willow twigs, which swayed alarmingly above the roaring torrent below. He and Freyre were surely the first Europeans to witness the Balti national game of polo, for he relates how a Muslim 'Kinglet' who entertained them and helped them on their way, invited them to accompany him 'to see an exhibition of cavalry exercises and games'.

Desideri's account of Ladakh deserves quotation *in extenso*. He first describes the extent of the country—'two months' journey in length'—and enumerates the territories on its borders. He goes on:

It is mountainous, sterile, and altogether horrible. Barley is the chief product; a little wheat is grown, and in some places apricots. Trees are scarce, so wood is hard to procure. There are many sheep, especially very large geldings; their flesh is most excellent, and their wool extraordinarily fine. Musk deer also exist. In valleys at the foot of mountains, and also near streams, the natives find a good deal of gold, not in large nuggets, but as gold dust. They eat meat, and the flour of roasted barley, and drink Chang, a sort of beer made from barley, which I shall mention hereafter. Their clothes, made of wool, are of suitable shape and make. They are not at all arrogant, but rather submissive, kindly, cheerful and courteous. The language of this country does not differ much from that of [Tibet], and the Religion and books relating to religion are similar. There are numerous monasteries and a great many monks; their superior is a chief Lama, who, to qualify for the post, must have studied for some years in a University in [Tibet], as must any monk who aspires to be promoted to a higher grade. A number of merchants from Kascimir engaged in the wool trade live in this Kingdom, and they are allowed to have mosques and openly to hold their religion. Occasionally merchants come from the kingdom of Kotan with well-bred horses, cotton goods and other merchandise. Some come from [Tibet] by way of the great desert and bring tea and tobacco, bales of silk, and other things from China. There are villages but only one city in this kingdom, Lhe or Lhata,

which is the capital where the Grand Lama and the absolute Sovereign
live. It is situated in a large plain surrounded by mountains, and dotted
with villages. The city at the foot of the hill gradually extends upwards
until you reach the Residence of the Grand Lama and the Royal Palace,
both large, fine buildings. Above, nearly on the summit of the hill, is a
fortress, while the city is defended by walls on either side and below. The
houses, strongly built, are roomy and well adapted to the country.

This corroborates at almost every point both what we know of
Ladakh today, and the scattered hints we have relating to its
history. The fact that a necessary qualification for priestly
advancement was to have studied at a university in metropolitan
Tibet; the presence of Kashmiri merchants engaged in the pashmina trade, and the religious tolerance extended to them and
other Muslim merchants; the caravan trade from central Asia
(though he mentions Khotan rather than Yarkand) and Tibet—
all these we know from other sources, but it is useful to have them
confirmed by an independent outside observer. The mention of
barley, wheat and apricots as practically the only crops; the diet
of wheat and *tsampa*, washed down with *chang*; even more the
assessment of the Ladakhi character—these, to anyone familiar
with present-day Ladakh and its background, inspire confidence
in Desideri as an observer possessed of the two cardinal qualities
of objectivity and sympathy. The modern student of Ladakh has
good reason to be grateful to him and his predecessors.

Appendix II

Information for Visitors

The intending visitor to Ladakh must make sure he is physically fit. Altitudes of 3,000 m and over are definitely contra-indicated for anyone with high blood-pressure, or heart or chest problems. This is true even for a visit to Leh to see the *gompas*; much more so for the traveller who intends to leave the beaten track and take to the mountains, where he will be out of reach of medical help should emergency arise. Intending trekkers, and anyone over the age of 45, are advised to go in for a thorough medical check-up, with particular reference to blood-pressure, heart and lungs, making sure that their doctor knows their intention to stay at a high altitude for several days or weeks, before embarking on the enterprise.

Even the most physically fit are advised to take things easy on their first arrival in Ladakh, particularly if they have flown in. The recommended minimum acclimatization period is a week to ten days, and this means that many visitors who stay for shorter periods never have the chance to acclimatize properly. However short the visit, strenuous activity should definitely be avoided for the first two days at least. Trekkers should plan to spend at least four or five days before they set off on their march. Ideally these might be spent in Leh where there is plenty of interest to be found in the bazaar, or the alleyways of the old city, and many good walks in the neighbourhood.

Travel

Air. Indian Airlines have scheduled flights to Leh three times a week from Srinagar, the flying time being 35 minutes. There are also two flights from Delhi, via Chandigarh. A magnificent panorama of ridges and peaks is obtained from the aircraft but this is, particularly for the one-time traveller, no substitute for the slow unfolding of the landscape on the ground. Also, acclimatization problems are likely to be greater. However, the option exists, and is the only one available to winter visitors.

Road. State Transport buses ply daily between Srinagar and Leh, with an overnight halt at Kargil. The 'A' class bus service, which is likely to be preferred by most travellers, is not a daily one, but goes about five days a week—the booking offices in Srinagar and Leh, or the Tourist Information Offices, will be able to advise. In contrast to the truck drivers, many of the bus drivers display all the desirable qualities of care, courtesy and consideration for other road users, which are even more essential on mountain roads than on the flat. In my five years' experience of Ladakh, I have not heard of one bus going off the road.

The ideal way to come is in your own vehicle, which gives you the freedom to stop where you will, get out, take photos, and drink in the landscape and the sun and the pure air. Driving time is approximately seven hours Srinagar–Kargil, and nine hours Kargil–Leh. The road is black-topped throughout, except over the Zoji-La which, being under snow all winter and requiring bulldozers to clear it at the beginning of summer, would have to be resurfaced every year. A stretch of about twenty kilometres, from the Captain Bends up and over the top of the pass, is therefore rough. For the rest, the road is under a constant process of maintenance, and there will always be patches whose surface leaves something to be desired—next on the roadmenders' agenda. There will also be diversions, round the construction of new bridges and culverts. Ordinary saloon cars can and do travel to Leh, where in 1977 a sensation was caused by the arrival of a diplomatic Rolls Royce; but ordinarily it is not advisable to take in anything so low-slung. A rugged vehicle with plenty of clearance—a jeep or a Dormobile—will prove the most useful, in terms of not only the journey from Srinagar, but also visiting *gompas*, and negotiating other unmade roads—e.g. that to Zanskar. People driving their own vehicles must make sure that they carry enough petrol or diesel to see them through the whole journey. Fuel is only available at Leh, nowhere else in Ladakh.

Another thing that drivers may do to minimize the rigours of the journey is to check with the tourist authorities in Srinagar, Kargil and Leh, as to the timings of the military convoys. With three of these in each direction on the road every day from June to October, it is difficult to avoid them altogether; but at least it is better to organize one's timing so as to meet one coming in the opposite direction, when it is possible to pull in and let it pass by, than to come up on its tail, and be faced with the prospect of overtaking anything from 30 to 100 slow-moving trucks, every one of them belching nauseous diesel fumes.

Accommodation

Leh and Kargil both offer a variety of accommodation, to suit every pocket and standard of luxury. Hotels are divided into 'A' and 'B' classes, and in both the prices quoted will include full board. At the far end of the spectrum, rock-bottom prices obtain in dormitories, which provide sleeping-space but little else. Best value in the middle range is obtained in Government tourist bungalows and rest-houses, but these have a limited number of rooms and bookings are hard to get. Facilities in the smaller hotels and guest-houses vary, as do prices; but as many of them consist of little more than a couple of rooms added on to a family home, they offer perhaps the most authentic experience of Ladakh available to the visitor. Some give half or full board. For those whose lodgings do not provide food, there are a number of eating houses and restaurants in both Leh and Kargil. Standards vary, but there is a choice of several where a palatable and cleanly cooked meal may be had.

At the height of the tourist season—that is, the three months June, July and August—it is advisable to book accommodation in advance. Failing a personal recommendation to any particular establishment, the intending visitor may write to the Tourist Officer, Leh, or the Tourist Officer, Kargil, explaining his requirements and the sort of prices he is willing to pay, and his request will be passed on to an appropriate hotel or guest-house. In September and October, as the weather turns chilly and the tourist rush declines, advance booking is not necessary. Winter tourists planning to fly in are also advised to book in advance through the Tourist Officer, as many of the hotels and guest-houses close for the winter. Anyone planning a winter visit should, when he books the room, check up on the heating arrangements, and whether there will be an extra charge for this, or whether it is included in the tariff.

Gompa visits

The *gompas* within easy reach of Leh and Kargil may be visited either by local bus, or by taxi. There are local buses to most of the surrounding villages, and the timetable may be consulted in the Tourist Office. During the season, a special bus for tourists runs to Hemis only.

Taxis are expensive, with varying rates for metalled and un-metalled roads, and stiff waiting charges. These rates, which may be verified at the Tourist Office, are officially sanctioned rates and not subject to negotiation.

Only a few of the *gompas* have special opening hours—those within reach of Leh being Sankar, Namgyal Tsemo and Shey Palace, also the Stok Palace Museum. The Tourist Officer will be able to advise. Other *gompas* are theoretically open all the time, but some of the smaller ones, with only a few monks who may not be resident all the year round, may be found empty and locked up if there has been, e.g., a death in the village, or any other occasion for a religious ceremony, at which the monks are required to officiate.

For those wishing to stay overnight in order to attend the early morning *puja*, there is accommodation at only a few *gompas*. There are small private hotels at Hemis, Alchi and Lamayuru, and Government tourist bungalows in Sakti (for Thak-thak), Saspol (for Alchi) and Mulbekh (also at Panikar, up the Suru Valley, for views of Nun-Kun). Elsewhere, visitors must make their own arrangements, either renting a room in the village, or camping. Either way, they should carry their own supplies and sleeping bags.

Trekking

The easy way is through an agency, but this is very expensive. The less affluent trekker can make his arrangements through the Tourist Office in Leh, which maintains a register of reliable guides at fixed and reasonable rates. The guide, in consultation with the trekker, will then arrange for pack animals, tents and supplies. The price of pack animals is said to have become exorbitant due to the increasing demand; and expeditions may find it necessary to arrange to have them brought from outside—e.g., from Kulu. No register of guides exists in Kargil, where the trekker who wants to avoid an agency will either have to make his own arrangements, or get in touch with a Leh-based guide.

Trekking in Ladakh is as safe as it can be anywhere in the world. There is no danger of encountering bandits, and precious little of wild animals. (There are said to be bears around Rangdum, but Rangdum is not a trekking area.) Mountain weather can never be guaranteed absolutely, but the Zanskar range, in the rain-shadow of the Great Himalaya, offers a better chance of perfect weather, with less danger of freak storms or flash floods, than almost any other mountainous area in the world. The main possible hazard is sudden illness—something that can occur any time, any place, the possibility of which is hardly going to deter the hardy trekker. But he should realize that, several days' march away from medical help, and at altitudes of over 3,000 metres, its consequences may be serious, even fatal; and he should take reasonable precautions. An emergency medical kit should be carried, and at least one member of the party should know clearly how to use it. For the trekker, even more than the ordinary tourist, a medical check-up and acclimatization are vital parts of his preparation, and should not in any circumstances be omitted or skimped.

Every precaution must be taken against losing one's way, for in this inhospitable and sparsely-populated terrain such an accident could be fatal. The danger is obviated by employing a guide, but there is no reason why the fit and experienced trekker, equipped with a large-scale and reliable map, should not dispense with a guide, particularly if he has been over the ground before. He will however do well to pay heed to local advice, especially on the state of the bridges which are regularly swept away as snowmelt increases the volume of the streams in summer, and regularly rebuilt as the waters subside. With or without a guide, every expedition should be self-sufficient in food, as villages deep in the folds of the mountains are too poor to provide anything in the way of supplies.

A few of the more popular treks are as follows:

1. Markha Valley—the valley behind the Zanskar Range and Stok Kangri, just across the Indus from Leh.   10 days.
2. Saspol to Lamayuru.   5 days.
3. Lamayuru to Padam.   11 days.
4. Likir–Ri-dzong–Hemis Skurbuchan–Tingmosgang. 3 days.

   This follows the old foot- and pony-trail from Leh to Khaltse, which was the usual route before the construction of the motor road.
5. Kishtwar to Padam.   8 days.

6. Manali to Padam.   8 days.
7. Pahalgam to Panikar.   7 days.
8. Dras to Shergol, via Sankhu.   7 days.

Nos. (5), (6) and (7) start south of the Great Himalaya in respectively the Jammu, Kulu and Kashmir areas. All except no. (4) involve the crossing of passes between 4,000 and 5,000 metres.

As opposed to the trekker who is concerned mostly with the valleys and passes, the climber who is interested in getting to the tops of mountains may also find Ladakh attractive. The giants of the Karakoram are closed to the ordinary public (Saser Kangri and Teram Kangri have both recently been climbed by Indian Army expeditions); and there have been numerous expeditions to Nun-Kun the last few years. But major peaks apart, there is a lot of scope especially in the Zanskar Range for the climber who wants to practise his skills in a remote area, but who is not interested in chalking up 'firsts'. With proper acclimatization, a small expedition could from a base camp at about 5,000 metres, find a number of ascents to give them the satisfaction of having reached 6,100 m (20,000 ft). This will mostly not involve much in the way of 'technical' climbing, as the quality of the rock is poor, but it can still be a source of great enjoyment. The mountains to the south of the Zanskar and Suru valleys, on the north face of the Great Himalaya, have heavier snowfall than those of the Zanskar Range, and thus a lower snowline and longer glaciers. They offer a greater variety of technical problems. An article by Mark Dravers in the *Alpine Journal* 1980, reviews possibilities open to both climbers and trekkers in Ladakh.

The Inner Line

Ladakh is bounded by some of India's most sensitive borders—with Pakistan-occupied Kashmir, China and Tibet—and great tracts from north-west to south-east are closed to visitors through a device known as the Inner Line, which they are not allowed to cross. The detailed alignment of the Line is kept under review by the Government of India, but the foreseeable future is not likely to bring any major change in its effect of closing the Indus valley below Khaltse including Da-Hanu, Nubra, the area beyond the Chang-La—Chushul, Tang-tse and the Pang-Gong Lake—the Indus valley above Upshi, and the eastern part of the Zanskar range. Foreigners wishing to visit these areas will be granted permits only in the most exceptional cases. They should apply well in advance to the Government of India, through the Deputy Secretary (Foreigners), Ministry of Home Affairs, Government of India, New Delhi. Indians wishing to visit areas beyond the Line may apply to the Secretary, Department of Home Affairs, Government of Jammu and Kashmir, Srinagar, J&K (or Jammu Tawi, J&K, if the application is made between November and April inclusive).

Clothes and equipment

The summer visitor to Leh will need basically warm-weather clothes, with a sweater for evenings and mornings when it may be chilly. Temperatures begin to fall around the second half of August, and though cottons continue to be worn during the day until mid-September, a heavy sweater or an anorak or coat will be needed in the mornings and evenings. From mid-September it starts getting distinctly cold, and woollens are needed even during the day, though in the sun it is still hot. Winter visitors—which means November to April—will need to equip themselves with heavy woollens, anoraks or tweed coats, gloves, balaclava helmets or equivalent, and warm boots.

High summer—roughly the second half of June to the middle of August—is no problem; neither, in its own way, is deep winter, November to April. In the intervening months it is advisable to adopt the layer system of dressing so that as the sun's warmth increases in the middle of the day, layers of down and wool can be discarded one by one, to be resumed as temperatures fall towards evening.

At any season of the year, the visitor who plans to depart from the more or less beaten track and the relative comforts of Leh and Kargil, or even to live on the cheap in the two towns, is advised to carry a sleeping bag.

The atmosphere of Ladakh is extemely dry, and the sun, because of the rarefied air, very fierce. It is absolutely essential, therefore, to carry skin conditioners, whether in the form of sun-tan lotion, moisturizer, or straightforward cold cream. Skin creams are available in Leh bazaar, but visitors who prefer to use their own brand should be sure to bring enough. This is especially important for those with sensitive skins. Although little Ladakhi boys disport themselves in the nude in the summer sun, sun-bathing at 3,000 metres is contra-indicated for white skins. Even brown ones can burn at high altitudes.

Lists of equipment for trekkers can be got from the Tourist Officers in Leh and Kargil, or from agencies specializing in mountain treks. Intending trekkers should remember that nights in the mountains will be chilly at any time of year, and make sure that they have adequate bedding. They must also bear in mind the impossibility of living off the land in Ladakh—the occasional village will be able to provide them with no more than a little *tsampa* if they do run short; they must therefore plan to carry enough food for the whole trek. Basic supplies, including fruit and vegetables in season, can be bought in Leh and Kargil, but the bazaars of these places may be a little short on variety as regards tinned foods, or any kind of delicacy, and expensive as well, so it is a good idea to stock up in Srinagar or any other big city. Dried apricots, one of the Ladakhi staples, are plentiful, especially late in the season after the new crop comes in—say from the beginning of September on; they are easily portable, and an excellent form of instant energy.

Every visitor to Ladakh should keep a good torch handy. It is essential for making the most of the *gompas*, whose shrines are often ill-lit; and also for any night sorties, if only into the streets of Leh and Kargil, in both of which the electricity is switched off at 11 p.m. (10.30 in winter). Buses both ways leave Kargil well before dawn; and many a visitor's main memory of that town will be of stumbling through dark uneven alleys in the small hours—agony which a torch can mitigate.

Glossary

Arhats   The sixteen original disciples of Gautam Buddha.

Bodhisattva   A concept in Mahayana Buddhism. A soul that has by its merits gained in innumerable incarnations, reached enlightenment, but forgoes *nirvana* out of compassion for all the other souls not yet so blessed, in order to work for their enlightenment and liberation.

Bon, or Bon-chos   A blanket term for the religion prevailing in Tibet before Buddhism. Probably embraced many cults, varying from place to place. Pantheistic and shamanistic, probably included the cult of ancestors. Various elements taken over by Tibetan Buddhism.

Buddha   A soul that has achieved enlightenment, and accepted *nirvana*. Originally applied to Gautam, founder of Buddhism; later the concept elaborated in terms of both time—series of Buddhas in history, one for each aeon; and space—series of five Buddhas symbolizing the cosmic system.

Chang   Mildly alcoholic drink, brewed from barley: fermented barley-water. Slightly sourish taste; when fresh an excellent summer drink. Drunk in great quantities by the Buddhists of Ladakh (as by all the Tibetan peoples) on all festive occasions.

Chogtse   Low table, usually carved and painted.

Chorten   Religious structure, found at the entrance to villages or *gompas*, or almost anywhere. The *stupa* of ancient Indian Buddhism, by origin believed to refer to the grave-mounds erected over the divided ashes of Gautam Buddha. Its different forms symbolize different religious concepts. It should always be passed keeping it on the right—i.e. any circuit or part-circuit of it should be in a clockwise direction.

Chuba   The Tibetan dress, word applied to both men's and women's gowns.

Dharmapalas Guardians of the Law: fierce divinities of Tibetan Buddhism, probably originally demons of the Bon religion.

Du-Khang Assembly hall; main temple of a *gompa.*

Dzo Offspring of the male yak and the common cow. Bred mainly for the plough: combines the strength of the yak with the docility of the cow. The female, called *dzomo,* is kept as a milch animal. This hybrid is not sterile, but the *dzomo's* progeny is not viable.

Gompa Lit. solitary place: Buddhist monastery.

Goncha The Ladakhi dress, word applied to both men's and women's gowns.

Gon-khang Temple of the Guardian Divinities.

Grim Naked barley, the staple crop of the whole Tibetan plateau, including Ladakh.

Gur-gur Onomatopoeic word: the cylindrical wooden churn in which butter is made, and the ingredients of Tibetan tea— the infusion of tea itself, salt, milk and butter—are blended. Hence *gur-gur* tea.

Jalebi Sweetmeat made of batter piped into convoluted shapes.

Jehad Holy war of Muslims against infidels.

Jhoola Swing; hanging rope bridge.

Jooley Greeting of the Ladakhi Buddhists, on both meeting and parting. Also means thank you. The *oo* sound is more closed than the English *loom,* more open than the French *tu.* Approximates the.Glasgow pronunciation of *book.*

Kafila trade caravan.

Khang Building, house, edifice, e.g. *Lha-khang,* temple.

Khang-bu Lit. little house: social custom by which the ownership of a piece of property is transferred to the heir, on his reaching years of discretion, the parents retiring to a little house adjoning the main property, keeping only enough land and livestock for their own sustenance.

Khar Palace. *Khar-Mon*—Musicians of the Palace, title given to Gyal Katun's personal musicians and their descendants.

Kushok An incarnate lama, the head of a monsatery; he achieves the title of Kushok only after undergoing a long and rigorous course of training in the theory and practice of Buddhism.

La Mountain pass.

Lama Term ordinarily applied to all Buddhist monks, and so used in this book. Strictly speaking should apply only to the *Ge-long*, fully ordained senior monks qualified to act as spiritual teachers.

Lha- Prefix meaning 'of the gods', e.g. *Lha-khang*, temple.

Losar The new year festival. Celebrated in Ladakh not at the time of the actual Tibetan new year, towards the end of February or early March, but on the first day of the eleventh lunar month, usually in December. This is said to be due to the fact that when Jamyang Namgyal decided to take the field in western Ladakh—a decision which led to the great Balti invasion of the beginning of the 17th century—he was advised to wait till after the new year celebrations. Being unwilling to submit to the two or three months' delay this would mean, he advanced the date of the new year festival. In spite of the unfortunate results of this, the Ladakhis have continued to celebrate Losar two or three months in advance of the actual new year.

Mahayana Lit. the Great Vehicle: historically the second school of Buddhism, the first being the Hinayana, or Lesser Vehicle, implanted in Ceylon and south-east Asia. Distinguished from the Hinayana by a greater elaboration: idea of the Bodhisattva. Gautam Buddha considered not merely as a spiritual teacher, a human being among humans; but as a manifestation in time of a primordial principle of Buddhahood. Erection of a complex system, basically of supports and aids for the individual soul to reach enlightenment.

Mandala A square or circular design, seeking to illustrate the relationships of various symbolic concepts in the Buddhist cosmic order.

Mani Wall. A long wall, faced with stones engraved with some text or *mantra*, most often *Om Mani Padme Hum*. Usually found on the outskirts of a village. Like a *chorten*, it is to be kept on the right in passing, hence the footpath inevitably bifurcates around it.

Mantra An invocation, the power of which resides not in the meaning so much as in the sound. A particular *mantra* may be associated with a particular deity, and constant repetition of it is an important part of meditation.

Mudra A symbolic hand-gesture.

Mok-mok   Steamed dumplings stuffed with chopped meat.

Nirvana   The final state of the soul's release from the endless cycle of mundane existence in incarnation after incarnation: merging of the individual soul with the Absolute.

Om Mani Padme Hum   Mantra associated with the Bodhisattva of Compassion, Avalokiteswara. Literal meaning is 'Hail to the Jewel in the Lotus', which may have a secret tantric significance.

Pashmina   The fine soft wool which is the winter growth, under its shaggy hair, of the pashmina goat. The raw material of the cashmere shawl.

Pattu   Coarse homespun woollen cloth.

Perak   The turquoise-studded headdress of Ladakhi women.

Sakyamuni   One appellation of Gautam Buddha, referring to his family connection with the Sakya clan.

Tamasha   Spectacle, fair, amusement.

Tantra   That aspect of the Vajrayana which distinguishes it from the Mahayana. The tantra are a series of secret texts, of mystical and esoteric significance, in which sexual symbolism plays an important part, and which are revealed to the aspirant only after appropriate initiations.

Thangka   Scroll-painting on cloth, of a religious subject, used in worship.

Toosh   The winter under-coat of the *stos*, or Tibetan antelope. Softer and finer than pashmina, and even more prized, it is the raw material for the finest shawls in the world.

Tsampa   Parched barley flour, the staple food of the Tibetan peoples.

Vajrayana   Lit. Vehicle of the Thunderbolt: historically the third school of Buddhism, a development of the Mahayana. The masculine principle of compassion expressed in the concept of the Bodhisattva complemented by a feminine principle of wisdom, personified in the female deities, the Taras. The way of enlightenment lies in the union of these principles, often shown by a symbolic representation of sexual union called in Tibetan *Yab-Yum*. The means of achieving this expressed in the secret texts of the *tantra*.

Yab-Yum   Symbolic representation of sexual union between some deity and his female counterpart. See Vajrayana.

Select Bibliography

The Tibetan Background

Clements Markham (ed.). *Narratives of the Mission of George Bogle to Tibet, and of the Journey of Thomas Manning to Lhasa*. London, 1876.
Heinrich Harrer. *Seven Years in Tibet*. London, 1953.
Michel Peissel. *Mustang: A Lost Tibetan Kingdom*. London, 1968.
Rinchen Dolma Taring. *Daughter of Tibet*. London, 1970.

The Historical Background

Luciano Petech. *The Kingdom of Ladakh 950–1842*. Rome, 1977.
The most scholarly and up-to-date work.
A. H. Francke. *History of Western Tibet*. London, 1907. Reprinted, with a critical introduction by S. S. Gergan and F. M. Hassnain, as *A History of Ladakh*. New Delhi, 1977.
——— *Antiquities of Western Tibet*, 2 vols. Calcutta, vol. I 1914, vol. II 1926. Reprinted New Delhi, 1976.
C. Wessels. SJ. *Early Jesuit Travellers in Central Asia*. The Hague, 1924.
Ippolito Desideri. *An Account of Tibet*, ed. Filippo di Filippi. London, 1937.

The Cultural Background

A. H. Francke. 'A Lower Ladakhi Version of the Kesar Saga'. *Bibliotheca Indica*, new series, Nos. 1134, 1150, 1164, 1218. Calcutta, 1905.
——— 'The Eighteen Songs of the Bonona Festival'. *Indian Antiquary*, vol. XXXIV. Calcutta, 1905.
Madanjeet Singh. *Himalayan Art*. UNESCO, Paris and London, 1971.
David Snellgrove and Tadeusz Skorupski. *The Cultural Heritage of Ladakh*. London and New Delhi, 1977.

19th and Early 20th-century Accounts, and Travel Books

William Moorcroft and George Trebeck. *Travels in the Himalyan Provinces of Hindustan and the Punjab, & c.* London, 1837, reprinted New Delhi, 1971.

The most detailed and careful of all the accounts, which still retains much of its relevance.

Frederic Drew. *The Jummoo and Kashmir Territories.* London, 1875, reprinted New Delhi, 1976.

A different emphasis from Moorcroft and Trebeck's, but equally valuable. These two are incomparably the best accounts of Ladakh published up to the present.

G. T. Vigne. *Travels in Kashmir, Ladak, Iskardo.* London, 1842.

A useful account of Baltistan; disappointing on Ladakh.

Alexander Cunningham. *Ladak, Physical, Statistical and Historical; with Notices of the Surrounding Countries.* London, 1854, reprinted New Delhi, 1970.

The first attempt at a general account of Ladakh. Tends to be diffuse, and not always accurate; but useful within limits.

E. F. Knight. *Where Three Empires Meet.* London, 1893.

Sven Hedin. *Central Asia and Tibet,* 2 vols. London, 1903.

———. *Transhimalaya,* 3 vols. London, vols. I and II, 1910; vol. III, 1913.

Jane E. Duncan. *A Summer Ride in Western Tibet.* London, 1906.

Arthur Neve. *Thirty Years in Kashmir.* London, 1913.

A. Reeve Heber and Kathleen M. Heber. *In Himalayan Tibet.* London, 1923, reprinted as *Himalayan Tibet and Ladakh.* New Delhi, 1976.

The Hebers lived as medical missionaries in Ladakh for several years, and their account is careful and accurate.

Peter Fleming. *News from Tartary.* London, 1936.

Ved Mehta. *Portrait of India.* Penguin, London 1973.

Recently Published Works

Thomas J. Abercrombie. 'Ladakh—The Last Shangri-La'. *National Geographic Magazine*, Washington DC, March, 1978.

Superb photographs.

Geraldine Doux-Lacombe. *Ladakh.* Paris, 1978.

A thoughtful and well-informed guide, particularly strong on the Buddhist angle.

J. N. Ganhar. *The Wildlife of Ladakh.* Srinagar, 1979.

A useful preliminary survey, the only one available.

Prakash Gole. 'A Birdwatcher at Large—Ladakh, June–July 1976'. *Hornbill*, the Journal of the Bombay Natural History Society. Bombay, October–December 1977.

Unpublished Work

Cambridge Undergraduate Ladakh Expedition 1977. Matho—Continuity and Change in a Ladakhi village.

The only in-depth study of its kind related to Ladakh.

Index

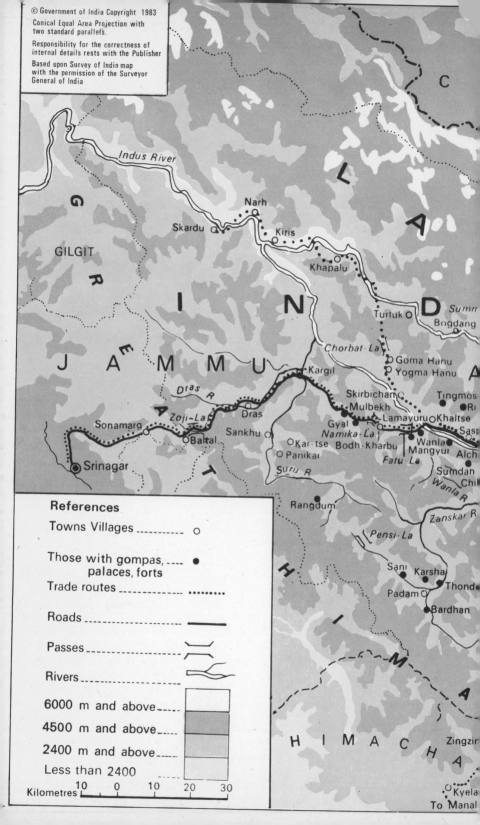

© Government of India Copyright 1983

Conical Equal Area Projection with
two standard parallels.

Responsibility for the correctness of
internal details rests with the Publisher

Based upon Survey of India map
with the permission of the Surveyor
General of India

Indus River

G
R
E
A
T

J A M M U

GILGIT

L A D A
N

Skardu
Narh
Kiris
Khapalu
Turtuk
Bogdang
Summ

Chorbat-La
Goma Hanu
Yogma Hanu

Kargil
Skirbicham
Mulbekh
Tingmos
Ri

Dras R
Zoji-La
Dras
Sankhu
Gyal
Namika-La
Bodh-Kharbu
Lamayuru
Khaltse
Sasp

Sonamarg
Baltal
Kar-tse
Panikar
Fatu-La
Wanla
Mangyu
Alch

Srinagar
Suru R
Sumdan
Chi
Wanla R

Rangdum

Zanskar R

H

Pensi-La

Sani
Karsha
Thond
Padam
Bardhan

M

I

A

L

A

References

Towns Villages	○
Those with gompas, palaces, forts	●
Trade routes	••••••
Roads	——
Passes	⌒
Rivers	⌇
6000 m and above	
4500 m and above	
2400 m and above	
Less than 2400	

Kilometres 10 0 10 20 30

HIMACHA

Zingzir

Kyela
To Manal